STAINLESS
SURGICAL
STEEL
JAPAN

OINK

An introduction to charcuterie butchery and other related matters including techniques for tying, curing, tools, theorems, expectations, hypothesis, anecdotes, narratives, fear and much loathing, both pictorial and otherwise, at all times for both domestic and commercial, together with applications with literary references as appropriate and necessary.

PJBOOTH

(In collaboration with A-R C F Booth and N J D Booth, on a loose and ad hoc basis, to a greater or lesser extent. Mostly lesser)

pjboothoink.com.au

OINK

Published in 2024 by Peter John Booth

Copyright © Peter John Booth 2024

ISBN 97800648459552

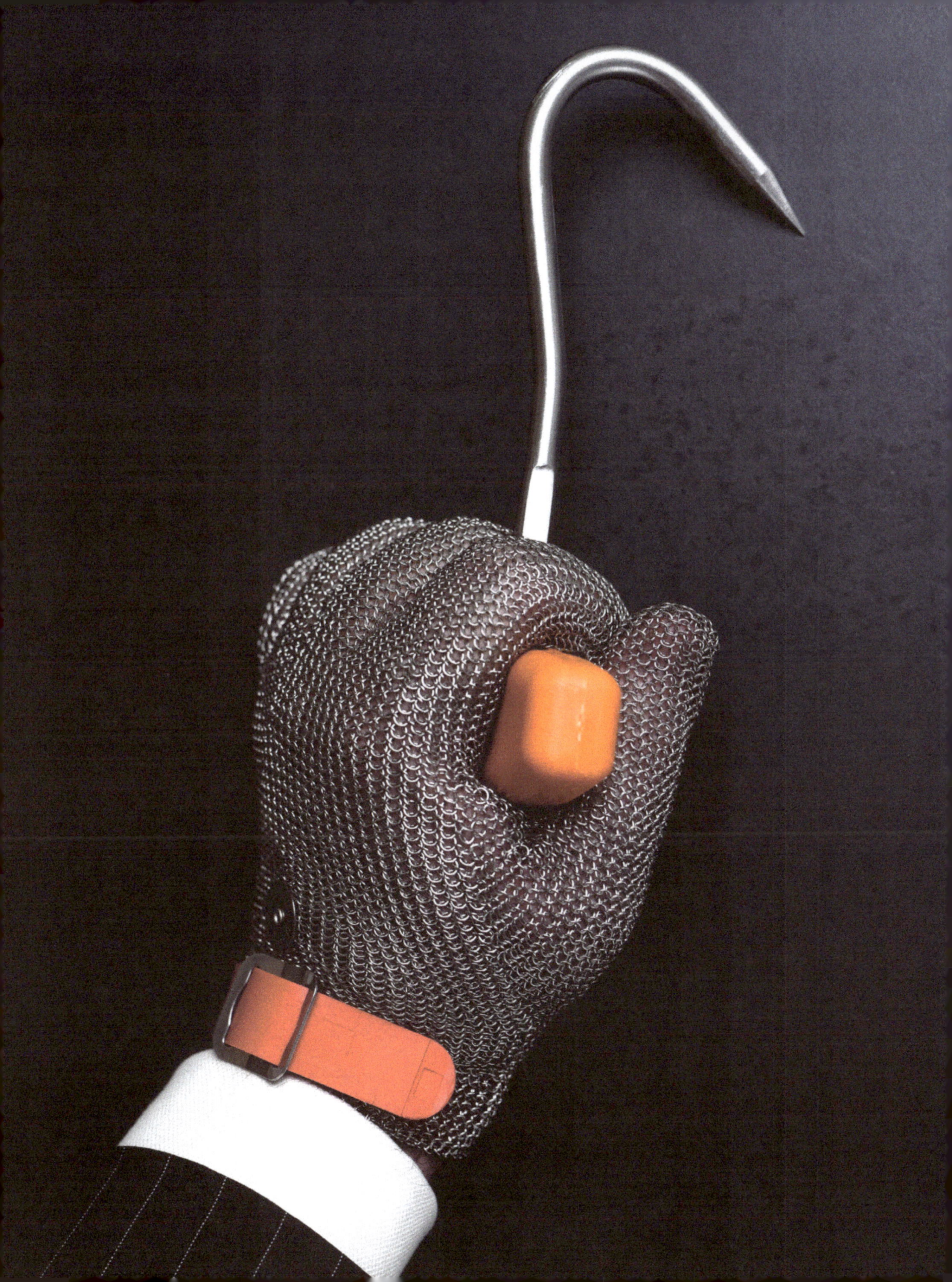

THE DEDICATION

For Helen, Amelia-Rose and Nicholas.

THE FOREWORD

It seems fitting that I met Peter Booth on my 30th Birthday. Peter visited Oakridge winery to teach my kitchen team how to cure meats and make salami. How could I know that stuffing sausages, tying bubble knots and lathering fat and flour onto a leg of pork would drastically influence the way I cook and think about food. Entering my thirties would become an exciting new chapter. The fundamental skills and techniques that I learnt that day have become my portal to ultimate creativity.

We live in the information age. We're bombarded with data, facts and opinions. It's ubiquitous. Ironically, a quick internet search tells me that 'Knowledge goes a step beyond information. It encompasses the understanding, interpretation, and application of information. Knowledge is information that has been processed by the human mind through learning, experience, or instruction.'

Enter the 'knowledgeable' Peter Booth and his most recent publication, OINK.

As with Peter's other books, OINK is an act of generosity. We can be confident that the hard work has been done. We can access the important information at a stage when we're not even sure what's important. There is no "fast" way to learn. From my experience it's about finding a reliable source of information or teacher. Someone who can communicate meaningfully so that you get successful results and gain understanding.

I am obsessed with books and learning new skills. I carry books in my car and bag just in case I get a moment to indulge my addiction. Peter's books are in high rotation. I constantly refer to them.

Peter's passion for learning and teaching is evident in the way he communicates in his books. His preparation and techniques yield consistent results. His understanding of fundamental skills and meat is something that only comes with experience. When you taste his cures and ferments or witness his butchery skills, you know that he knows!

Butchery is an art form that has been passed on through the ages. OINK is a timely publication that helps to preserve this traditional craft, reduce waste and save money.

I have an endless respect for Peter and his passion, experience and generosity to write these books. OINK is a 'must have' addition for the curious foodie, chef or person who loves to learn.

Jo Barrett, Charcutier, Patissier et Fromagier.

Melbourne 2024

THE CONTENTS

Goupil Frères
A

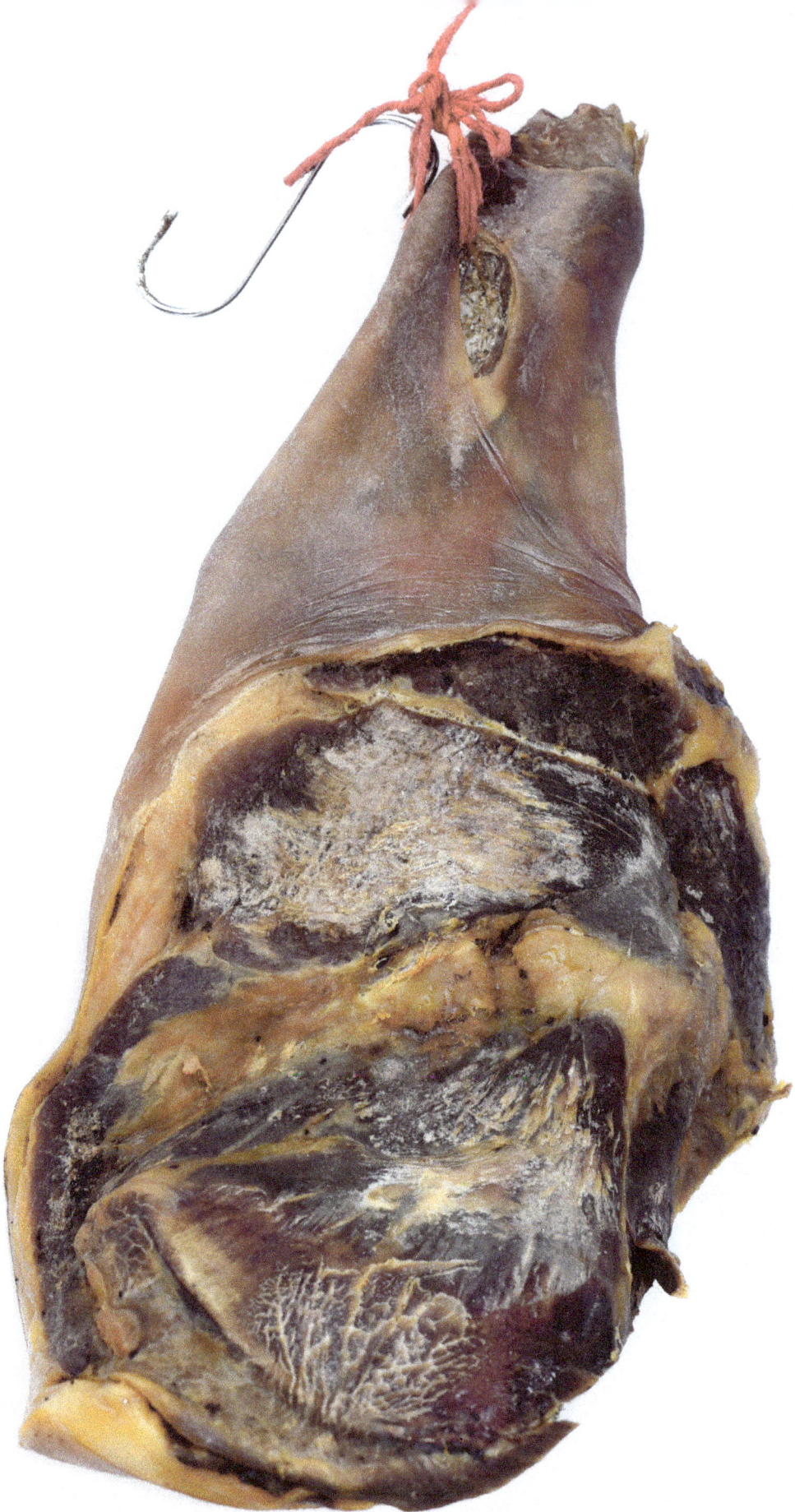

THE PROLOGUE

THE PROLOGUE

It is my habit to take detailed notes especially in this area. I have taken notes of my experiments in charcuterie for a very long time. I note that the first entry in the first notebook was made in January 2013. This became the foundation for the first book, hence the title. I have continued with my habit of recording notes since that time. You will recall that one of my concerns in this area from the very beginning was the paucity of information regarding the methodology and other aspects of this craft. It was because of those concerns that I decided to turn the first notebook into the first book," A Charcuterie Diary" was the result. That book has had some modest success. There have been many notebooks since. The other thing which I had found was most unsatisfactory in the available texts was the instructions as to how to butcher the meat. I have not written of this before in the previous books. The reason was that I was more concerned about recording my observations in the area, and the recipes, which I had discovered. However, the process of making charcuterie meant that I had to teach myself how to butcher the various cuts of meat. The recipes would only describe in narrative form how to go about these tasks but not the butchery which was required. I have taught myself how to approach the task of butchery over many years. The purpose of this book is to fill another gap in the market, that is to say, describe in a pictorial narrative how to achieve the cuts of meat required in order to carry out this back water, of butchery and culinary expertise. There is no other book available, to my knowledge, which explains in a pictorial and narrative sense, how to achieve the specialized cuts of meat required for charcuterie. There is no other book which also explains the equipment needed to explore this culinary backwater. It is for that reason that I had once again embarked on the arduous task of recording my observations.

This book represents more than 11 years of self-education, an abundance of fear and loathing, and of conducting charcuterie classes in various places in Australia.

However, I have long had an aversion to cookbooks which are essentially "meat on a plate " iterations but with a sparse narrative.

The challenge with this book was to provide "how to "instructions, which must always be prosaic, with some artistic flair both in a narrative and photographic sense.

This book is the result.

I hope that this may be of interest to you.

I am for the very last time, a river to my people. Ignore previous statements to that effect.

Suck it up cupcake.

> *Do not imagine, comrades, that leadership is a pleasure. On the contrary, it is a deep and heavy responsibility. No one believes more firmly than Comrade Napoleon that all animals are equal. He would be only too happy to let you make your decisions for yourselves. But sometimes you might make the wrong decisions, comrades, and then where should we be? (George Orwell, Animal Farm)*

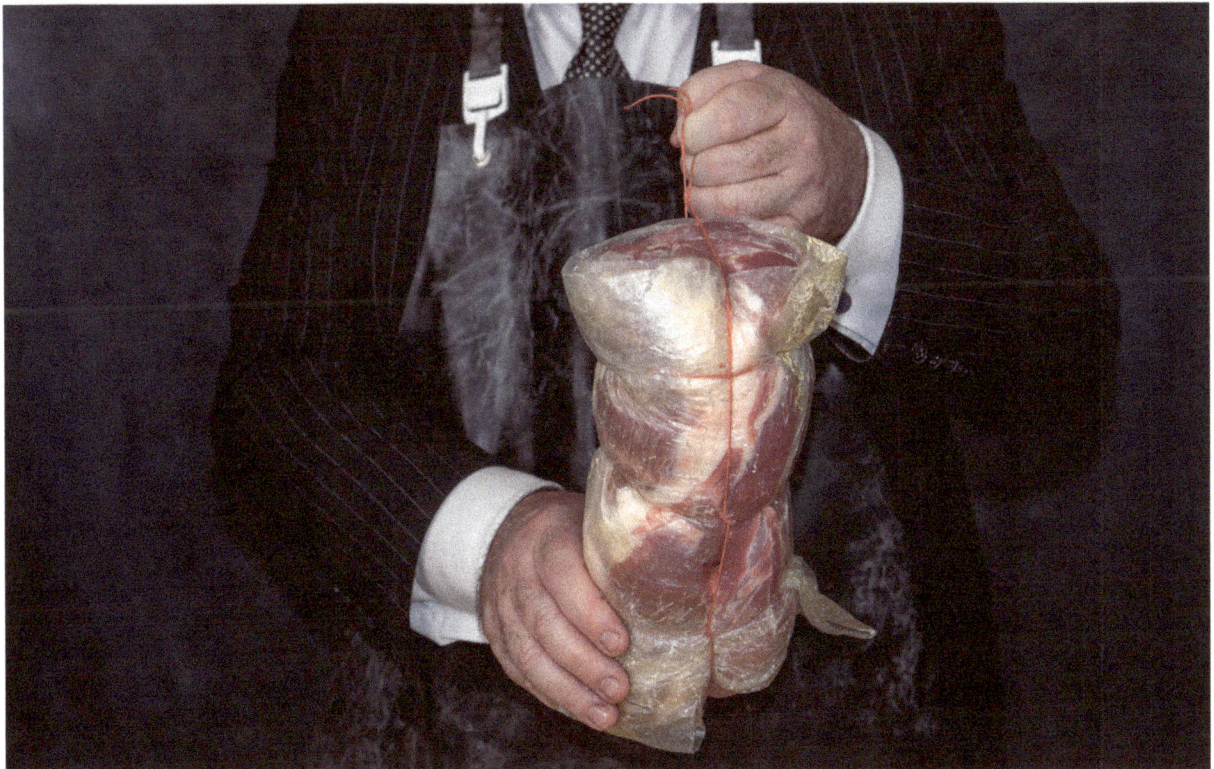

THE
TECHNICAL
THINGS

THE TECHNICAL THINGS

THE EQUIPMENT AND OTHER STUFF

a) Knives

You will need good knives in order to undertake basic butchery tasks. This may or may not be an oxymoron, but it is worth stating in this area. I have many knives. I have always had many knives. Some knives I like more than others. Although I do not tell the other knives this. I like them because of their weight, blade length, ability to sharpen, or just because I like them. You will need to decide what knives are important to you and which are useful for your intended tasks. Let me explain the types of knives that I use, and which are important to me for a variety of reasons. I like knives which will assist me in everyday use in butchery terms, that being the essential subject of this book.

I address this topic further below, however for present purposes is important to have knives which are easy to sharpen, retain a sharp edge for a relatively useful period and which are convenient to use both in weight, length, and size.

It is a matter for you which brand or type of knife you choose. I have chosen a particular brand which I use every day on which I find to be satisfactory. That does not mean that I do not use other different brands, weights, and lengths of knives for different purposes. A heavy Japanese chef's knife, a deba, is something that has a particular use with particular types of meat and for particular cuts. I use such a knife as and when it is required. Similarly, long bladed flexible filleting knives are very useful for specific applications. I also have a very useful, purpose designed, rabbit boning knife which probably has little application outside its particular purpose or perhaps for poultry, of the smaller persuasion. It is not unusual for me to change the type of knife that I am using during the process of breaking down a carcass whether it be beef, pork, lamb, poultry, or rabbit. It is important to be versatile in the process and recognise when a different tool needs to be implemented in order to achieve the task.

Be open-minded about the knives which you will use in the task of breaking down a pork carcass as with any other carcass.

Adapt, improvise, overcome.

I am a river to my people. Do not ask me why. I do not know. Perhaps I do , although maybe not. This, like many other things, is subject to The Need To Know Principle. If you need to know, then you will be told and therefore will know. If one does not need to know then one will not know. Henceforth and hereafter, the NTK principle. What vouz needs to ask is whether vouz needs to know. Too often in this life vouz and votre presume that vouz and votre need to know. Moi is here to inform vouz and votre that this is rarely the case. Moi decides the application of the NDK principle. More of this later.

Over and out.

c) Bone saw

It is in the nature of butchery that one will need to cut through bones. If you are butchering correctly, then this will not happen very often. However, it is necessary and unavoidable. You should not be afraid of this. Consider it a cardiovascular workout and hopefully there is someone younger, stronger, and fitter in the room who can step up. This is only for experience and training purposes. You need to explain to them that you can do it faster, better, and more efficiently than they can, but you choose to give them a once-in-a-lifetime training opportunity. In my experience they generally accept this as an explanation.Do not disabuse them of this.

There are several things to remember when cutting through bone. First, use the saw only to cut through bone, never to cut through flesh. Use a knife to make an incision to expose the bone and then use the saw to cut through the bone. You will hear the change in pitch once the saw has progressed through the bone and is starting to progress through the flesh. You must stop at this point. Cutting through the flesh with a bone saw will give a jagged edge, heat the meat unduly and is generally not accepted in the refined world of butchery. I know that you will not do this. If you do, then I will find you. There will be nowhere to hide.

Bone saws can range in length and height but generally they are approximately 40-50 cm long and 10-12 cm in height. They will range in price substantially. I have 2 bone saws. They are approximately the same length and height, however one cost a reasonable amount of money whereas the other cost considerably more. Initially I thought that a cheaper bone saw would be just as good as a more expensive bone saw. I was conceptually correct but not in practice. The cheaper bone saw does work the same as the more expensive product. However, the cheaper bone saw has considerably more flex in both the structure and in the blade. This means that the saw does not cut in a straight line as one needs it to do. The flex in the saw and in the blade, especially, means that it does want to move straight through the cut but wants to change direction. This is inefficient and undesirable. The more expensive bone saw is much more rigid in its construction and in the blade . Accordingly it cuts in a straight line and with less effort than the cheaper, more flexible, bone saw in my experience.

Assuming that a tool like a bone saw should only be a once in a lifetime acquisition, I encourage you to look at a more expensive bone saw rather than a cheaper bone saw. In my experience the cheaper bone saw is a lesson in false economy. At least it was in my experience. There is truth in the old adage that a bad tradesman blames his tools and that good tools are cheap because they last a lifetime.

> *His face was like the autumn sky, overcast one moment and bright the next. (Conrad, J, "Heart of darkness")*

d) String

Once the meat is prepared in the desired fashion it is often advantageous to tie the meat so that it cures evenly or smokes evenly. Therefore, string is needed. Do not use garden twine, waxed string, or synthetic strings. They will melt, muck up the whole thing, and will end in tears. Use cotton butchers string.

Trust me on this.

Butcher's string comes in different diameters. String for trussing larger pieces of meat needs to be thicker. This is because you will apply more force to it in order to truss the meat properly. If you use a finer diameter string it will cut through the meat because of the force that you apply. Therefore, for smaller, lighter, pieces of meat then one can use a finer diameter string because the force applied will be correspondingly less. If you use a thin string and apply significant force, you will cut into the meat.

Larger pieces of meat can tolerate, and require, significantly more pressure in the tying and therefore a larger diameter string will be useful and will not cut through the meat.

Tip of the spear, edge of the knife.

e) Butchers' hooks

The butcher's hook is nothing if not synonymous with the art of butchery. The meat needs to be hung to tenderise, it is also a very useful part of butchery because gravity can assist in separating meat from bone as a part of the butchery process, and dismembered pieces of meat can be hung on hooks awaiting further processing.

Classically a butcher's hook is in an " S " type configuration, it is blunt at the upturned end and has a sharp pointed end at the bottom of the " S "upon which the meat is hung.

They are manufactured in different sizes and in different thicknesses depending on the application, the thickest and largest meat hooks being used for the heaviest pieces of meat.

For the purposes of hanging a small piece of meat or a small salami some other variations can be considered. Your local hardware shop will have a variety of " S" hooks which are used for hanging tools, but which can very easily be used for hanging meat. They are much cheaper and do the same job equally as well as very expensive stainless steel butchers meat hooks. I have used them for many years without any regrets.

TRAYS AND OTHER CONTAINERS

Once you have butchered the meat you will need to salt cure it in the refrigerator. It is best to place it in the refrigerator on trays. Do not use metal trays, the risk is that the meat will react with the metal and absorb some metal flavors. Use plastic trays with a significant edge so that the meat juices, especially if the meat is being cured using salt, can be contained and do not contaminate the refrigerator.

If the meat is to be salt cured for a period, then it is desirable that it is in a container in the refrigerator with a lid, this contains the water which will be extracted from the meat by osmosis but also will prevent the meat from drying out in the especially dry conditions to be found in a domestic refrigerator.

"The creatures outside looked from pig to man, and from man to pig, and from pig to man again; but already it was impossible to say which was which." (George Orwell, Animal Farm)

g) Mincers

If you are serious about preparing your own meat for the purposes of charcuterie, then a mincer is essential. I have many mincers which been have acquired over the journey. The very first mincer was a hand

operated cast-iron mincer which clamped to the bench, very similar to the one that my mother used so many years ago. I have used it on a few occasions but in modern terms, and by reference to readily available electrically powered mincers ,it is somewhat anachronistic. The next mincer was an attachment to a well-known American stand mixer. It was reasonably powerful but, as I have written before, it did not like meat, sinew and especially did not like fat. It ended up being a terribly exasperating process, but I must say that it was a process which was undertaken in the very early years, and which may have reflected my naïveté in the whole damn thing. But the experience was so traumatic that I have not returned to it.

My next experience with a mincer was with a small domestic mincer which I came across in a kitchenware sale and which, it must be said, performed very well but only on an extremely small scale. If one wanted to make small quantities of minced meat products, then this would be a very good machine. However, I had aspirations which were somewhat more significant.

The next acquisition was a mincer of presumably Asian origins, it being an unknown brand to me, but it was of commercial quality, with replaceable mincing plates or dies and of one horsepower in magnitude. I pause to reflect on the power of mincers, most are stated in power in terms of horsepower. I do not know why this would be the case except that they are intended for a North American market. In Australia we do not use horsepower and we have not done for decades; the traditional form of power is either kilowatts or perhaps watts and they are not powered by horses. It is therefore difficult to understand or appreciate the power of the product which one is considering purchasing because the nomenclature is utterly foreign.

Returning to the Asian mincer it is of very good quality, very heavy perhaps 15 or 20 kg weight and does a very good job. There was probably no need to replace it. The reason being that I usually acquire meat which the butcher has minced to order rather than mincing it myself. But there is no doubt that if one is butchering a significant carcass then the meat needs to be minced at home during the process.

The next mincer which I acquired is of Italian ethnicity , smaller and more elegant design than the Asian designed mincer. That is not to say that it is either better or worse than the Asian mincer. It just means that it is nicer, smaller, and perhaps quieter. I use both interchangeably. They are of approximately the same power and diameter in terms of the mincer throat. That is to say that both are of one horsepower in power terms and identified as "22" in terms of throat size.

I pause to observe, without any admission of liability, that a mincer of one horsepower capacity will comfortably mince vouz mother-in-law should the occasion arise.

The singular benefit of the Italian mincer is that it can be used to produce tomato sauce by the replacement of the J curve mincer head with a specialised conical sieve and auger which separates the juice of the tomato from the skin and seed. I have used this on many occasions. But I digress.

The only thing that can defeat us is ourselves.

h) Stuffers

Let me turn to the topic of sausage stuffers. A topic which could require some ingenuity, pathos and mostly fear and loathing if one does not have the correct machine. In order that there should be no doubt there is really no alternative for stuffing a sausage casing unless one has a sausage stuffing machine. For domestic purposes, and that is what I will only consider in this book it is a hand cranked sausage stuffing device. They come in many different sizes and in two different orientations ,but the purpose of any of these devices is only to push the minced meat into a casing to create sausages either for fresh cooking purposes or for air drying purposes. There are two variations in the machines. First the capacity and secondly the orientation. The capacity is generally between 3 kg and about 10 kg for domestic purposes. The real issue is the orientation. Domestic sausage stuffing devices are either vertically oriented or horizontally oriented. My sausage stuffing device is approximately 4 kg capacity and is horizontally oriented. There was no reason for this acquisition other than I thought that about 4 kg capacity was about what I would need for research and consumption purposes. The real issue for me was the orientation of the device, either horizontally oriented or vertically oriented. Professional sausage stuffing machines do tend to be vertically oriented, no doubt to take advantage of gravity and also for the purposes of storage in the butcher's shop. For similar reasons I opted for a horizontal orientation of the sausage stuffing machine because it would fit more naturally in my available shelves. It also seemed to me that a vertical sausage stuffer, manually operated, present some problems because of the natural tendency of the mince to undergo a 90° transformation in orientation, and which would, it seemed to me, provides some difficulties in the stuffing process. Nonetheless I have been very content with my 4 kg, horizontally oriented sausage stuffer for many years and I do not intend to change it at all.I add that it is Italian, and it is red.What more needs to be said?.

At all events I am pleased to say that my choice of a 4 kg horizontally oriented sausage stuffing machine has been very good. Although I have to say that a sausage stuffing machine of a significantly larger quantity would, on occasion, be more beneficial. How was I to know this when I acquired this machine nearly 10 years ago, when I knew nothing of this area?.

I am a river to my people, and I do so for the last time.

i) Casings

Whether it be salami or a fresh sausage the product needs to be wrapped in a casing which will enable it to be contained and or air dried without disintegrating. The traditional method of encasing a minced meat product was to use fresh intestines of the pig, lamb, or cow. These are ubiquitously referred to as casings because they are a method of encasing the minced meat such that it can be either used as a fresh product or used as an air dried, cured, product.

This was, of course, a traditional method of using all the available parts of the animal to achieve a holistic view of the available products. One could not get through the winter and then the ensuing warmer months without available protein.That is what this is all about, maybe not so much now.

Casings for minced meat products, whether of the fresh sausage variety or the air dried variety are of varying diameters and lengths according to the animal. That is to say that the diameter of a beef intestine is much larger than the diameter of a pig intestine and, in turn, of the diameter of a lamb intestine. Beef intestine is of a such significant diameter that with one exception, of which I will return to later, they were not really used very often. Conversely the intestinal diameter of lamb casing is of such a small diameter that for similar reasons, it was not used very often. This means that one returns to the intestines of the pig which was of a very convenient diameter, is to say roughly about 30 or 35 mm. This is the classic natural casing which is used to produce fresh cured sausages. It is the convenient standard for fresh pork sausages and for cured and thereafter air-dried style sausages.

The lamb intestines are somewhat underutilised. They are approximately one third of the diameter of pork intestines, but are nonetheless used for fresh sausages, usually of pork stuffing but also of lamb stuffing. They tend to be very fragile and very difficult to use but small diameter, chipolata type pork sausage or small diameter merguez type lamb sausages are reasonably common. They are very good also.

There is no doubt that the classic fresh intestines have been used for fresh pork sausages and fresh air-dried type products. However, I can tell you that they are nasty, slippery, slimy suckers, particularly small diameter lamb intestines, and extremely difficult to use.

When I started using these products there was no doubt in my mind that one must use natural casings and one must deal with the difficulties inherent in such products. This meant that I spent many hours grappling with nasty, slimy, slippery natural suckers that you call natural casings, and it was a source of much frustration to me. You may say that Moi is easily frustrated. This may well be correct.

There is no doubt in my mind that those who were making these products all those hundreds of years ago would have been very, very interested in different alternatives had they been available.

This leads me to the next topic, which is natural collagen casings, but which are manufactured to create much more user-friendly products in modern times.

Let me introduce you to the future.

Over the journey, of which you have been a participant, I have found that there are wonderful new products, and they are no less traditional than the old fashion fresh products, indeed they are derived from them, but they are so much easier to handle.

Let me introduce you to the casings made from natural collagen, in some artificial formed way which I do understand and do not care about, which are dried and present the really, easy method of encasing minced meat products, and other products, in a very user-friendly and time efficient manner. Allow me to introduce the formed collagen casings, and the collagen wraps.

> *"Man is the only creature that consumes without producing. He does not give milk, he does not lay eggs, he is too weak to pull the plough, he cannot run fast enough to catch rabbits. Yet he is lord of all the animals." (George Orwell, Animal Farm)*

j) Formed collagen casings

These are casings formed from natural collagen but manufactured into a variety of shapes and sizes. The best iteration, and the one I use most times when I am embarking on this type of venture is a sausage style casing of approximately 35 mm in diameter, but it only has one open end. The lower end is occluded but the upper end is open such that it can be inserted on a sausage stuffer nozzle and filled. This means that only one end needs to be tied. They are quick, they come in various diameters and lengths. They enable one to move through a significant quantity of minced meat very efficiently whether to produce fresh sausage or air-dried sausage type products.

k) Collagen wraps

For larger pieces of meat it is often more convenient to have a sheet of naturally formed collagen so that the raw meat, albeit cured, can be wrapped, such that it is not overly dried out during the air-drying process. Collagen wraps are specially useful for larger pieces of meat such as a capocollo or lean pieces of meat such as a beef loin .

They are also very useful for lean pork cuts such as pork loin which is devoid of significant intramuscular fat. Although careful butchering can mean that the lean piece of meat is protected by rib bones, fat, and skin as is the case of a pork loin.

Synthetic collagen wraps are a very, very, useful part of the charcuterie armory. You should use them as often as you can.

l) Labels

It is important that one records the weight of meat, the type of meat, and the date upon which the meat is consigned to the curing cabinet. As you are aware it is my practice to allow the meat to air dry until a weight loss of approximately 40% is achieved, sometimes this may require some more air drying up to 50%. Therefore, it is important to record the date upon which the meat is consigned to the curing cabinet, its raw or wet weight and the desired target weight. After tying the meat and wrapping it in collagen or elastic netting I will record its circumstances on a cardboard luggage tag. These are readily available from stationery providores and extremely cheap. You can also make them yourself from cardboard or thick paper. More resilient products can be obtained of a plastic variety but in my view they are unnecessary.

What is important is that one can identify the cut of the meat, its wet weight, the date upon which it was consigned into the curing environment, and, if possible, the target weight.

This enables one to quickly review the progress of the progeny and discern how the progeny is enduring the process of air drying.

These are important parameters to monitor.

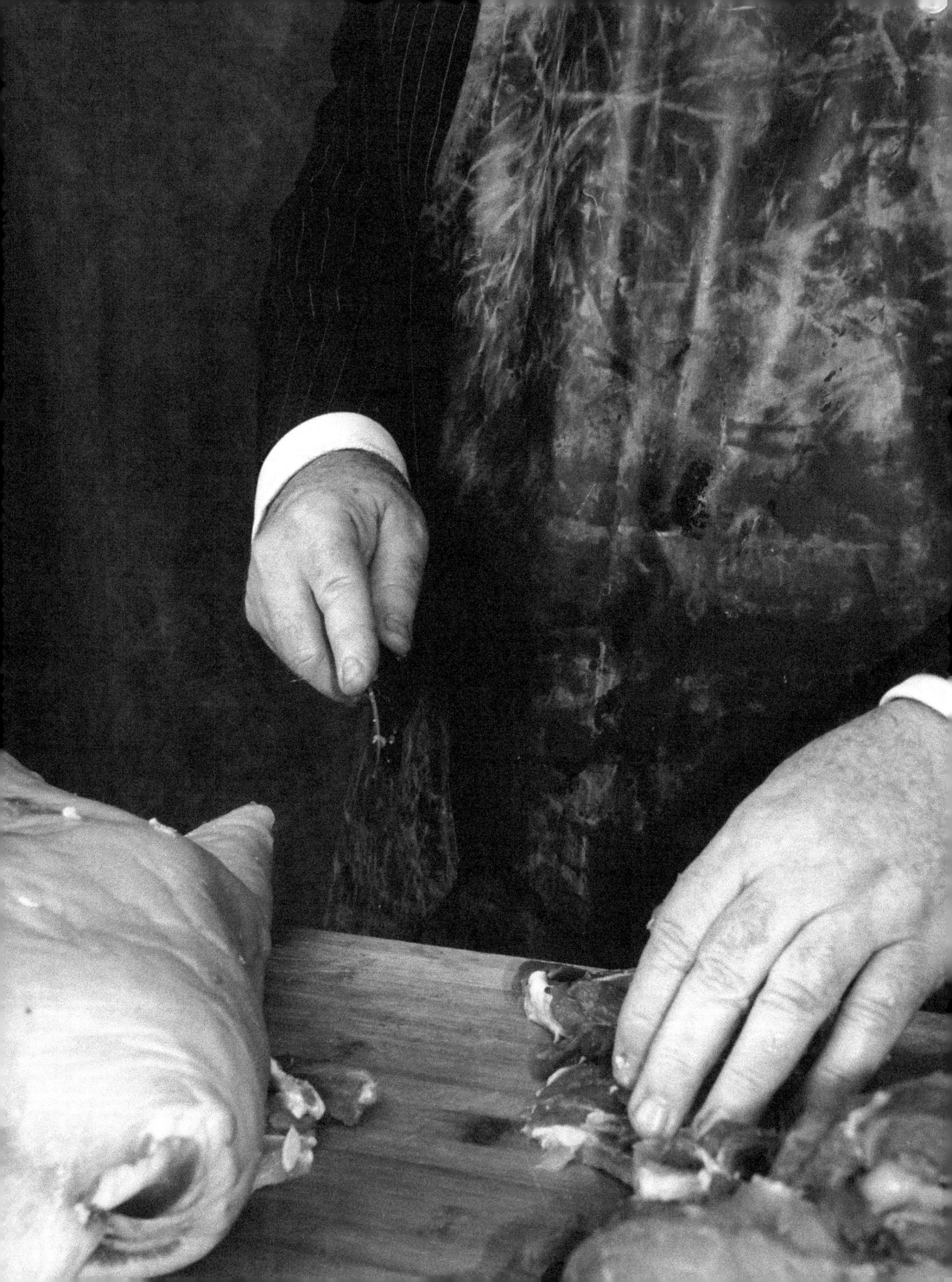

m) Resealable plastic bags

Re sealable plastic bags are an essential part of the charcuterie armory. They are very important for the dry curing meat in the refrigerator. They are useful because they take up very little space, they can be shifted from side to side for, the so-called overhauling, or curing piece of meat, to evenly distribute the cure through the meat. Yes, they do tend to leak at unfortunate times. However, if placed in the refrigerator on a plastic tray then the almost inevitable leakage is contained and is manageable. In my view the ability to rotate or overhaul the meat in a plastic bag is very important and gives an even cure. I have written about this issue before. Clearly the vacuum sealing of meat, together with dry curing agents is a more robust method of ensuring that there is no leakage in the refrigerator. However, I think that the pressure under which the meat is subjected, and therefore the cure, means that it is very difficult to rotate the meat and expect a redistribution of the cure. One needs the liquid to distribute, to achieve an even penetration. I acknowledge that many advocate the idea of vacuum sealing meat in order to undertake the initial curing process. My point is simply that the pressure to which the meat is subjected does make it a lot more difficult to achieve an even penetration of the cure by means of rotation. This does not mean of course that the pressure to which the meat is subjected does not mean that the dry cure ingredients are forced inevitably into the interior of the meat. All I mean to state is that it has not been my experience.

I guess at the end of the day this means that I am much more traditional than you may expect.

I can only record my observations and hope that they provide some assistance to you.

n) Containers (including the wooden boxes)

An essential part of charcuterie preparation is the step of salt curing. Most of the preparations that you will undertake will be dry cured, namely with the addition of salt and dry spices to the raw meat. This process results in the salt drawing out liquids from the meat in the process of osmosis. A container is required such that the extracted liquid does not flow through your refrigeration chamber. I use a variety of different shaped plastic and non-reactive containers for this purpose. It is important to use nonmetallic containers because the metal can react with the salt and create a metallic taste in the meat which is undesirable. Plastic, glass, or ceramic containers are therefore best. A container with a lid is most desirable because the meat will not dry out unduly in the harsh conditions of your domestic refrigerator. If there is no lid, then wet baking paper can be applied to the surface of the meat which is exposed to the ambient air to protect it from unnecessary drying.

A question which often arises is what to do about the resultant liquid in the curing container. Some in this area advocate draining off the liquid at regular intervals during the salt curing process. I prefer not to drain off the liquid for a simple reason. You have carefully prepared the ratio of meat to salt and of dry spices to meat. You have also carefully prepared the minimal amount of curing salt by reference to the wet weight of the meat. If you drain off the resultant liquid and you are necessarily removing the cure compound including, importantly, the curing salt. Therefore, one has gone from a carefully prepared environment of curing agents to a much-reduced environment of curing agents and into the realms of uncertainty, botulism, death, and tears.I add fear and loathing also. This is not an area which I recommend you investigate. Rather I suggest that you treat the liquid in the bottom of the curing container as a transition from a dry curing environment into a wet curing environment. Consider it this way, if you were curing meat in a wet environment, one would not pour off a portion of the brine after a period of time because you thought that it was bad brine.

There is another alternative. During the global pandemic, because I was extremely bored, I investigated the use of wooden boxes, predominantly wine boxes, for their use in dry curing. There are some obvious issues. The wine boxes tend to be of fragile construction. They therefore needed to be strengthened with the addition of stainless-steel screws at appropriate locations. The second issue was that I did not want the extracted liquid to leak through the refrigerator. This presented some technical challenges. The result was the use of waterproofing preparations derived from organic materials such as orange oil and carnauba wax. After some experimentation I have found these to be good products and I have used them when the occasion has arisen. Rope handles make the wood boxes easy to manipulate. They are not the most practical of curing containers, I acknowledge, but I really like the process of using them, the process of investigating how to waterproof them without using nasty chemicals and the inherent pleasure of using them.

o) Butcher's needles

Once the meat has been butchered and prepared in the appropriate form. It is often useful to tie it into a particular shape or to add strings for the purposes of hanging and/or smoking. There are several useful butchers' tools which can be used to assist in this process.

The most useful tool in my armory is a stainless-steel needle with a handle, the business end is arrow shaped with a hole in the center. This is sometimes called a butcher's needle or a bacon needle. It is very useful for passing a string through the meat such that the meat can be hung or rolled. Let me explain. When I prepare pork bellies for smoking as with bacon or other preparations it is necessary to pass string through the meat such that it can be hung in the smoker. The same is true if I am preparing meat, in whole muscle form, to be air dried once it has been cured. The challenge is making a hole in the meat and passing a string through it. This often results in the skewer passing through the meat and through the palm of one's hand. Easter jokes aside this is not a desirable result. Although I add that it perhaps, possibly, on a without prejudice basis has happened to Moi. The bacon needle is the answer. The needle is passed through the meat, the string is then passed through the eye of the needle on the other side and the needle withdrawn. The string is removed from the eye of a needle and then the needle removed from the meat. All that remains to be done is to tie it off into loop. This is safe, quick, and very easy. This can be used to create hanging points for meat which can either be air dried or smoked. The loop of string is also a convenient place to attach a label which will record the type of product, the date, and the wet weight.

These also come in smaller iterations, from the world of leatherwork, they are smaller and shorter but essentially the same, and often referred to as awls. I have several of them, but the longer more substantial needles used in butchery are much preferable.

The other thing that is of some use are other butchers' tools, again often referred to as rolling needles or tying needles. These are more substantial stainless-steel needles which are used to secure, for example a full rolled pork belly prior to the meat being tired. They are used for the purpose of securing it in an even shape so that it can then be tired. Once tired the securing needles are removed and the meat roasted.

I also have a small needle which was referred to as a prosciutto needle . It is about 6 inches in length with an offset, blade shaped The eye of the needle is in the rear of the needle not the blade end. The closest cousin to this is probably a sewing needle. This is used to literally stitch up a piece of meat such that it is joined as one would do with a piece of fabric. It could be used to stitch a rolled piece of meat for the purposes of roasting or even smoking, or air drying.

The last product which I use, reasonably often, are weaving needles, which are not really needles at all. They are ice cream stick shaped wooden devices with a hole at the rear and a tapered point at the front which are used in tapestry making. The idea is that the tapered point is used to slide under a vertically opposed strand to create the weaved product. I use these when I am tying a product like culatello to create the circular, spiderweb, net which is required to hold the product together.

These matters are somewhat difficult to describe in words, hopefully the pictorial and tutorial is of more assistance.

Battle is the fiery crucible in which only true heroes are formed.

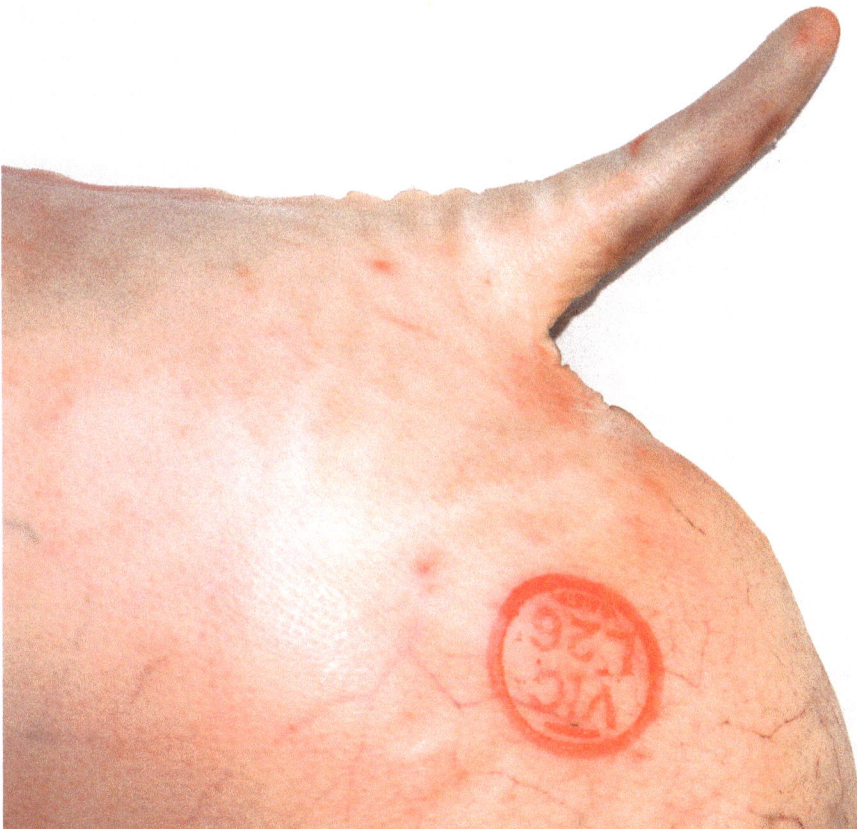

p) Cryovac

Vacuum sealing of meat is a significant advantage in terms of extended longevity of the meat in the refrigerator. I will often purchase meat at the markets on a Saturday morning and vacuum seal the meat when I come home on that day. This is because my circumstances at home are not as regular as they once were. This means that I do not know whether my fellow travelers in the house will be engaged for dinner on every night of the week as I would expect them to be. This is especially the case for those fellow travelers, called children, who occupy the house on a semipermanent but ad hoc basis to which we have become accustomed.

In my experience vacuum sealing fresh meat will give it a longevity which is surprising, fresh meat will last at least for 10 days if not longer once cryovac sealed.

Vacuum sealing of raw meat is also of assistance in the curing process, although in my experience the assistance can be of limited value. Let me explain. The process but involves usually curing meat in a zip lock bag such that it is dry cured in the beginning but, almost wet cured, in the end. The air is expelled from the bag as much as possible, however not exclusively. This means that the air is present in the bag so that it can be overhauled or rotated from side to side in order to ensure that a good even cure is effected.

On the other hand, vacuum sealing the meat together with the curing agents, in my view, is antithetical to the process of distributing the cure throughout the meat. The vacuum pressure applied to the meat means that it is extremely difficult for the fluid and therefore the cure to be distributed across the surfaces of the meat.I acknowledge that the vacuum force does assist but I like turning the meat and observing the cure distribute. It is for that reason that I do not vacuum seal dry cured meats during the curing process.

In other respects, the cryovac machine is a very good piece of technology. Without a cryovac machine it would be difficult to achieve many of the products which I have undertaken for example, hot smoked pork shoulder, porchetta de testa, and hot smoked beef tongue, to name a few.

q) Vacuum bags

It follows that vacuum seal bags are very useful things with fresh, especially meat. They are a very convenient way to extract the air from fresh meat and therefore extend its shelf life for a considerable time. Vacuum seal bags can be used if one has too much fresh meat to process in the short term. I have done this many times.

Vacuum seal bags come in various sizes and dimensions which will be convenient depending on what size and of meat you are processing.

A common problem which I have encountered is that meat on the bone can have sharp bone bits, such that the pressure of the sealing may result in puncture of the bag. This is most undesirable because it may occur sometime after the meat has been sealed in the bag and placed in the refrigerator. Accordingly, one may not know   of the depressurisation of the bag until sometime later when it is all too late and ends in tears.Some baking paper or blue kitchen paper inside the bag will help.

However vacuum seal bags are also essential process to slow poaching in water in the technical process referred to as sous vide.

Doubt kills.

r) Sous vide

Sous vide is a French technique for cooking food, best realised in modern times. The term literally means "under vacuum", which means that the meat must be vacuum sealed as an essential part of the process. The vacuum sealed product is then immersed in a water bath and cooked very slowly, over a long period of time at a very precise temperature. Commercial iterations of this concept were a quite large water bath which is integrated with a system for maintaining a very precise temperature, utilising an immersion heater and an impeller to distribute the hot water evenly. They were commercial products which were very expensive and out of reach for the domestic user. Relatively recently domestic versions of the same concept have become available. They closely resemble a stick mixer used to mix semisolids such as cooked vegetables and the like. However, they are adapted to being inserted into a normal cooking pot and will maintain the extremely accurate temperature required for such a cooking technique. More recent iterations acquired a Bluetooth facility which means that one can monitor the circumstances of the ubiquitous mobile phone.

In charcuterie terms they are extremely valuable, let me outline some of the applications. Slow cooked meat such as beef tongue can be cooked in a vacuum sealed bag such that the good stock and other circumstances of the cooked meat are not lost into the water bath but are retained . The tenderised and cooked meat can then be hot smoked, after having been peeled to remove the extremely tough outer layers of the tongue. Another product, of which I am extremely fond, is the boned, rolled, tied pig head which becomes the Italian product known as *porchetta de testa*, or the French iteration, *porc de tete farci* or its closely related British cousin, *haslett*.

There is quite simply no better way to prepare these products than by using the low and slow water bath technique of sous vide.

It follows, of course, that one needs a vacuum sealing machine to commence the process. I assume that you have embraced technology, in the absence of which you would not be interested in this topic.

I commend this technique to you and in particular the recent domestic iterations of the machine. They are cheap, reliable, and do not take up much room in the pantry, which is a desirable thing in my household.

Rosebud (Citizen Kane)

r) Muslin and other cloth wraps

Very often there is an imperative to wrap your whole muscle preparation in a protective layer. This can be an issue when one has meat which is in whole muscle preparations. Whole muscle preparations very often do not have an external skin layer to protect them from excessive desiccation. Therefore, extra protection is required. This wrapping can be in the form of a breathable fabric, the cheesecloth or muslin type of fabric is most useful. This was the way, I infer, that it used to be done many years ago. The fabric wrapping creates a barrier to excessive desiccation and therefore is quite useful. I have used muslin cloth to wrap prosciutto and other whole muscle preparations. It seemed to me, in the beginning, that this was paying respect to the history and culture of this culinary backwater. I still think that their use has a place. However when I have done so it vastly reduces the airflow across the surface of the meat. This, in turn, encourages the growth of moulds, often nasty, evil moulds, which has not been a happy result. Therefore, I suggest to you that you may care to experiment with breathable cotton fabric wrappings but in my experience, there are better alternatives.

One useful alternative is an elasticised cotton fabric, mostly used by our North American cousins, called a ham sock. These are very tightly stretched across a prosciutto or what the Americans call a ham and does create an external barrier which is advantageous in discouraging excessive desiccation. However, the fundamental problem remains which is meat which is wrapped in these products does tend to acquire mould. Our North American cousins seem to embrace the resultant mould, but I am yet to be convinced. I acknowledge that a degree of mould on a whole meat preparation can mostly be a good thing.

I can only suggest that you try these products and see which works for you.

In my view modern products are more useful, namely elasticised netting and pre-formed collagen sheets or wraps. I deal with each in turn.

I love the smell of napalm in the morning (Apocalypse now)

s) **Netting and netting tubes**

You have all seen the classic Italian or European air-dried sausages which are encased in a tight elasticised netting. The netting performs two functions. First it compresses the meat notwithstanding the meat is drying and therefore shrinking. This type of elasticised net maintains an even pressure on the meat and it assists in the drying of the product. It is therefore beneficial.

The next benefit of elasticised netting is that it forces the sausage shape to be maintained and therefore an even cross-section which encourages even drying across a section of the sausage. This is another benefit and results in, usually, an evenly air-dried product. A most desirable result.

However, these elasticised nettings, which come in a variety of diameters, are only useful if they are tight on the sausage. This means that a device is required to expand the net such that the preformed sausage can be inserted into it and then the net returns to its original, smaller, diameter. The device is very simple, called a netting tube. They come in various diameters into which the sausage is inserted, the netting is stretched across the exterior surface and then once the sausage is passed through the tube the net closes around the sausage. They have a flat end for the purposes of assisting the stretching of the elasticised netting over the exterior, the open end of the tube has a removable cone, again to assist in stretching the net beyond its normal diameter, over the exterior surface of the tube. Once sufficient length of netting is stretched over the netting tube, the netting is cut, pulled further down, the cone removed and then the open end of the net is tied off. The sausage is then pushed through the tube, and out of the tube, it is then tied off at the other end. This results in the classic method, air dried sausage, with which we are all familiar.

If you want to achieve the classic look, and a degree of certainty about the end product, then elastic netting and netting tubes are the way to go.

Round up the usual suspects (Casablanca)

t) Collagen wraps

Whole muscle products do not generally lend themselves to netting although there are some limited exceptions depending on the size and therefore diameter of the meat. But it is nonetheless desirable to take steps to avoid excessive desiccation particularly when the whole muscle product does not have a skin or rind covering on the exterior. A good way to do this is by using collagen wraps. These are sheets of natural collagen, but which are manufactured into a convenient shape. They come in various sizes, for use with various sizes of meat. Consider them to be like baking paper, with which they share some similarities. The sheet is placed on the bench and the meat is wrapped such that it is evenly covered by the collagen sheet. It then needs to be tied and secured such that it does not come loose from the surface of the meat. Once this has been done is often convenient to net the product to give it even contact between meat and collagen wraps and for the associated benefits of the elasticised netting creating a uniform or semi-uniform shape in the whole muscle preparation.

Open the pod bay doors, Hal (2001: A space odyssey)

u) Chopping boards

A good chopping board is an essential part of the tools required for basic butchery. Traditionally they are made of wood, but modern chopping boards are often made of plastic. Each has downsides and benefits; each has attributes and disadvantages. I deal with each in turn.

I like wooden chopping boards; I have many of them and I like them all. I like the look of them, the feel of them especially as they grow old, developing a patina which makes them much more attractive. Just like me. There are probably 3 basic types of wooden chopping boards. First a single piece of wood usually of relatively substantial thickness , say, 40 mm. These are the single sheet of timber where you are cutting across the grain. They are the cheapest type of wooden chopping board, and the price will vary depending on the quality of the timber. A pine chopping board will be cheaper than a hardwood chopping board, but each will achieve the same purpose. They are nice to use, they are kind to the edge of your blade because the wood is much softer than the edge of the blade and will not damage it. Conversely, depending on the species of board they will wear out relatively quickly, pine would therefore wear out more quickly than a hardwood board. The disadvantage of boards like this is that, depending on the thickness, they tend to warp and will not lie flat on the bench top. This can often happen, particularly with softwood boards if the board is left in contact with water, staying in the sink awaiting cleaning and drying prior to the next use. The board will absorb water and in so doing it can expand unevenly. A board which has warped or developed a curvature is difficult and dangerous to use. They are unstable because they are not flat and can move significantly when you are chopping. This is dangerous and should be avoided. There are several ways that such a board can be remediated if not tolerated. The board can be placed on a wet tea towel, this will very often overcome a slight warping of the surface. It is often good practice with any board because it stops the board from moving across the bench surface at an inconvenient moment. An alternative is to wet the board thoroughly and then place it between two tea towels and apply and even pressure, for example another board with a weight on top. This will often encourage the board to return to a flat surface.

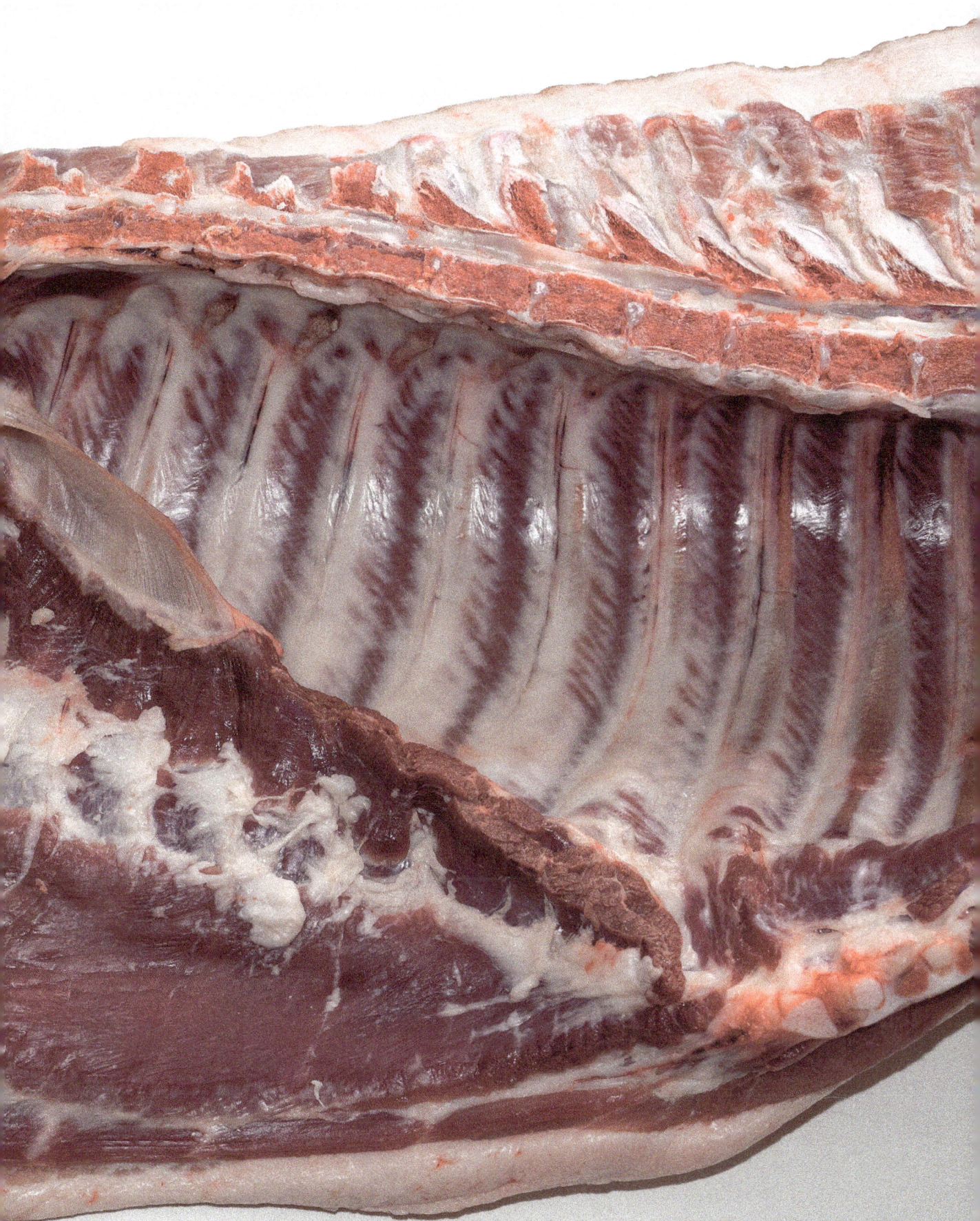

The second type board is a variation of the first. It is made with timber, the fibers of which traverse the length of the board. However, unlike the first type is made with several pieces of timber which had been dove tail jointed or glued together along the length of the board. These are usually made from hardwood; they are more expensive than the first type but had significant advantages. Mainly they are more resistant to warping because of the lamination of timber through the length of the board. They are less likely to warp because of this method of construction. However, it is not a common way to make boards.

The third type is much more common, much more expensive, and offers significantly more advantages. This is the so-called end grain cutting board. This involves a completely different method of manufacture such that individual, long square sections are glued together to create a long-laminated block. This long-laminated block is cut in sections across the grain such that the end result is a board of required thickness, they are usually quite thick, but the cutting surface is the end grain of the timber rather than the long grain. Cutting on the end grain is a much more robust surface, slightly harder on the cutting edge of the knife, but therefore has more longevity. They are also very visually attractive once easily individual pattern of the end grain and usually with some colour variation. Particularly expensive versions use the end grains to create patterns of shape and colour. Ohey are also less prone to warping because the timber fibers are much shorter. These boards are usually made from hardwood and overall are probably the most robust boards which will give years of use.

The last type are end grain boards which are not made in the laminated form described above. These are made by cutting a cross-section of the tree trunk such that the only surface presented is the end grain surface. They tend to be usually circular in shape, for obvious reasons, often banded with a metal strip to ensure their structural integrity and are quite thick. They are common in Asian cultures and can be found in Asian kitchenware shops in Australia. They are good, easy to use , but tend to be very heavy and cumbersome because they are made extremely thick for the purposes of heavy cleaver chopping of meat on the bone. For that reason, they are often to be seen in Asian butcher shops or barbecue restaurants which serve cooked meat on the bone. I like them but unless they retain a position on the bench and not be put away their size and weight make them difficult for everyday use and then replacing them in storage. The size and weight often make them somewhat cumbersome to wash and clean.

Plastic boards are very different. They tend to be rectangular in shape, of varying sizes but usually quite thin. The advantages of a plastic board are quite significant. They do not acquire the flavour or smell of the product which is being chopped, they are also resistant, to a significant degree, to staining. They are therefore hygienic, easy to clean, and do not require any maintenance. The plastic is reasonably soft and kind to the knife edge so your knives will be very happy. They do tend to warp in my experience, probably because I put them in the dishwasher. The very large boards which I use for butchering a half pig or similar do not fit in the dishwasher and have not warped to any significant degree. There is no doubt that they are light, durable, hygienic, easy-to-use, and come in a variety of different colours. You may smirk at the idea of the board coming in different colours but it enables one to dedicate a particular colour to a particular use, for example red boards for red meat, white boards for pork, a yellow board for fish, and so on. This avoids cross contamination, which is particularly important in a commercial environment, not so much at home.

I have boards of each persuasion as described above. For quick tasks I will probably reach for a plastic board, for other tasks where I take some more time and enjoy the process I will always reach for a wooden board.

It goes without saying that I really, really, want a butcher's block made from end grain timber, on wheels, preferably antique. It also goes without saying that I will probably never acquire such a piece of history. Such is life.

v) Wooden chopping board maintenance

It may surprise you to learn that wooden chopping boards do require some maintenance.

Obviously after every use they need to be washed in hot soapy water. This is because wood is porous and will take up meat juices and if not washed properly, they will become evil, and you know the rest. Do not let them sit in water for a long period of time, this results in the boards warping and a curved, wobbly chopping board is just as dangerous as blunt knives if not more so.

However, beyond the obvious washing after use the boards, being natural products do require some maintenance. During Covid I had time to contemplate these matters. Some modest research, Internet-based as always, disclosed that there are many products available which are safe to use with food preparations. Chopping board oil is useful to rejuvenate the board and give it some essential items. Classically they are made as a preparation of citrus oils and beeswax. Other similar products are wax preparations to rejuvenate wood, usually based on beeswax, orange oil and carnauba wax. Cleaning products can also be found, often described as cutting board cleaners. These are based with different preparations, often lemon oil and coconut oil. All these products are applied to dry boards in modest amounts and then buffed with a soft dry cloth.

I found two suppliers to be useful and conveniently obtainable in Australia, Howard and Gillys. I have not been paid to promote either, sadly.

These products do not need to be applied regularly but on some occasions after some use, they refresh and rejuvenate.

Another aspect is that on a cold wet winters' afternoon in the study, the simple pleasure of rejuvenating a wooden board is not to be underestimated. It is right up there with bringing back your knives to a lovely edge and shine in the case of carbon steel blades. It is a pleasure which is hard to describe in words.

If you appreciate the look and feel and joy of using natural wood chopping book boards, as I do, then if you look after them, they will last you at least one lifetime. I don't know about you, but I suspect that I have only one lifetime in me. Although time will tell.

Do not use ammonia-based kitchen cleaning products. They will permeate the board and ever after flavour the meat. Not a good result.

You will have critics and naysayers in votre ranks. All Vouz must do is look them in the eye and lie.

x) Fridge maintenance

I have two dedicated charcuterie fridges. I use them for dry ageing meat, storing meat whilst it is being salt cured and before I air dry it. This means that the meat is often leaking from containers, I should be more vigilant, but I am not such that these fridges need to be cleaned regularly.

Over the years I have developed several solutions to this problem, usually arising from leaky plastic bags from the butcher. First take the meat out of plastic bags as soon as possible. Then place it on a plastic tray with raised edges such that while it is being rested in the fridge until required, the leakage of liquids does not permeate the shelf and create issues insofar as cleaning and maintenance is concerned.

Meat which is to be used fresh I cover lightly in vegetable oil and wrap in baking paper. Baking paper or silicon paper is breathable and allows you to wrap the meat such that it does not dry out unduly. This is a good thing. I can comfortably keep fresh meat for 7 days in my refrigerator once it has been lightly oiled and wrapped in baking paper. Sometimes I will place it on a rack over a plastic tray to keep any leakage away from the meat.

The other technique which I use very often is to cryovac the meat as soon as I return from the market. This is especially valuable if the meat is on the bone. I often do not know when I will use the meat that I have chosen for the week, largely dependent on the movement of my knucklehead home share dependants otherwise known as number one son and number one daughter. Once sealed in the cryovac the meat is comfortably safe for 5 days in the case of meat on the bone and 10 days in respect of bone less meat.

However, from time to time the refrigerator does need to be cleaned because of unexpected or unintended liquid leakage from meats in various states of resting, curing or otherwise loitering.

Ammonia-based kitchen cleaning products should be avoided at all costs. Whilst they are very efficient in cleaning. They have the obvious disadvantage of the ammonia smell permeating through the refrigerator. In the case of difficult to move detritus, hop soapy water is the preferred method of operation. For all other things vanilla based preparations, whether commercial or home-made, are the best solution. Vanilla has a unique property of absorbing bad smells. Commercial vanilla-based kitchen cleaning sprays can be obtained. They are very useful in cleaning a refrigerator. The other very useful preparation which my mother explained to me many years ago was to put a glass or a cup with a small amount of vanilla in the bottom into the fridge. The vanilla will permeate the refrigerator and absorb any nasty evil odours.

It helps that vanilla is one of my favorites and all-time best smells.

y) Freezing meat

It follows from the thesis of this book that it is most desirable to use fresh meat which has not been frozen when preparing charcuterie. This does not mean that charcuterie cannot be prepared using frozen product. Of course, it can. The authorities in the area, notably McGee suggest that the quality of fresh meat, after freezing is somewhat diminished. I do not disagree with this proposition. However, there is no arguing with the result which is that if one does not have the time on a Saturday or Sunday to prosecute preparation of charcuterie, whether whole meat or minced meat, deciding to do some preparation and freeze the results is not a wholly unacceptable state of affairs. I have done this many times because the intervening events meant that I was not able to carry out the plans which I have made for the weekend which largely revolved around the preparation for charcuterie and the necessary consequences.

On many occasions I have prepared the meat for processing on a Saturday with a view to its final processing on a Sunday morning only to have those plans cast aside by extraneous factors. The partly prepared meat and fat would be packaged and frozen to be dealt with on a later date. I do not consider that this is a significantly detrimental practice having regard to the end product. I assume there is some loss of quality compared to the fresh product. Nonetheless the alternative of discarding several kilos of meat, fat, and preprepared spices is insignificant compared to the possibility of using these preprepared integers on a later occasion. I have done this on many occasions. You should not be afraid to do so. However, I acknowledge that unfrozen, fresh meat, fat and spices is the most desirable outcome.

The most you can hope from it is some knowledge of yourself. (Conrad J, "Heart of Darkness ")

z) **Spice grinders, mortar, and pestle.**

There are only a few things that one needs to make charcuterie. In no particular order one needs fresh pork, fresh pork fat, casings and salt. The spices are the extra part of the formula, they are added in very small quantities and are for flavoring purposes only. However, they should be added as a fresh product if possible. This means that freshly ground spices are more desirable than those which have been ground earlier and have become somewhat stale. The question which arises is how to grind the spices fresh as needed. There are many ways to achieve this purpose. In the beginning I used in a mortar and pestle which was a hard ceramic   and made in Britain. It is a very good thing. I have used it for many years. The ceramic is incredibly hard, and the wooden handle of the pestle is a delight to use. I fully expect it to last for a for a generation and that it will be passed on to the next generation.

The other mortar and pestle which I own is an Asian produced mortar and pestle made from granite. It is, as you would expect, extremely hard but also extremely heavy. It is an implement which I use not all that often, but when I have to grind a significant number of spices, perhaps for a significant amount of meat. I really like using it. It is much easier to use than the British, ceramic mortar, and pestle but the effort of bringing it from the cupboard to the table is much more significant. The truth is they are different pieces of equipment, each best suited to a different use and, accordingly, I use them differently.

The next spice grinding machine I use, and I must say I use this much more frequently than either of the proceeding implements, is a small electric powered spice grinder. It is extremely easy to use, it requires no effort on my part and produces , very good results in a very short period. Whole spices are added to the machine in whatever ratio is required. The machine then reduces them to a course grind or a powder if need be. On balance I use the electric spice grinder much more often than I use the traditional, manual, forms of spice grinding. There is not to say that I do not really enjoy using a mortar and pestle to grind spices. In any event the traditional mortar and pestle is irreplaceable when one is grinding a mixture of dry spices and wet spices. The electric spice grinder would have considerable difficulty in dealing with this. This means that if I am preparing a wet spice marinade, comprising dry herbs and wet ingredients such as coriander root or the leaves of whatever spice is relevant, my vehicle of choice would be a manual mortar and pestle. However, if I were to be processing dried spices for the purposes of adding to a dry spice cure, almost inevitably I would lean towards a dry spice preparation using the electric spice grinder.

aa) Meat presses, of various sizes.

In charcuterie it is often convenient to use a press of some description or mold to create the desired shape and texture of the product. There are many ways to achieve this.

In terms of minced meat, a terrine mold often in a long rectangular narrow shape, with a lid is useful. These are used to cook terrines in a water bath such that they do not dry out. Other varieties have collapsible sides such that with a removal of a locking pin the product can be easily removed. These are often used for pastry enclosed terrines, referred to as pate en croute. The ability of the mold to fall away from the product means that the pastry encased product can be easily removed without breakage.

Other forms of meat presses are usually circular in construction but can be rectangular. These apply pressure to usually a whole meat preparation, but sometimes a very coarsely ground preparation such that it sets under pressure and creates a cohesive product.

Round forms often have a circular press on top and are classically used for whole preparations such as beef tongue or coarse ham preparations which are cooked. Some other types have a lid which is compressed by means of springs. They rely on the physical pressure of the machine to create a cohesive product.

Sometimes these molds do not rely on pressure but are used to create a desirable visual shape such as in the case of soft pate type preparations or fish emulsions and the like. The resultant product is displayed on a plate and has a resemblance to the physical form of the original protein, whether it be avian or piscatorial. They can be very decorative and desirable as historical pieces, although not so much used currently. Such is the pity.

ab) Meat mixer

Mixing minced meat for the purpose of making air dried sausages is critical. This step achieves what is often referred to in the texts as a primary bind. Language does not matter. It is in the nature of minced meat to want to separate and to fall apart. This is antithetical to the idea of a cohesive, air-dried sausage. Therefore, this step is important when you are making an air-dried sausage. I have previously described a way to do this which uses an understanding of the characteristics of salt and meat proteins. You will find this in Squeal, in somewhat more detail. Shortly put the addition of salt to minced meat results in a chemical reaction between the proteins in the meat such that the meat proteins are broken down into smaller protein fragments which are inherently sticky and therefore create a very good bind, very easily.

The more traditional method is to manually agitate the mince, thereby breaking down the meat proteins into the sticky sub compounds which create the bind. This can take 20 minutes at least. In my view life is too short to spend 20 minutes mixing minced meat by hand, which is usually at an extremely low temperature.

There are alternatives and I have one of them. It is a manual meat mixer. It is a stainless steel box for want of a better description, it has paddles in the lower part of the box and an external manual handle with which to crank thereby causing the paddles to agitate the meat. It is of about 5 kg capacity, more than enough for domestic use. An advantage is the effort in cranking the panels is much less than manually, wrist deep, mixing the meat. However, the great advantage is that one does not get frostbite and lose 6 or

10 fingers because this is usually undertaken with really, really cold meat. You may laugh but until you have mixed 10 kg of ice-cold mince for 20 or 30 minutes you will never really understand the truth of what I am sharing with you.

I am a river to my people once again.

ac) Temperature probes

In some charcuterie it is important to keep an eye on the internal temperature of the meat. This is relevant regardless of whether the meat is to be used in air dried sausages or in hot smoking or to be properly cooked. There are many temperature devices which are available. Modern digital temperature probes are cheap, accurate and convenient. The stainless steel probe is inserted into the meat and a very accurate reading is obtained. I use them every day, they are dispensable because often end up being placed in the washing water by evil elements of my household. However, I digress.

Other variants are the new Bluetooth probes which can be inserted into the meat and the meat then placed into a cooking or smoking vessel. They are relatively impervious to the conditions, although in my experience in my house they do not survive being placed in the washing up water. But I digress. They can communicate with mobile phones and give a very accurate reading of circumstances of the meat together with warnings as they approach relevant temperatures. They are relatively expensive but a very useful investment if one is doing a lot of smoking. The limitation seems to be one of distance. They have difficulty communicating with you if your hot smoker is outside the house and you are several rooms distant in a house with significant construction.

In the beginning I used mechanical temperature probes, an analog device with a stainless-steel probe attached. In my experience they are most unreliable, and I quickly learned not to contribute much accuracy to them at all.

Thereafter I used digital probes which were attached to a reader by a wire. They were not bad but were not very robust. I replaced many because they simply died. I do not think that there was water involved. I do not recommend them, but they are very cheap.

ad) pH meter

Until recently pH meters were only available in commercial applications. However domestic pH meters are now available and of the affordable persuasion. It was lockdown, I was bored, and I purchased a relatively affordable pH meter.

This leads to the next issue; why would one buy a pH meter at all?

To answer this question, one must understand the nature of pH and its relevance to charcuterie production.

Allow me to provide some assistance.

McGee, ever helpful, pulls no punches and states that the pH of a solution is defined as " The negative logarithm of the hydrogen ion concentration expressed in moles per litre". Thank you, Harold, we can all sleep much more comfortably knowing that. He goes on to explain that the term for the class of chemical compounds which releases protons into solution are called acids whereas the complimentary chemical group which accepts protons and neutralises them are referred to as bases or alkalis. The pH scale is that convenient version of the molecules involved and runs from 0 to 14. The pH of neutral, pure water as explained by McGee is 7. A lower pH is an acidic solution whereas a pH above 7 is a basic or alkaline solution.

Feiner, not to be outdone, explains that the abbreviation (or is it acronym ?) "pH" stands for a Latin term "potential hydrogen" or "potential of hydrogen". He then descends into an esoteric but strangely fascinating exposition explaining the negative logarithm to the base of 10 of the hydrogen ions. But I digress.

Does this pH business matter? I hear you say. The point is explained by Feiner when he states that the pH value has a significant impact on colour, shelf life, taste, microbiological stability, yield and texture of meat and meat products. The pH value of meat and the product generally lies between 4.6 (raw fermented salami) and 6.4. He explains that at a pH value of around 6.4 the meat is spoiled due to enzyme activity which produces many metabolic products such as ammonia. He explains that the process of fermentation, where the meat is allowed to be in relatively warm ambient temperatures results in a pH of approximately 4.6. The acidification changes the flavour of the product, and an acidic or sour flavour is obtained. He opines that the strength of the sour taste is dependent on how low the pH value falls. Harmful bacteria such as salmonella are inhibited at below a pH value of 5.5, accordingly by reaching a pH value of 5.2 or below the product is microbiologically stable due to acidification. He also explains that low pH values results in high amounts of moisture being removed from the salami , that this causes other changes, and due to acidification, the salami becomes more sliceable.

McGee also has something to add to this point. He states that fermentation occurs from 18 hours to 3 days depending on ambient temperature and sausage size until the acidity reaches 1%, the pH is at 4.5 – 5. High-temperature fermentation, he opines, tends to produce volatile acids with the sharp aroma, while low temperature fermentation produces a more complex blend of nutty aldehydes and fruity esters. He describes the latter is the traditional salami flavour. He goes on to state that fermented sausages develop a dense chewy texture thanks to the salt extraction of the meat proteins, their denaturation by the bacterial acids and to the general drying out of the meat mass.

The point therefore is this (I think). Traditional salami or air-dried sausage flavour is achieved using a process of ambient fermentation. The chemical processes involved are extremely complicated and best explained by Feiner or Dr Mc Gee if you are interested. One way to conveniently monitor what is going on inside the sausage casing is to monitor the pH value. A pH value of 4.3 – 4.6 or so is the time at which you can reasonably reliably assume that the fermentation process is complete.

The way to test this is to use a pH meter.

I do not apologise for the complexity of the foregoing, try reading Feiner and try to make sense of it yourself.

I am a river to my people.

ae) The knots

i) the butchers knot

It is difficult to describe a butcher's knot, or any knot for that matter, in narrative form. However let me try. First cut a length of string sufficient to encircle the meat. Place the meat in front of you in an East/West orientation. Pass the string under the meat so that one length is under the meat and one is over top. The ends of the string will be towards you. Pass bottom length under the top string from left to right, then over the top string from right to left. This will make a loop fashioned by the bottom string around the top string. Pass the end of the bottom string through the loop and under the top string and pull tight. This can now be tightened down onto the meat. The knot will tighten on itself as you pull. When it is tightened to your satisfaction make a simple locking knot around the top string to secure the knot. Cut both strings. This story is finished.

ii) the slipknot

Slipknots are very easy and are useful knots for general purposes. First cut a length of string sufficient to encircle the meat. Place the meat in front of you in an East/West orientation. Pass the string under the meat so that one length is under the meat, and one is over top. The ends of the string will be towards you. Using the bottom string make a long "U" shape with the bottom of the "U" towards you and the end of the string parallel to the top string ,away from you. Pass the cut end of the bottom string under both the bottom string and the top string to form a loop, repeat the process several times. Pull the bottom string towards you such that the loops close over the top string, this will make a hangman's noose type configuration which can be slid down and tighten around the meat. A locking knot is a good idea.

THE EQUIPMENT TUTORIAL

THE EQUIPMENT TUTORIAL

The purpose of this section is to describe the tools that you need to make artisan charcuterie. They are as follows:

a) knives: these are some of the knives that I use, from left to right a steel, a steaking knife, a straight edge boning knife, a curved semi flex boning knife and a heavy cleaver.

b) skewers of various types: starting from centre-left – a short awl, longer butcher's needles some with a hole for string, some without; a butchers needle with a handle, some long butchers skewers for holding meat while it is being rolled and trussed, wooden tapestry needles which can be used to weave a spiderweb of string around a large piece of meat for example culatello.

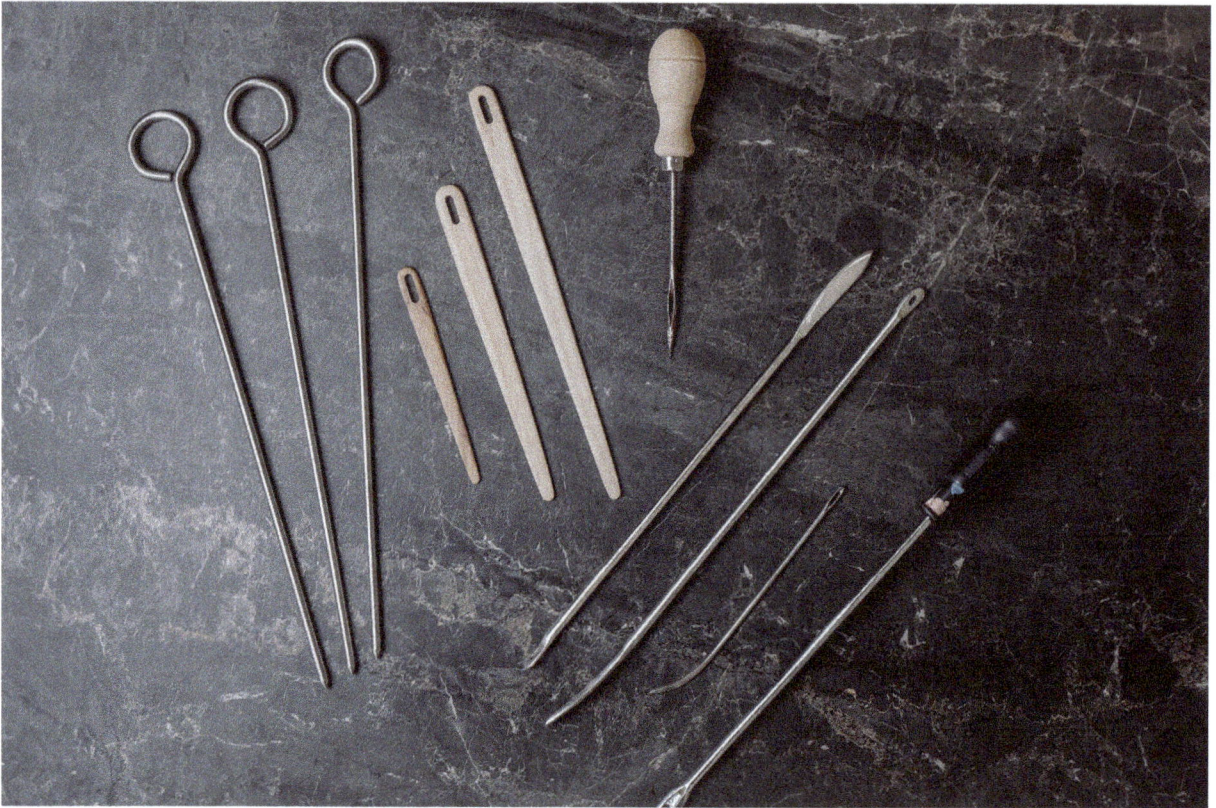

c) bone saw

d) string, netting, hooks and labels: I use white string for non-chili products and red string for those which have chilli, stainless steel hooks are useful for hanging products, small cardboard luggage tags are essential to record details of the product, the date on which it was hung and its original weight.

e) collagen wrap: it comes in various shapes and sizes and is useful for wrapping product which may dry out unduly.

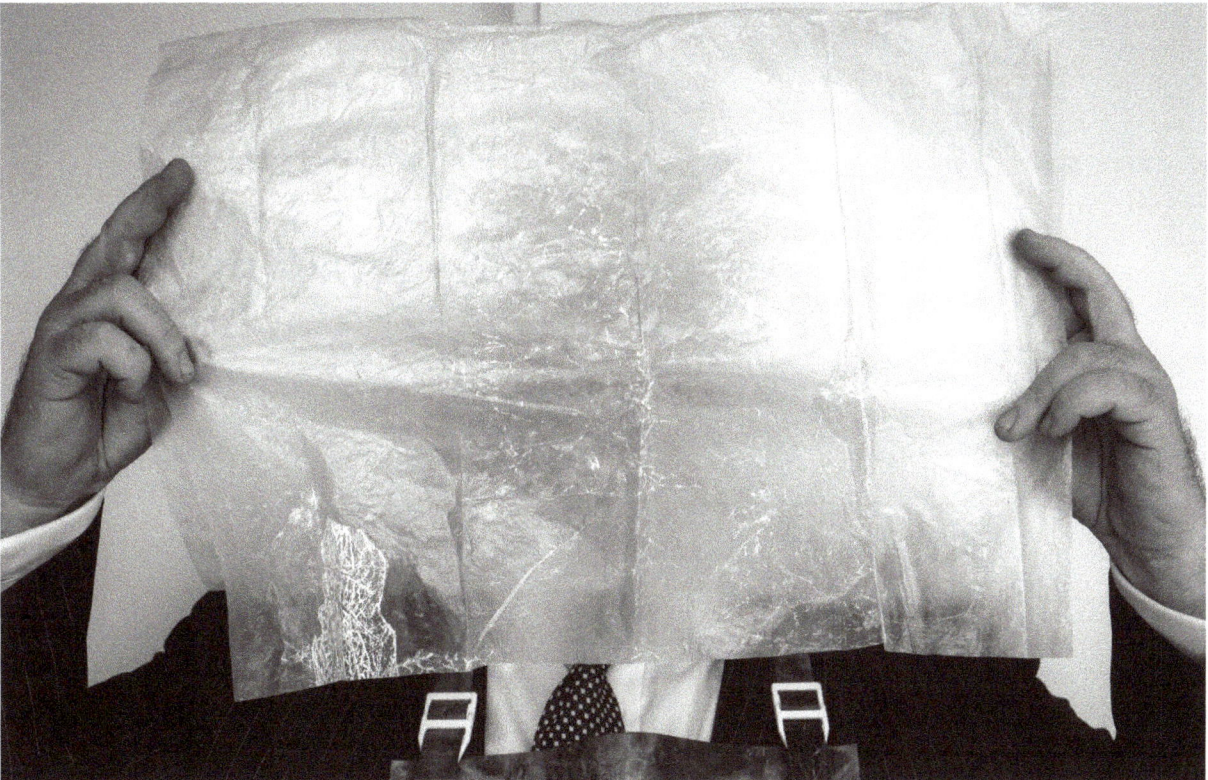

f) miscellaneous: from centre top, netting of various diameters, mincing plates or dies of various diameters, preformed dry casings of various diameters and collagen wrap. Always have a spare knife blade for the mincer in case of breakage.

g) stainless steel boning glove, boning hook and prickers for removing air from salami *(opposite page)*.

h) a good apron: either fabric or in this case, rubber.

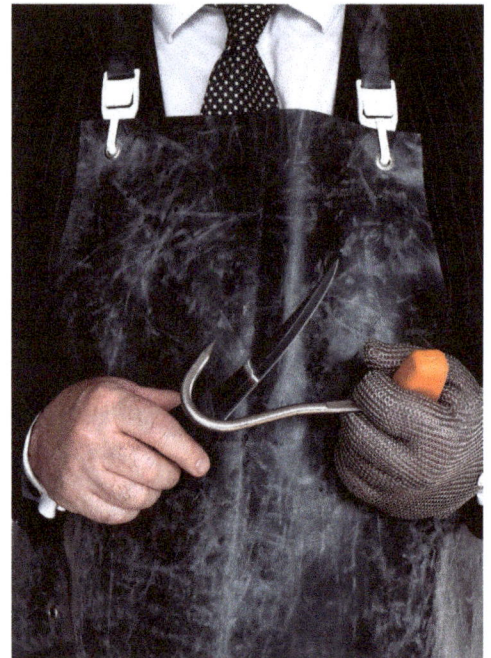

i) testing devices: from centre top, portable digital pH meter, Bluetooth digital temperature probe, handheld digital temperature probe, horse bone prosciutto tester, analog temperature probes, and wireless digital temperature probe *(below left)*.

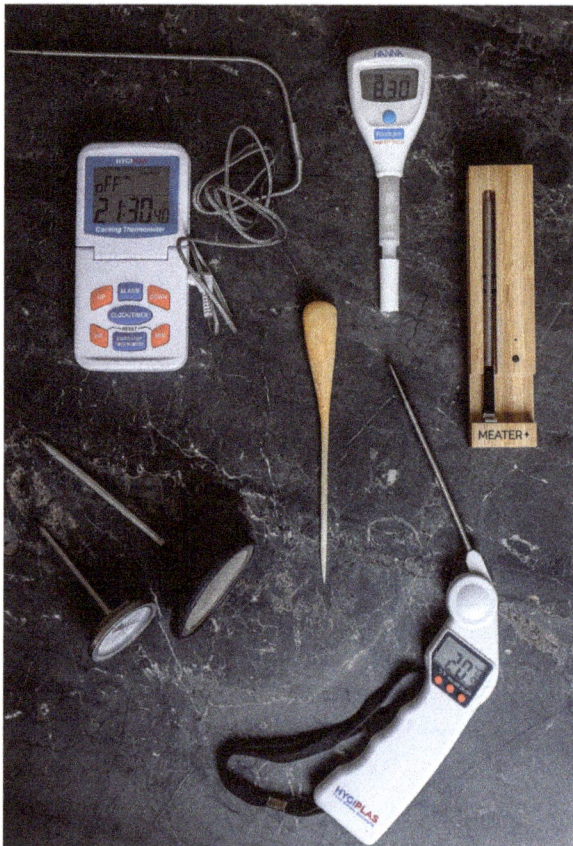

j) vacuum seal bags: preformed bags of various sizes and rolls in various widths *(above right)*.

k) other sharpening devices: whetstone's, oil stones and oil *(right)*.

l) spices: in convenient containers

m) meat presses of various types: these are useful for terrines, pates, pate en croute, fromage de tete, or pressed whole meat such as tongue, or ham.

n) vacuum sealer: very useful for precise cooking of, say, a porchetta de testa *(below left)*.

o) spice grinder and mortar and pestle *(below right)*.

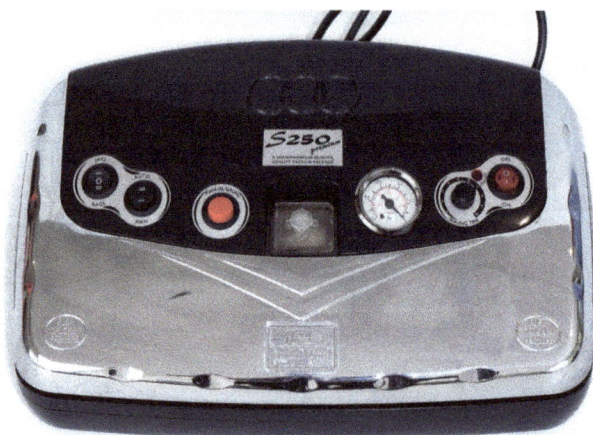

p) mincers

q) sausage stuffer

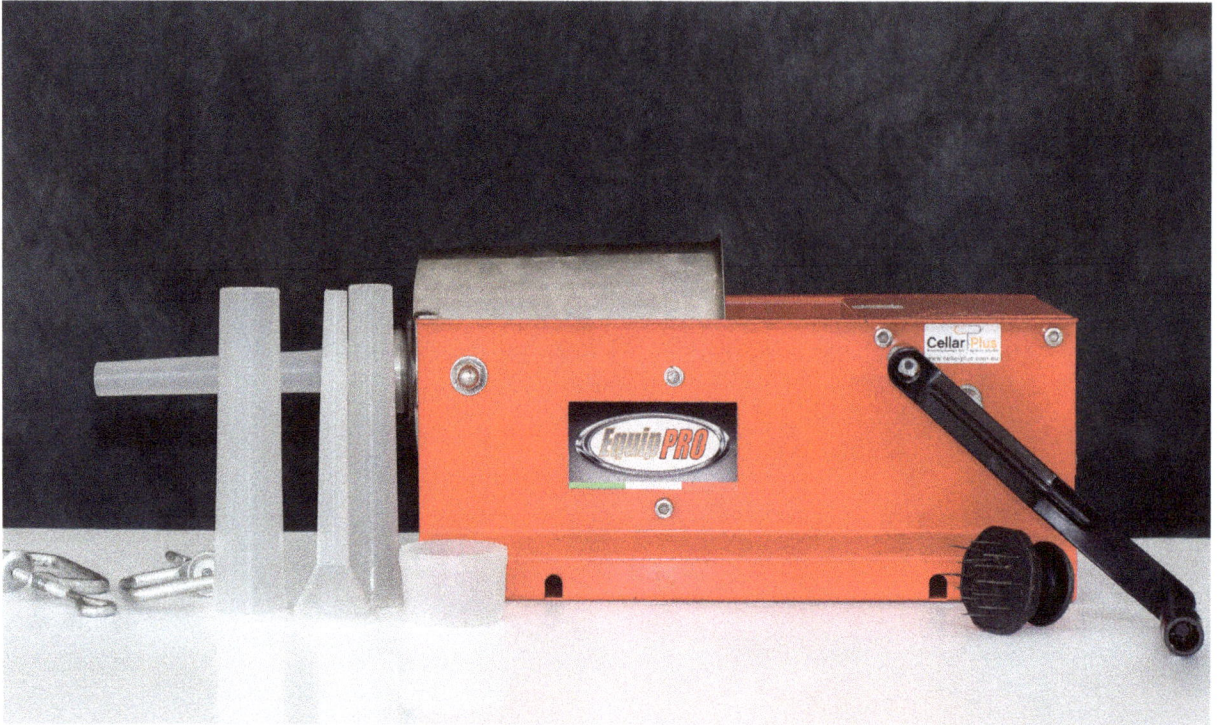

r) netting tubes - These are crucial for wrapping the meat in elastic netting

s) prosciutto stand - good to stabilse the prosciutto. They can be cheap or very expensive.

t) Salt, the critical element. From left to right - curing salt, coarse or rock salt, medium or flossy salt, and fine or table salt.

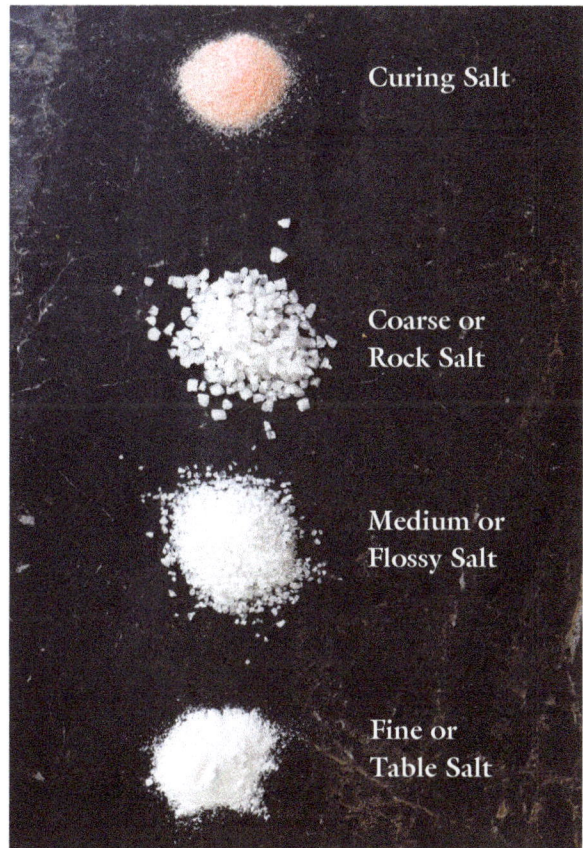

Curing Salt

Coarse or
Rock Salt

Medium or
Flossy Salt

Fine or
Table Salt

u) natural casings *(opposite page)* - These are preserved in salt and will last a very long time in the refrigerator. From top to bottom- sheep bung or appendix, ox bung, and another sheep bung. The bung is a one ended natural casing. Good for large diameter air dried sausage or soft products like ndjua or mortadella.

v) A meat or prosciutto press. Heavy steel with springs to compress the meat. Works best with boneless prosciutto unless you are The Hulk

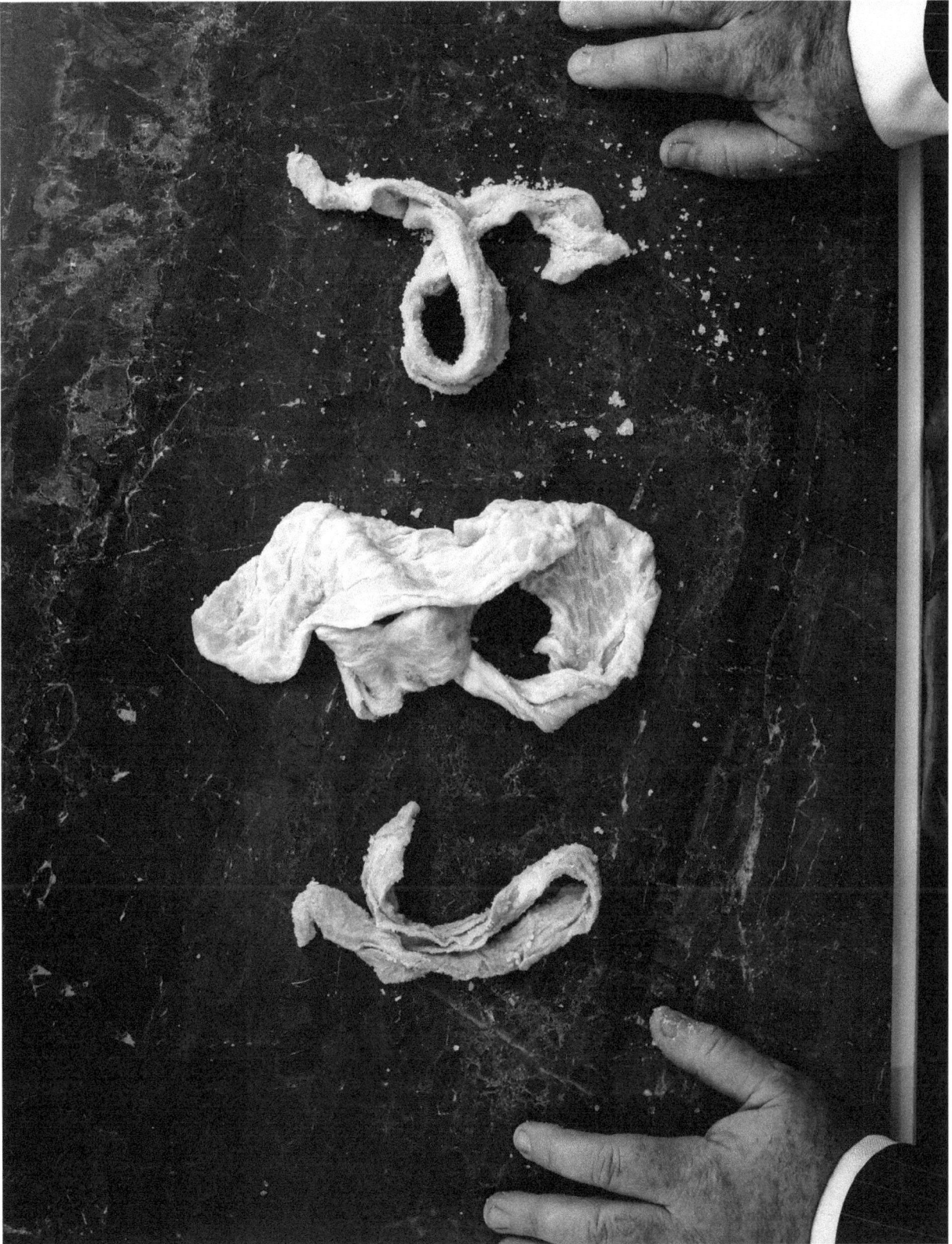

THE BUTCHERY STUFF

THE BUTCHERY NARRATIVE

A PORK CARCASS

At last, we get to the point of this book and the reason why I wrote it. It became apparent to me from the very beginning that this culinary backwater, so richly embedded in history, was all about preserving the abundance of meat which is achieved from a smallholder's livestock. In this case, the domestic pig. The domestic pig was kept from time immemorial as a food source but also as an animal which would thrive on waste food or the food which was not consumed by the human hosts. They are, I understand, relatively easy to look after, they eat most things, they occupy a small space, and as they say in the classics, everything but the squeal can be utilised. They are probably the perfect smallholder animal to be reared for meat, after the chook and probably the duck. The yield is significant, particularly if they are left to their own devices and to achieve significant dressed weights. This of course was the way that they were treated historically, the fatter, and heavier, the pig, the more desirable it was for the purposes of charcuterie production. As you may understand from my earlier observations in this book and the preceding two books on the subject, I am not so convinced about that. The other thing which should be mentioned is that the most economical way to approach charcuterie is by using a whole animal carcass or at least a half animal carcass. This way the butcher will sell you a whole or half carcass for the most economical rate per kilo. In this scenario you will pay the same amount for every cut of meat regardless of its market price. Let me explain further, pork belly is currently very trendy ,desirable and therefore very expensive. It is not unusual to pay $16 or $18 a kilo at the market for a cut of meat that, five years ago I would have paid $8 or $9 a kilogram for at the same market. The loin of the pig, of the boneless variety, is less desirable but one would still expect to pay in the order of $10 a kilogram at the market. The scotch fillet of pork, the so-called coppa, a reference to the Italian nomenclature, might be in the order of $10 or $12 a kilogram at the market. The leg, a less desirable cut in modern culinary observations, might be offered for sale at $8 or $9 a kilo, perhaps $ 6 or $7 on a good day at the market.

The offcuts of the butchery process, mainly from the shoulder and leg, form the foundation of mince which is, in turn, the essential ingredient for the purposes of making air dried sausages . This is offered for sale at the market for between $6 and $10 per kg, depending on quality.

 If you add these prices for the various cuts of meat and average them across the weight of the meat you will be paying more than the cost of purchasing a whole carcass or a half carcass of pork, the economy is clear.These are the economies of scale which applies to all purchasing, the more you buy, the less you pay on a unit price basis . A half pork carcass will cost about $8/ kg, a few years ago it was $ 5 / kg.

The head, trotters, bones, and skin are all desirable elements for the purposes of charcuterie and are effectively thrown in for free. Accordingly, if you have the capacity if not the fortitude to purchase a whole carcass or a half carcass then you are the beneficiary of the economies of scale and can afford to make risky decisions if not lose some elements by way of experimentation.

The easiest way to start is with a half pork carcass. If you want to double up on the quantities, then purchase a full pork carcass but instruct the butcher to split the carcass vertically down the spine. You can do this yourself, but it is logistically difficult if not physically a significant workout to do this at home. The butcher will do it with ease using his commercial circumstances.

The pork head is a vastly underrated cut of meat for the purposes of charcuterie. Do not overlook it, do not underestimate, and never, ever, acquire half a pigs head. A half pig head is more difficult to process than a full pork head. The benefits of acquiring a full pork head far outweigh the cost benefit of acquiring a half pork head. I will explain in due course.

Standby.

Therefore, my working assumption, moving forward, is that you have had the fortitude to acquire at least a half pork carcass and a full pork head.

The following is predicated on Vouz standing in front of a half carcass. Knife in hand. Poised like a leopard. Nimble as a gazelle. Vouz is strong. Vouz is beautiful.

Just like Moi.

Do not disappoint me on this. If you do, then there will be nowhere to hide.

Commit to this.

Moi has asked so very little of Vouz over the years.

Vouz owes Moi at least this much.

a) The three primal cuts

This book, being an instructional butchery treatise, is necessarily heavily layered with photographs and annotations on those photographs. The reason for this is obvious, it is extremely difficult to narrate instructions as to dismembering a pork carcass in the absence of some visual assistance. I often do this in classes, but it is with the assistance of and in the presence of, the recently departed. To do so in the absence of the recently departed is much harder. Allow me to try and do it in words but you need to match the words with the pictorial narrative with which we have taken so much care. Do not disappoint me on this.

You are standing in front of a half pork carcass. I like to arrange it in front of me with the head end to my left and the tail end to my right, this means that the limbs are facing away from you. This enables you to see the spine and the gaps between the vertebrae which are your target points for the initial dismembering of the carcass. The initial dismembering of the carcass is to render it into 3 pieces, the so-called primal cuts primal cuts comprising the forequarter, the loin, and the leg.

Thereafter each of these 3 primal cuts are further subdivided into desirable cuts for the purposes of charcuterie. I will deal with each in turn.

One simple rule must be adhered to from the very beginning. Use a very sharp semi-flexible boning knife for most of the work. Use this to cut flesh only. If a cut needs to be made through bone, then it should only be made with a saw. A commercial pig carcass will be of approximately 70 -80 kg in dressed weight. It is not a large or very old animal. In most situations a heavy steaking knife will be sufficient to cut through the gap between vertebrae. If it is not for you or you do not feel comfortable to do so, then use a saw.

Separating the forequarter is the first task. Count the ribs and mark the gap between the 5th and 6th ribs with your blade . Draw your knife through the flesh between the 5th and 6th ribs until you meet the spine and the gap between the vertebrae of the 5th and 6th ribs.

Use the steaking knife or a saw to cut through the spine between vertebrae number 6 and vertebrae number 5.

The reason for separating the forequarter between ribs 5 and 6, and vertebrae 5 and 6 correspondingly is peculiar to charcuterie butchery. Butchers will not usually do it this way. The reason is because in charcuterie one wants to maximize the length of the scotch fillet or coppa which is very desirable for charcuterie production and to maximize the length of the loin which is also desirable in charcuterie production. Each of these long muscles tapers over the other between vertebrae 5 and 6. Once you have made the cut between ribs 5 and 6 you can see in the profile the darker ruby red of the Scotch fillet and the correspondingly pale end of the loin in each cut. This tells you that you have made exactly the right cut and that you have maximized the length of each separate muscle.Cutting this way also maximises the size of the belly.

You now have the remaining part of the carcass which comprises the loin and the leg end. It remains to separate these 2 primal cuts. This is done by tracing the vertebrae where it curves down to the tail and counting back one vertebral joint. At this point you separate the leg from the loin section. Once again take a sharp knife to cut through the flesh up to the spine in line with the joint you have already identified. Using a heavy knife or a saw cut through that vertebral joint.

Therefore in a few economical and ninja like movements you now have created the 3 primal cuts which are essential for the preparation of charcuterie.

It remains to discuss the method to further dissect or subdivide each of the 3 primal cuts. Each is a different cut of meat; each has a different anatomical and skeletal structure. Each must be treated quite differently.

Vous est une charcutier (nearly).

b) The forequarter

The forequarter of the pig contains its most complicated skeletal structure and anatomy. There are several cuts of meat which are desirable for charcuterie purposes. The forelegs include the trotter, the scotch fillet, and the residual shoulder meat. Let me deal with them in turn.

The shank-The foreleg is attached to the body of the pig   by a ball-and-socket joint quite deep in the shoulder. The foreleg itself can have two uses. First it can be cut short close to the trotter and then reasonably high up where it joins the shoulder. The foreleg is then stripped of meat and becomes usable for sausage production. Alternatively, the whole foreleg can be removed from the shoulder quite high up. This requires a saw cut, the joint itself can be separated with a knife but it is quite difficult. This foreleg then, once removed and with trotter intact it can be tunnel boned. Care is taken to avoid piercing the skin, then separate from the bone, the bone is sawn off as close to the trotter as possible. This, once filled with a minced meat and spice preparation becomes zampone. This is generally poached and sliced in the style of a poaching sausage or cotechino.

The shoulder-This leaves the remainder of the shoulder which has several complex skeletal structures, the spine, the ribs attached to the spine, the scapula or blade bone and the residual part of the foreleg bone. The spine and ribs can be removed in one section. Alternatively, the ribs are sawn through about in the middle of the ribs this will expose the end of the foreleg bone and the scapula. The ribs and the ribs connected with the spine can then be removed. Care must be taken in exposing and removing the scapula for two reasons. First it is an unusual shape of bone which is flat on top but with a ridge underneath. It is therefore difficult to expose and remove. The second reason why care is needed is because a very desirable muscle or group of muscles is directly under the scapula. This would be called the scotch fillet in a beef carcass and is often referred to by its Italian name, coppa. This is a piece of meat which, when cured and dried, is referred to as capocollo. Care must be taken to ensure that it remains as intact as is possible.

The trim-The remainder of the meat in the shoulder is removed from the bone and diced. Its principal use is for fresh or air-dried sausage production. The reason it is useful for these products is because it has a very desirable radio of meat to fat, in the order of 80:20 or 75:25.

The products-The shoulder therefore produces very good trim which can be used for sausage production. It also produces capocollo, and zampone. The whole shoulder, minus the foreleg can also use to produce a whole piece of charcuterie, referred to by our Italian cousins as spalla. It is a bone in cured and air-dried product in the same vein as prosciutto.

Trust no one.

c) The loin

The midsection of the animal, often referred to as the loin section contains several parts which are useful. The boneless belly part is used for bacon, often referred to as streaky bacon, the loin and rib section is also used for bacon sometimes called back bacon. The loin, the circular muscle running along the spine and under the ribs is also used for lonza,bacon, kassler, or coppiette.

The loin-First separate the loin from the boneless belly, score a line with your knife parallel to the spine such that you can saw along the line and separate the belly, which will have a few rib bones, from the bone in loin section. The bone in loin can be treated several ways. If the spine ribs are removed the resultant meat can be cured and hot smoked to make bacon. I leave the bones and skin on. Once hot smoked the skin and bones can be removed and used for the purposes of flavoring soups and casseroles. If the spine is cut such that the ribs are no longer attached the bone in meat can be cured and hot smoked. This is the Austrian kassler or smoked pork chop.

The belly-Square up the belly piece and remove any rib bones. This can be cured and smoked to make streaky style bacon. It can be cured and air dried to make pancetta, the Italian unsmoked version of bacon. If the skin is removed the belly can be rolled, cured and air dried, this is rolled pancetta or pancetta arotolata.

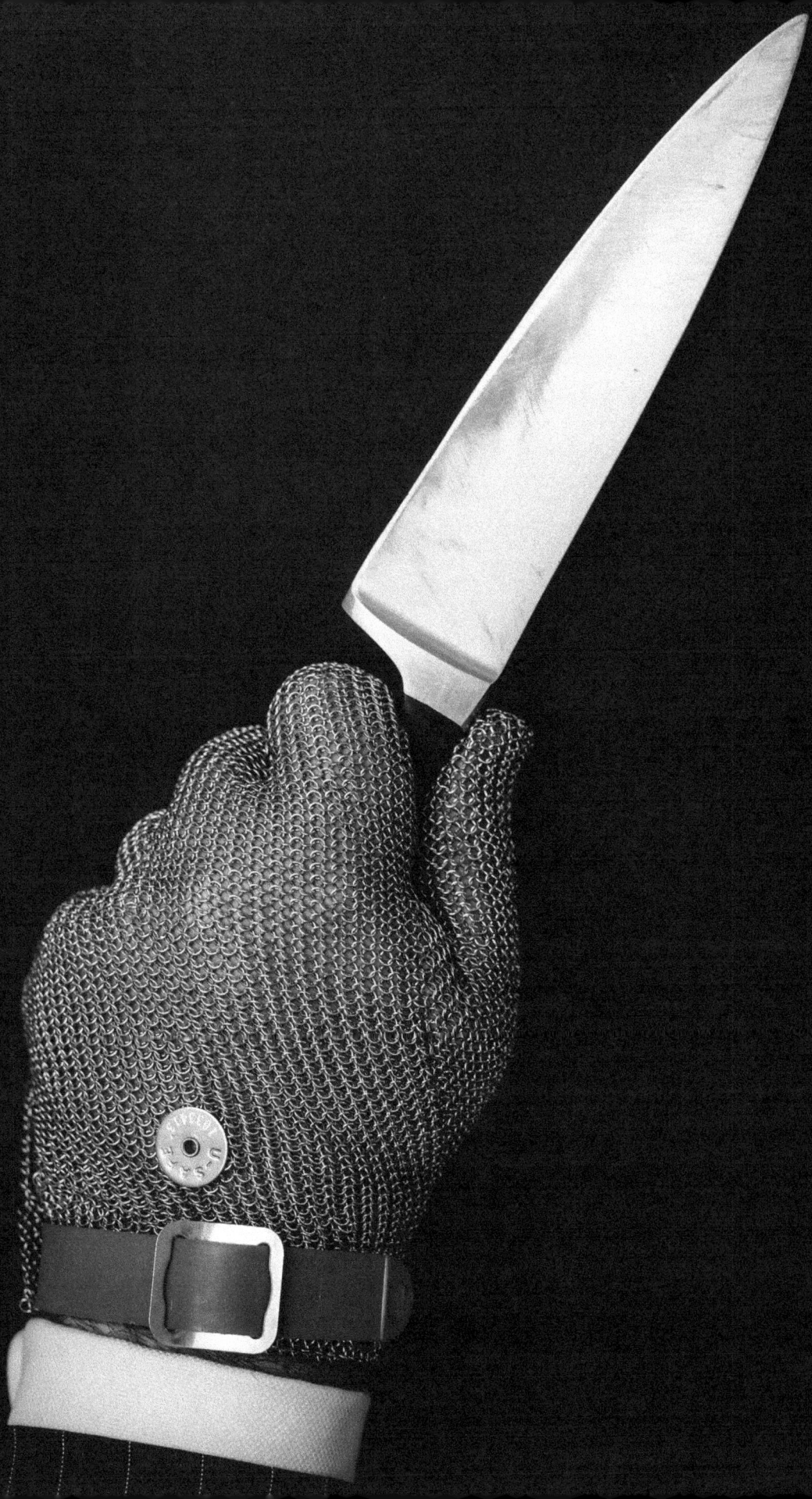

The fillet-The fillet or tenderloin is also to be found in this section, high up under the ribs. It can be removed and cured separately, to make a product referred by our Italian cousins as for filleto.

The fat-Some useful fat is to be found in the midsection. The hard, white, back fat is between the spine and the skin. This is very good for salami production. It can be removed and minced with the meat to create added fat content. It can also be cured separately to make lardo. A different type of fat is to be found inside the boneless belly, the flair fat is rendered and used in the production of terrines and pates. The intestines of the pig are encased in a lacy fatty diaphanous membrane, caul fat. You will only find this if you butcher your own pig, or the retail butcher is able to source it for you. It is used as a product to wrap around delicate minced meat preparations. It holds the product together and lubricates it as it dissolves during the cooking process. Some examples are faggots,a British offal meatball, or a similar French product the name of which I have forgotten.

The skin-This can be removed and for a variety of purposes. Finally minced and added to cotechino it contributes to its gelatinous properties. Salted and then cooked in fat, a process referred to by the French as confit, it becomes a condiment to be added to braises, confit de cauennes de porc.

The products-It can be seen that the midsection can offer several different products including many types of bacon, the tenderloin, the loin as a separate cut, the skin, and several types of fat.

d) The hind quarter

The hind quarter offers probably the most famous product in charcuterie, prosciutto. There are many other cuts however which should not be ignored.

The shank-The shank can be left intact together with the trotter and the whole leg used for prosciutto. This is my preferred use of the leg. If it is cut to produce a short leg, then its use is mainly for trim to be added to sausage and salami production.

The leg-The next step is to remove the residual hip bone where it connects to the femur, the long bone running down the leg. The hip bone takes some butchering to remove because it is an unusual shaped bone, and there is a tendon connecting the hip bone to the ball joint of the femur which is buried deep in the joint. Once removed the cut surface of the leg needs to be trimmed to remove messy or raggedy bits of meat which might provide convenient hiding places for nasty bugs. The ball joint of the femur is traditionally well exposed. An important point is to ensure that there is no blood left in the three main arteries which traverse the leg. The femoral artery tracks close to the femur and is the largest. The other two arteries are on either side of the femur. In commercially prepared pork it is unlikely that you will find much residual blood, domestically butchered pigs however can be a different matter. If not removed the blood can putrefy and spoil the meat from inside. The method of removing the blood is to push down very heavily and move forward from the shank end to the cut end. You may see a small amount of blood or frothy blood emerge from the femoral artery and the other two arteries. Keep doing this massaging until no more blood is observed. Wipe away any blood with a paper towel. Whilst on the subject of prosciutto I return to the issue of removing the shank or not. I have stated that it is my preference to leave the shank and trotter attached to that leg for decorative purposes. However, you may not have the available space to air dry a whole leg of pork together the shank and trotter. If so removing the shank from the leg is the only way to go. If this is done, then you are opening another avenue for nasty bugs to enter your meat during the long period of air drying. Be sure that a mix of salt and curing salt is worked hard into that cut end of the meat to close the door and deny the bad bugs an opportunity to spoil your hard work.

The rump-Depending on where the leg section has been separated from the midsection there may be quite a sizeable portion of the rump attached to the leg. This can be removed and cured up as a bone in piece of meat, referred to by our Italian cousins as rumpetto. In commercially sized pigs this piece is not large enough in my view to the treated separately. The very large, so-called prosciutto pigs present a different proposition.

Culatello , fiocco and noix de jambon.

As an alternative to prosciutto, the bone can be removed from the leg and the larger muscle on one side separated from the smaller muscle on the other side. The larger muscle is rolled and tied into a roughly teardrop shape; this is culatello. The smaller muscle is tied and becomes fiocco. Each is essentially a boneless prosciutto, a cured and air-dried product from the pork leg. Culatello appears to be more revered in Italian culture than prosciutto and is often cured for several years.

Yet another variation using a boneless leg of pork is to separate the many muscles contained within the leg along the seams. This produces a variety of different shaped muscles which are cured up and air dried in the same manner as prosciutto. Care must be taken to avoid the drying out, but they are a much quicker way to achieve a very similar product. This is referred to by the French as noix de jambon, literally ham nuts.

There is no courage without fear.

Welcome to the badlands.

As much as I do not like it, and I do not like it at all, charcuterie is often synonymous with the bad bits. Blood, organs, fat, skin, and everything else in between that I do not care to mention. There is no reason in modern times why charcuterie should be associated with the nasty bits. The association, in times past, was obvious. Protein was scarce, it needed to be preserved and conserved in all its iterations. The winters were long and cold. There was no refrigeration, freezing, canning, cryovac or anything in between. Life was hard. The fatted pig was a resource which would take the family or the village through the winter and into the relative fecundity of spring, summer and autumn. Accordingly, it would not be an accurate treatise on the subject to ignore what I consider to be the nasty bits and the unpalatable bits. However, there are some of them that I have some tolerance for if not some appreciation .However if you are looking for a book about offal then you and your evil thoughts need to go elsewhere.The pig head is a different matter, however.

The price of freedom is eternal vigilance.

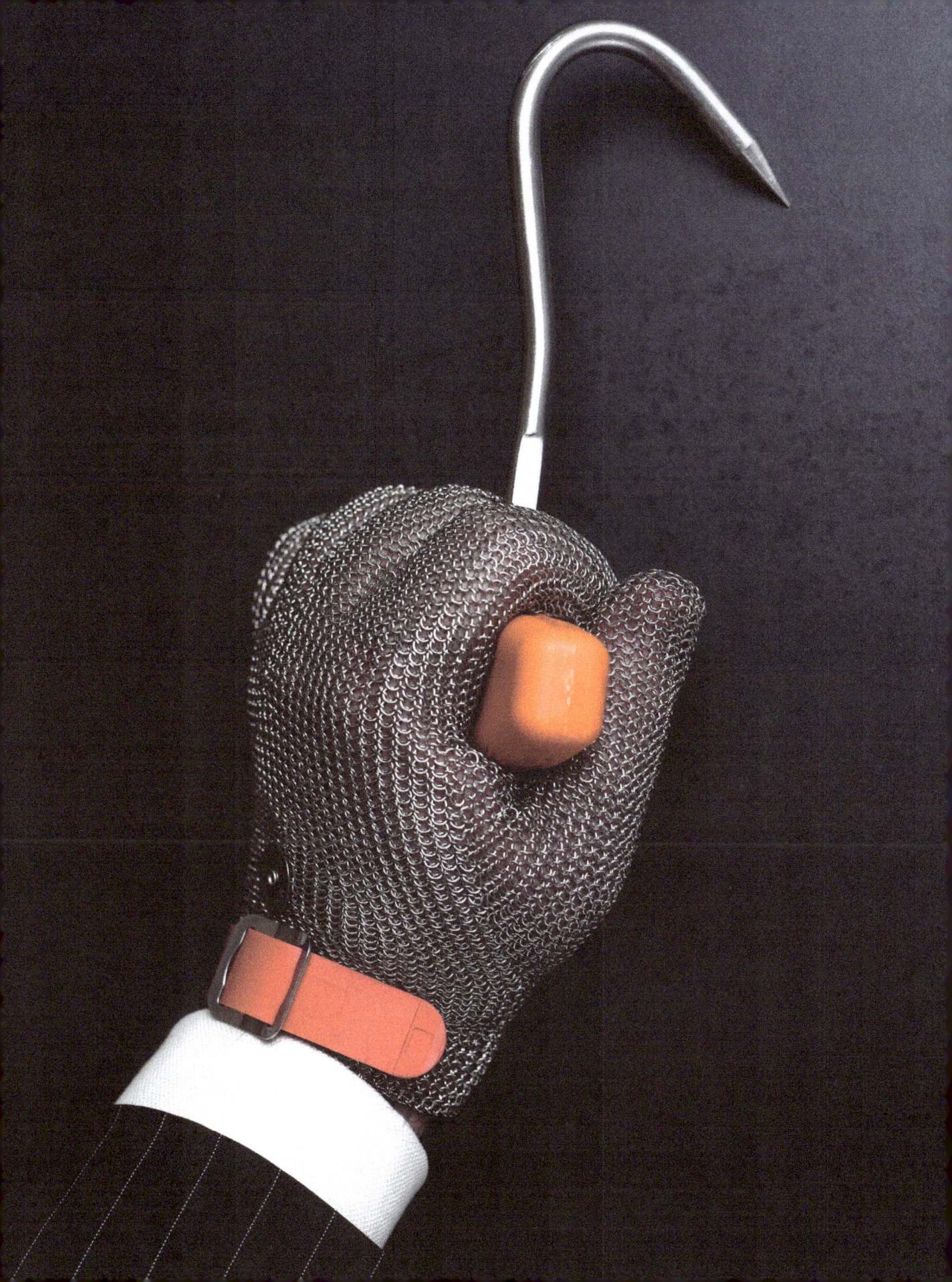

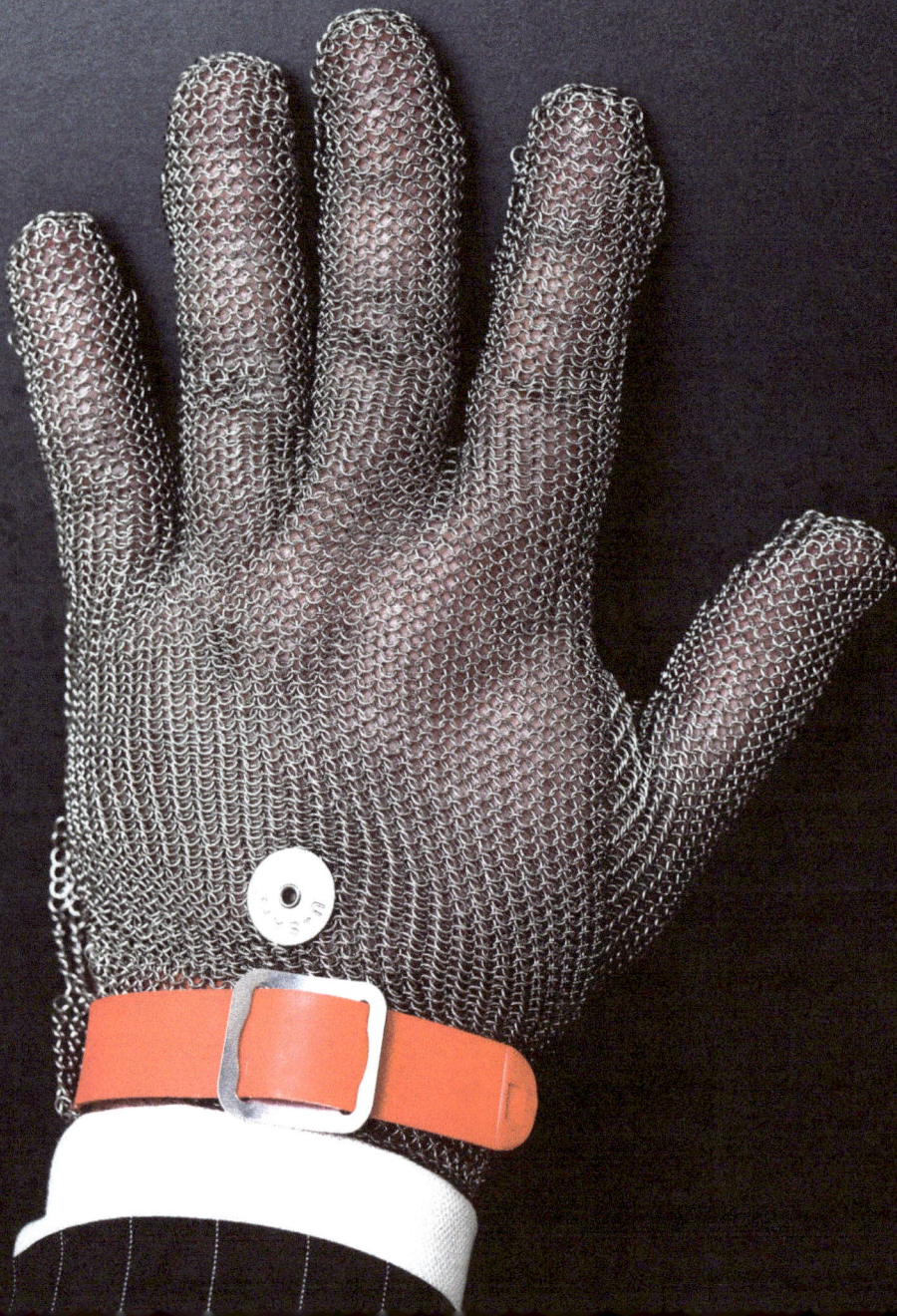

The head

A pig's head is a vastly underutilised resource. I do not why this should be so. The people who propound this culinary backwater are usually those who also extole the virtues of the nasty bits. The nastiest of all bits is the head. It is full of glands, bones, tongue, eyeballs, and ears just to name a few of the obvious and nastiest bits. Why would anyone think that they could make something remotely palatable if not enjoyable from the head. Indeed, it usually includes the brain and in one instance early on included the bullet which had dispatched the pig! On no view can anyone say that the pig head is a desirable part of the animal, I hear you say? Well, dear readers, I have news for you. The pig head is a good part of the animal. It is often discarded or used in pet food. It should not be discarded. It costs only a few dollars at the market and will create, with proper attention, love, care and all the other stuff, some good products. For example, fromage de tete, brawn, tete de porc farci, porchetta de testa, to name a few.

I have never met a pig whom I did not like.

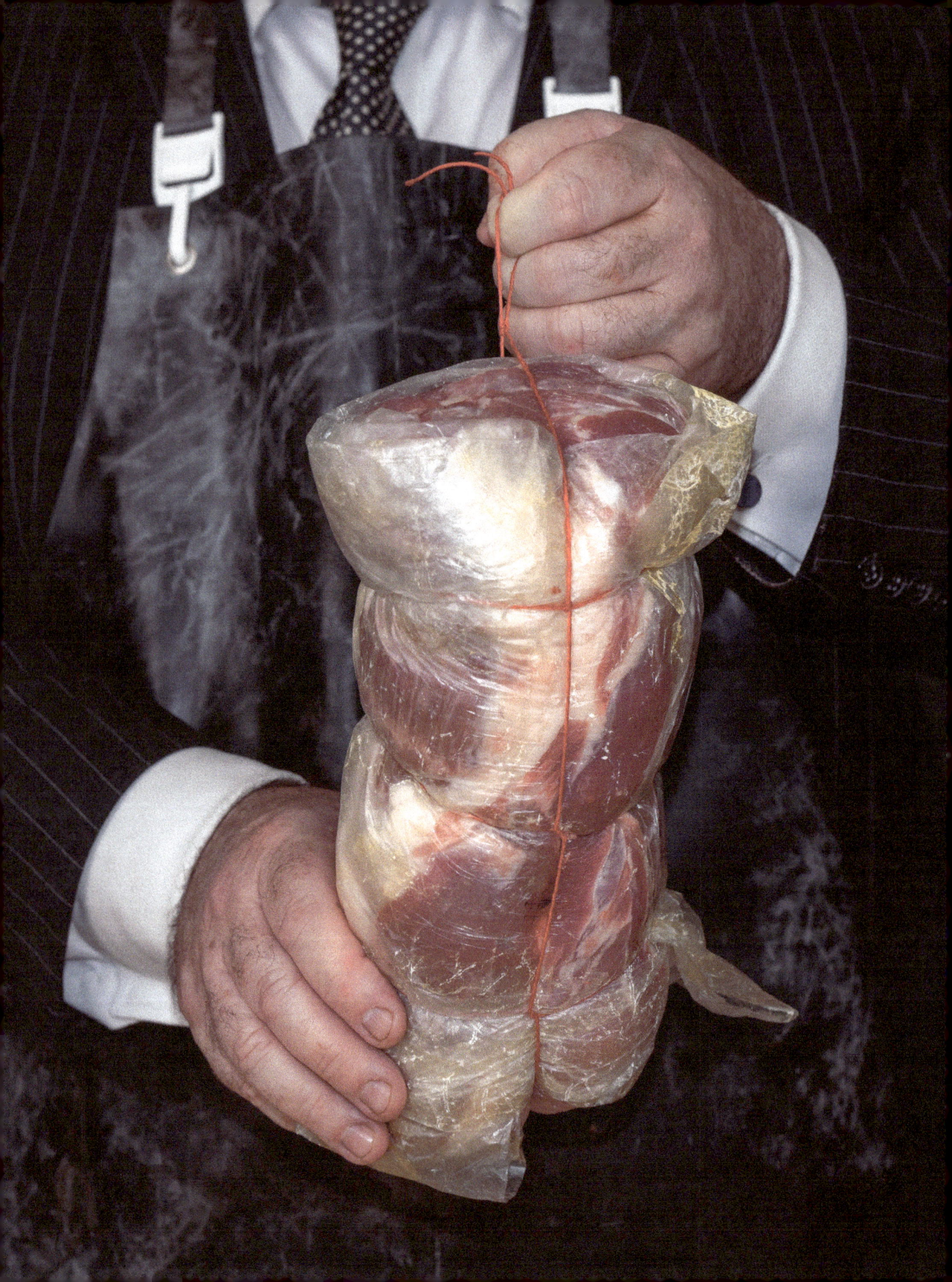

THE BUTCHERY PICTORIAL

THE BUTCHERY PICTORIAL

What follows is a brief narrative of how to go about basic butchery cuts for the purposes of various charcuterie production. The narrative is supplemented by images which hopefully make the point notwithstanding the clumsy narrative.Follow the pictures.

Remember, sharpen your knife every few cuts. It is easier to keep a sharp knife in good condition than to bring a dull knife up to a good edge. It is also much easier to cut with a sharp knife, and safer also. A blunt knife requires more effort and therefor more risk of cutting yourself.

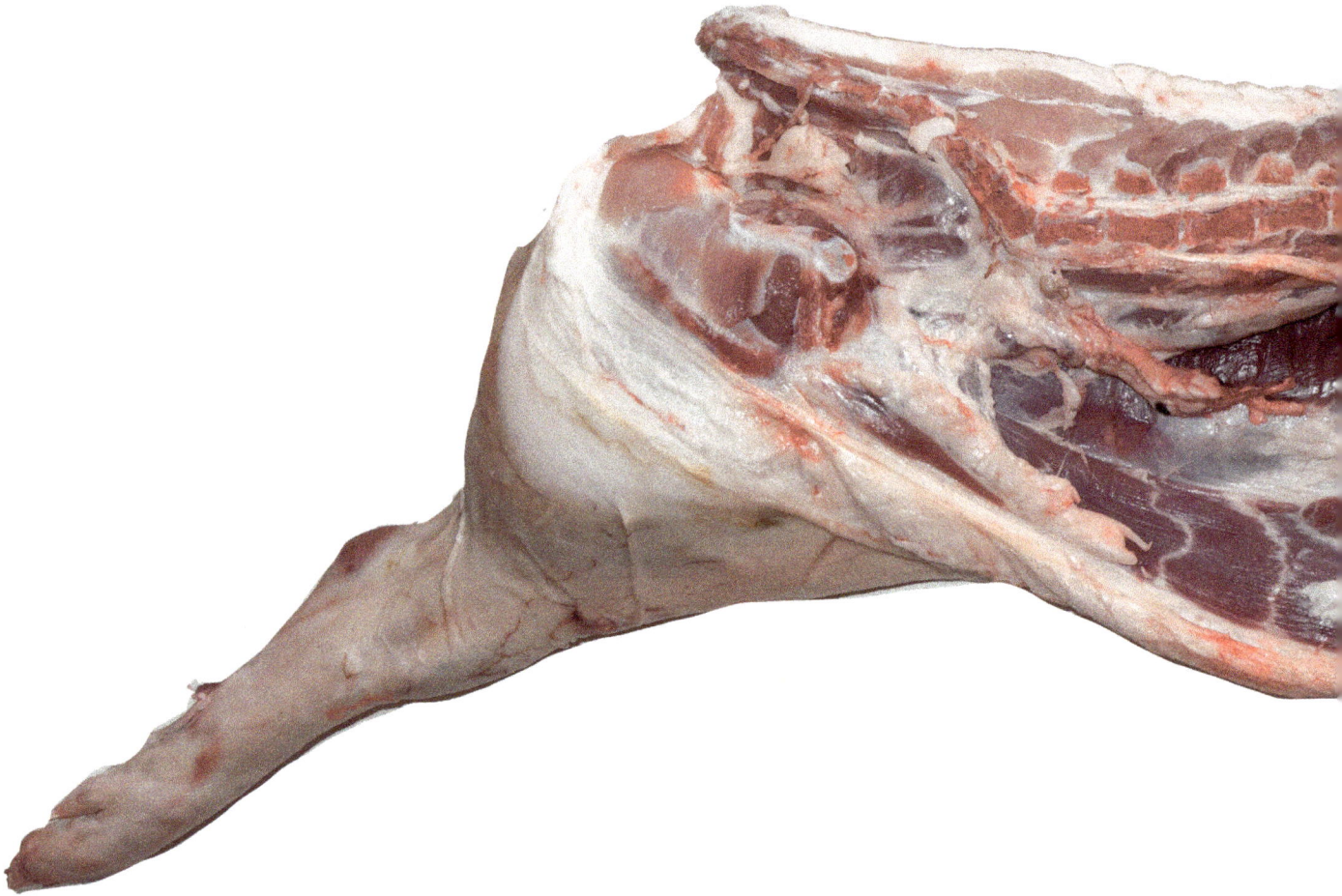

THE THREE PRIMAL CUTS

Start with half a pig. A commercial pig will be about 75 kg dressed weight, which means that the half carcass will weigh approximately 35 kg without the head. The head will be treated separately.

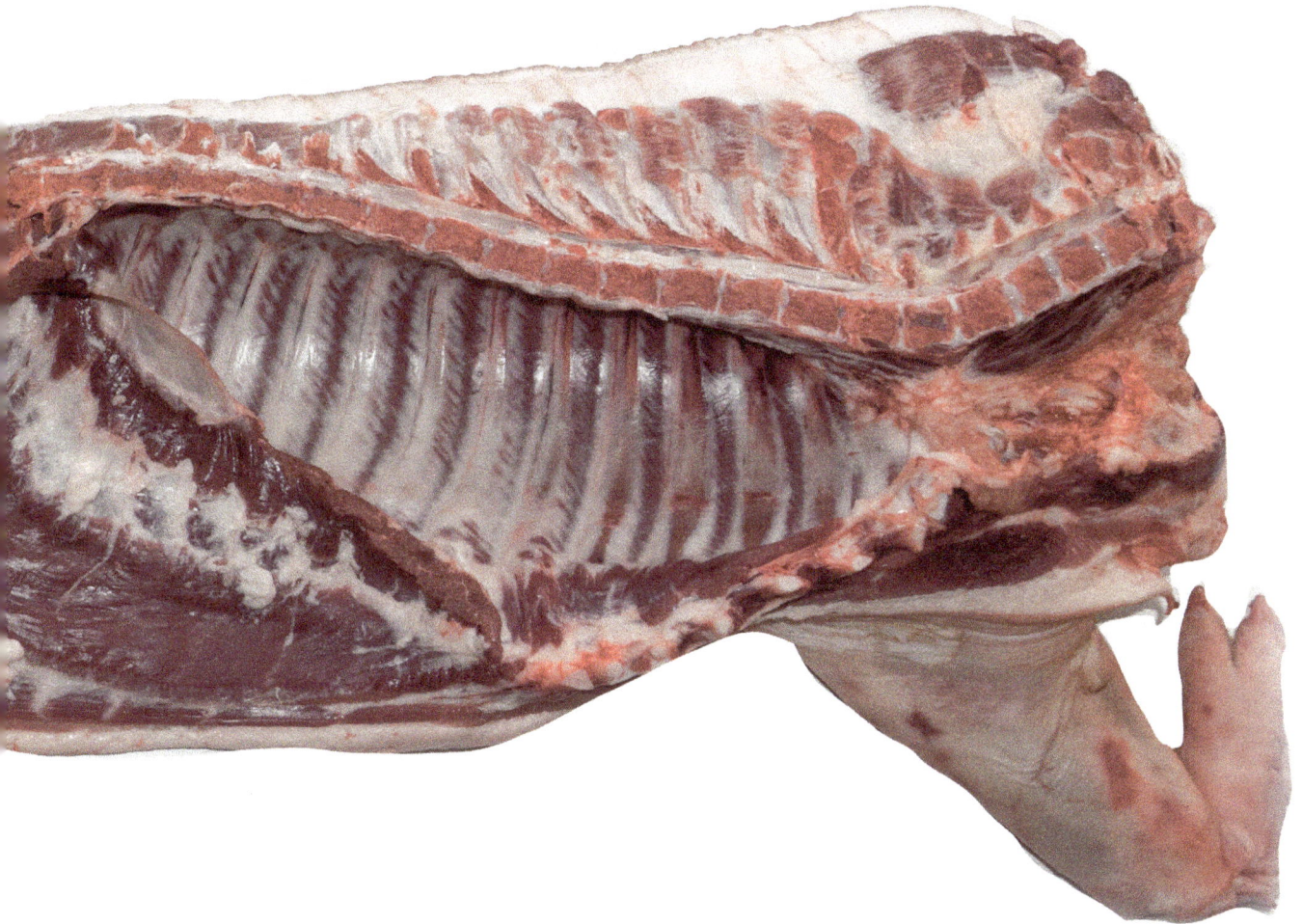

It is easier to approach the task from the cut side so that one can see the vertebrae and where to cut.

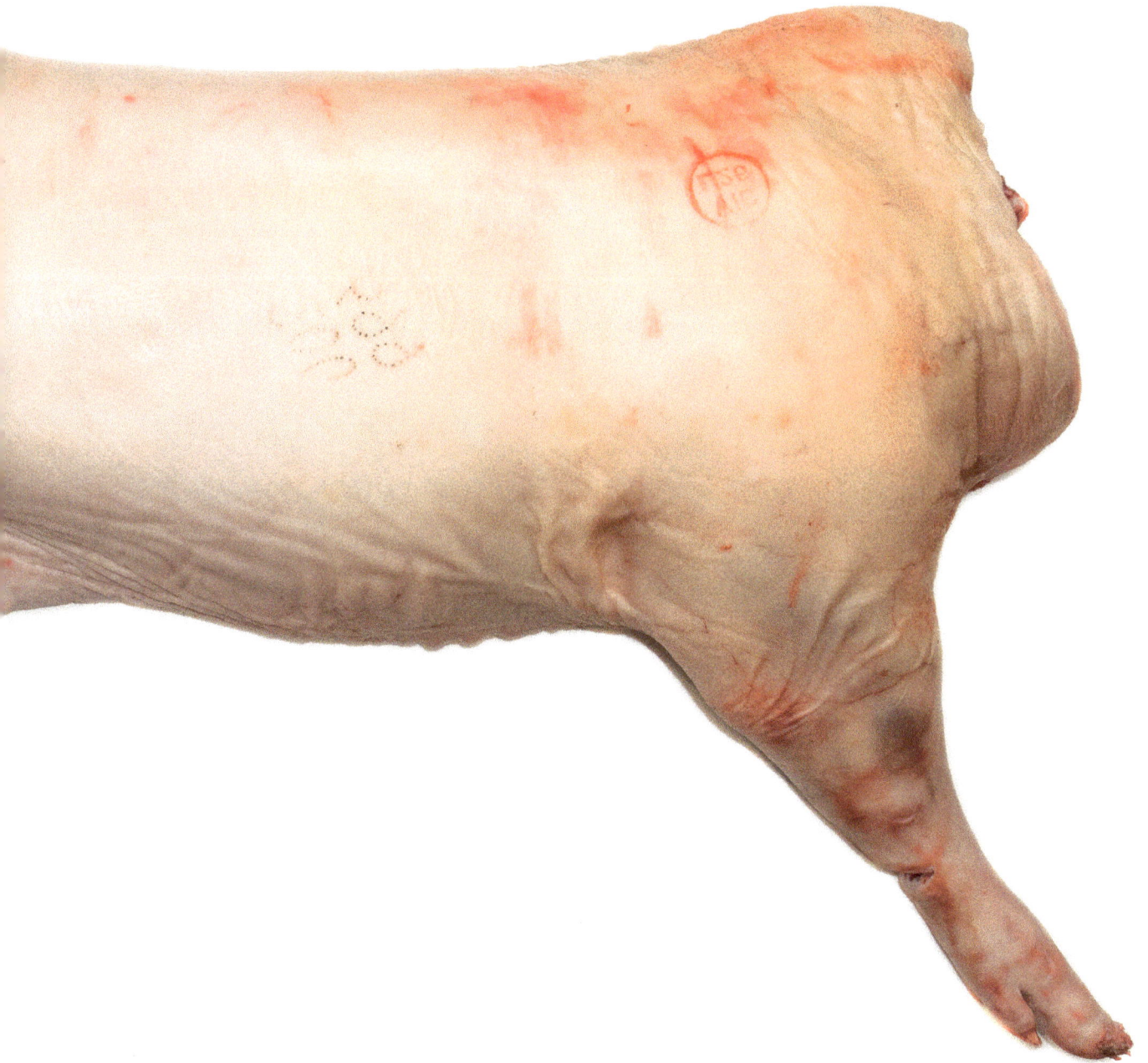

The first task is to separate the shoulder from the carcass. The first cut is between the fifth and sixth ribs. This is easily located from the cut side.

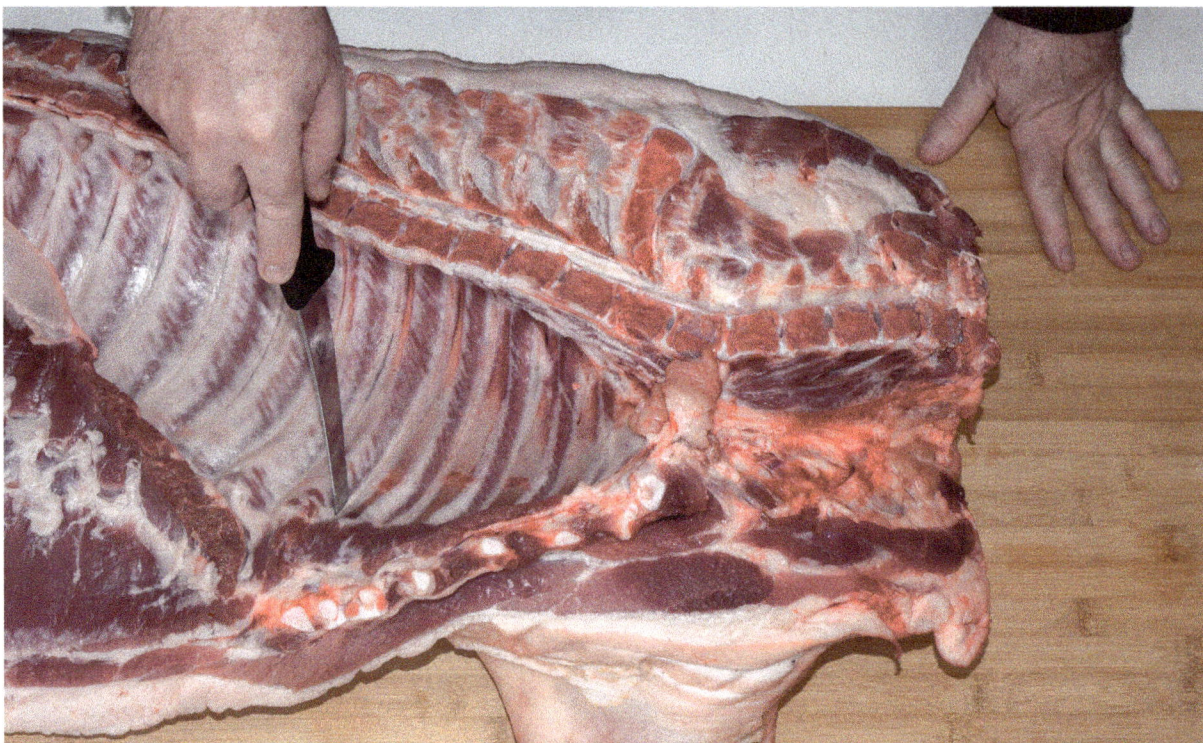

It can also be located from the skin side in the depression where the foreleg joins the belly.

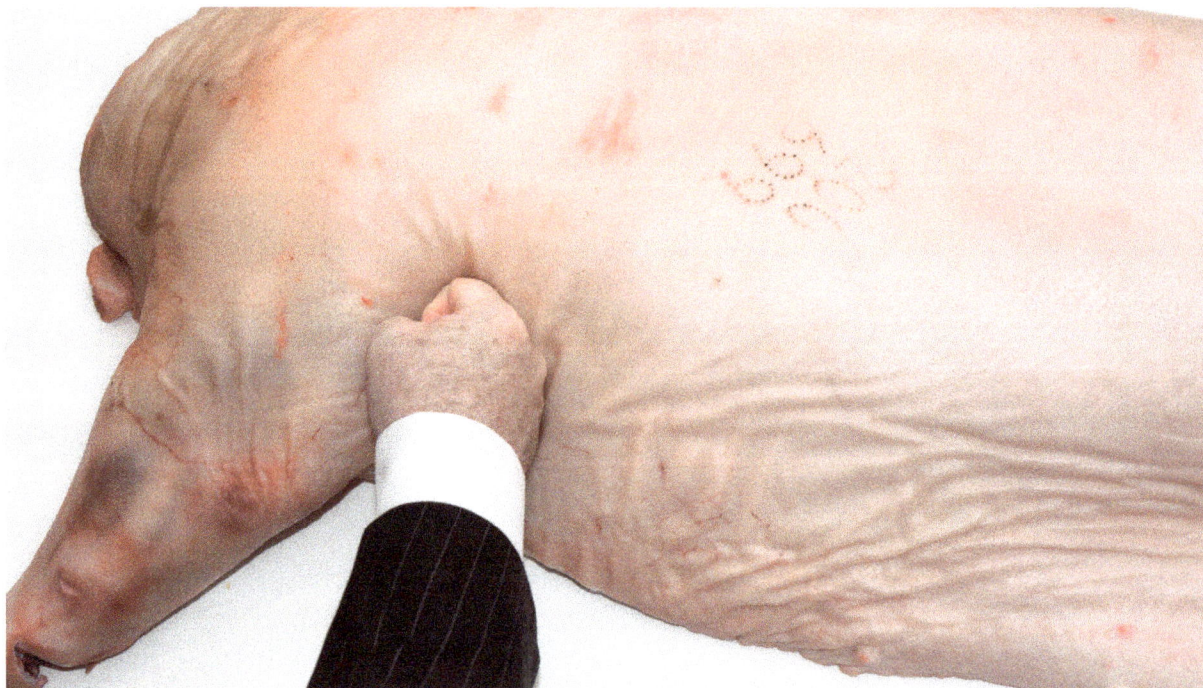

Cut through the belly and between the fifth and sixth ribs. You may need to use a bone saw to cut through the breastbone or sternum of the animal. Use a knife when cutting anything other than bone.

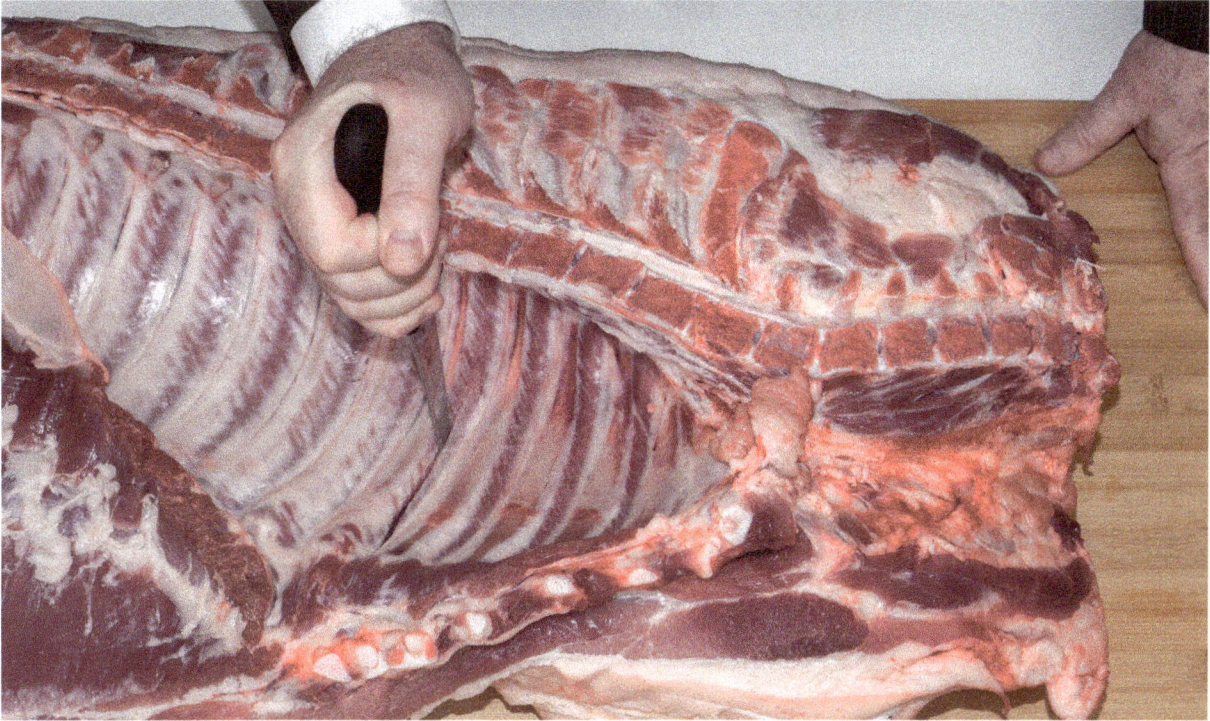

Cut through the vertebrae using a bone saw.

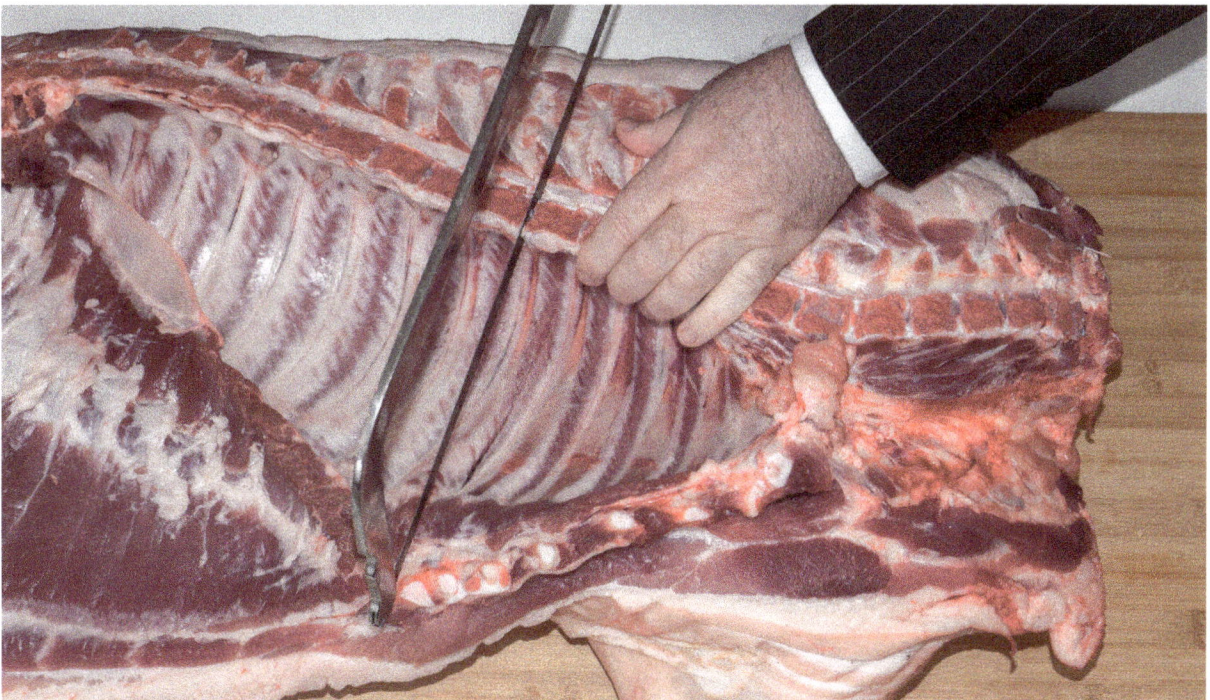

Once the bone saw has cut through bone return to the knife to cut through the meat.

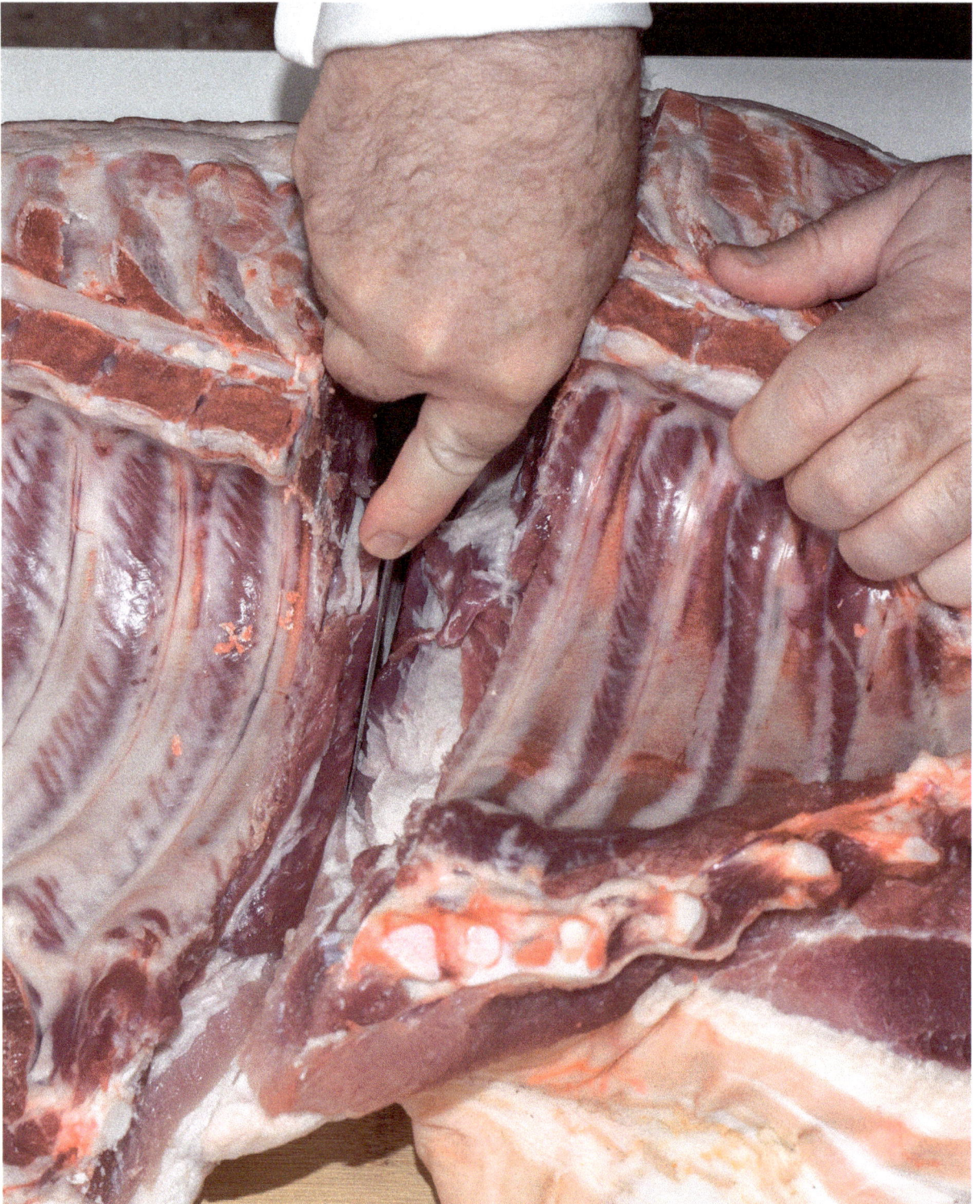

Now that the shoulder is separated you can see the point of cutting between the fifth and sixth ribs. It is to maximise the muscle within the shoulder called the coppa by the Italians, the pork butt by the Americans and the pork Scotch or neck by everybody else in the known Universe. It is also to maximise the pork loin. In other words, both those muscles crossover at approximately the location of the fifth and sixth ribs. The pork neck muscle is the darker colour because it is more hard-working and contains more myoglobin, the pork loin is the paler muscle which is less utilised and contains less myoglobin. Cutting at this point also maximises the belly, a good thing.

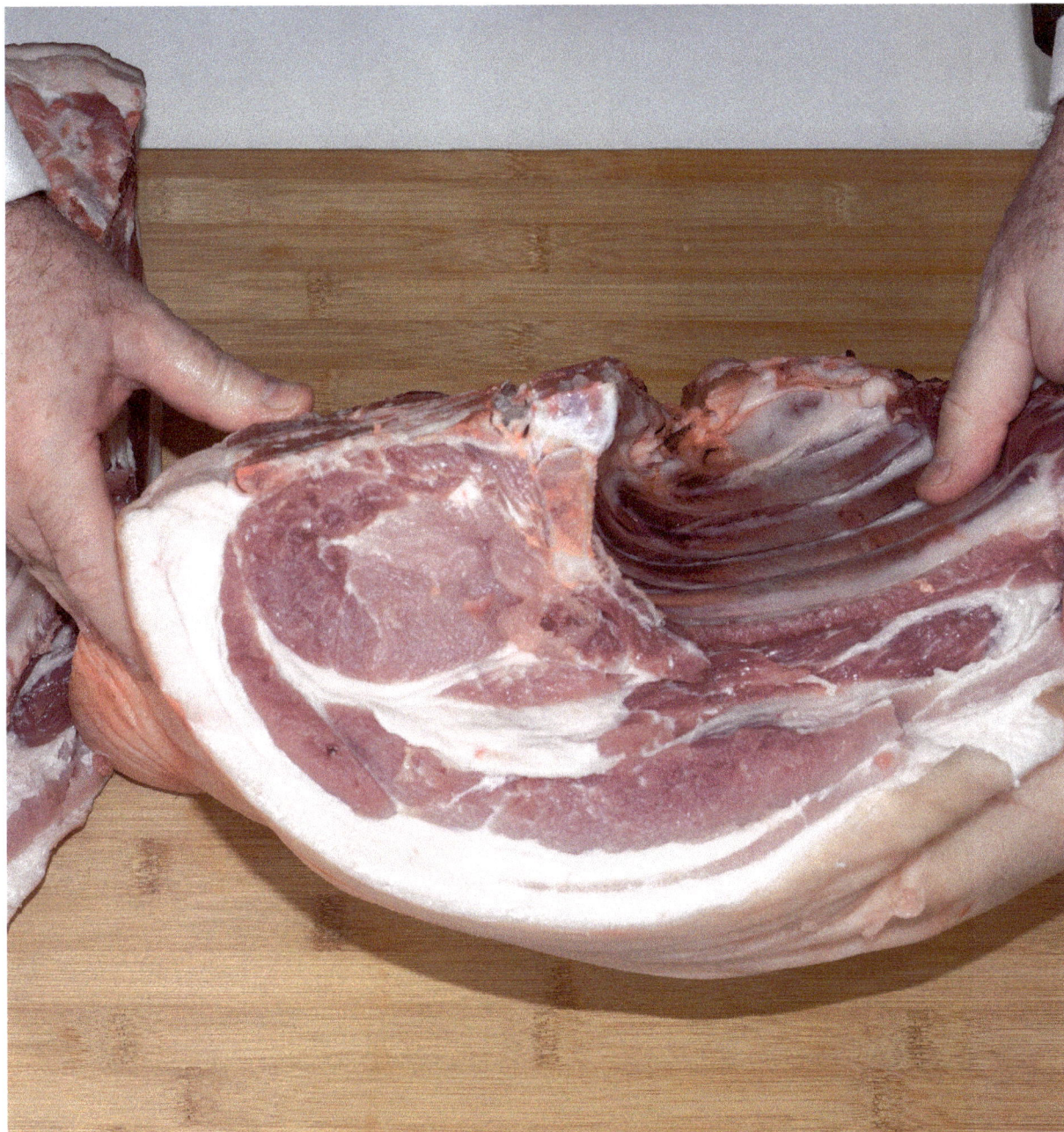

Remove any remnants of the diaphragm, this will be used for sausage production or mince.

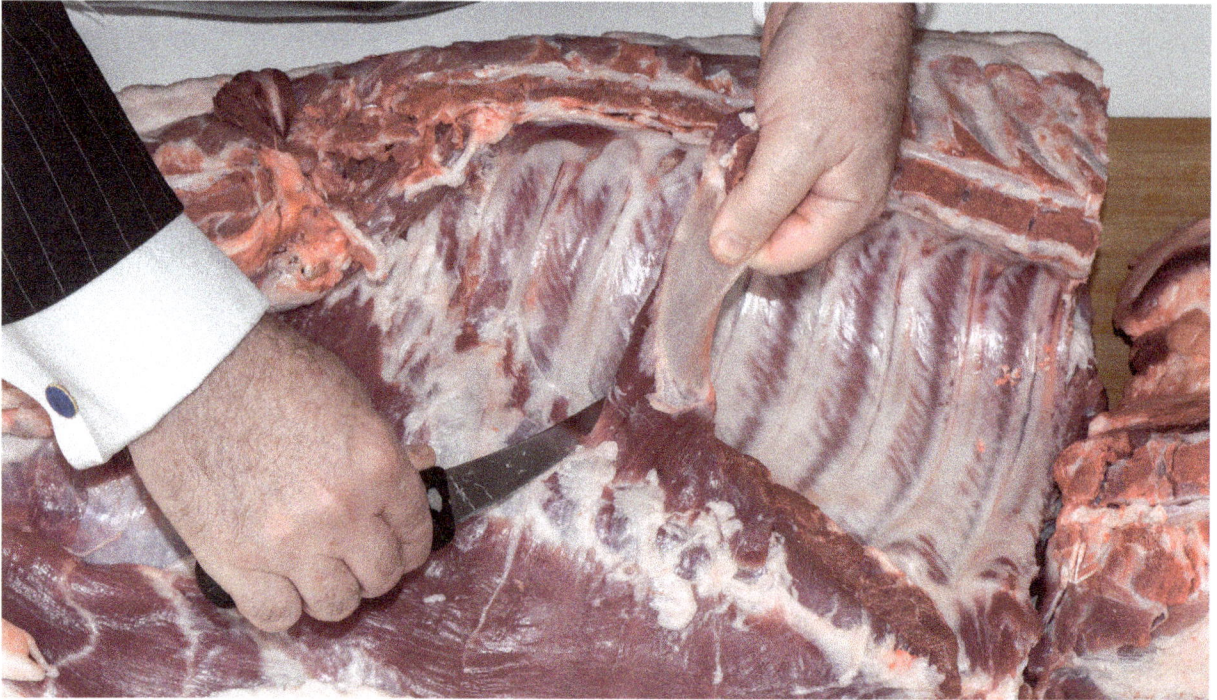

Remove the fillet or tenderloin as it is described by our American cousins from under the spine. It is thickest at the head end of the animal and tapers down to a fine a point as it gets to the hip. This can be used for charcuterie production in the form of being air dried on its own, minced for the making of air-dried sausages or included as a whole piece inside an air-dried sausage. Quite often however I grill it for lunch while doing the butchery.

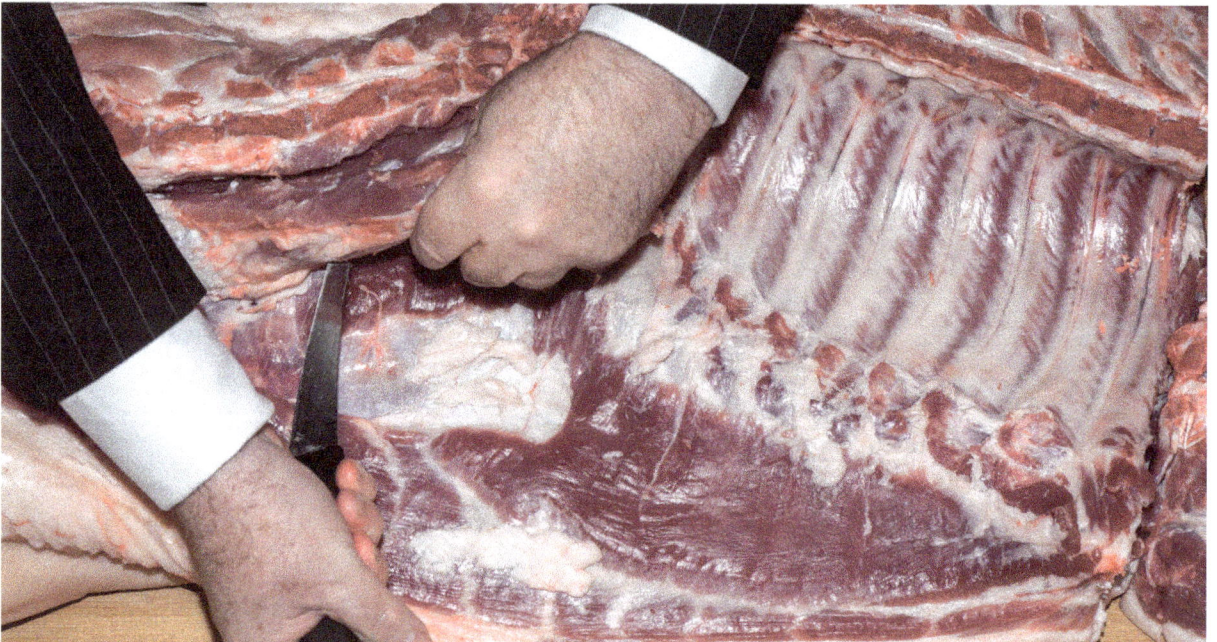

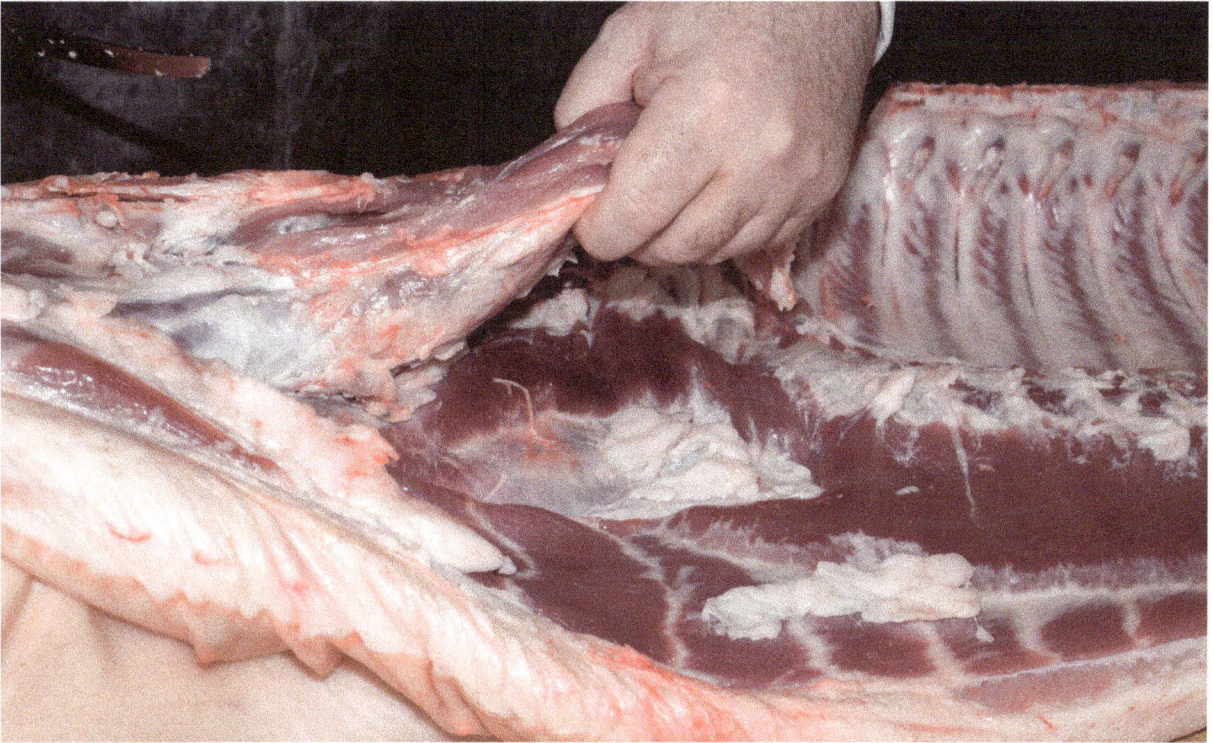

Now separate the leg from the carcass. This is best done by locating the point where the spine curves down and forms the tail. Count back one vertebra towards the shoulder from that point. This is the place to cut. Again, use a knife to cut through meat and the bone saw for everything else.

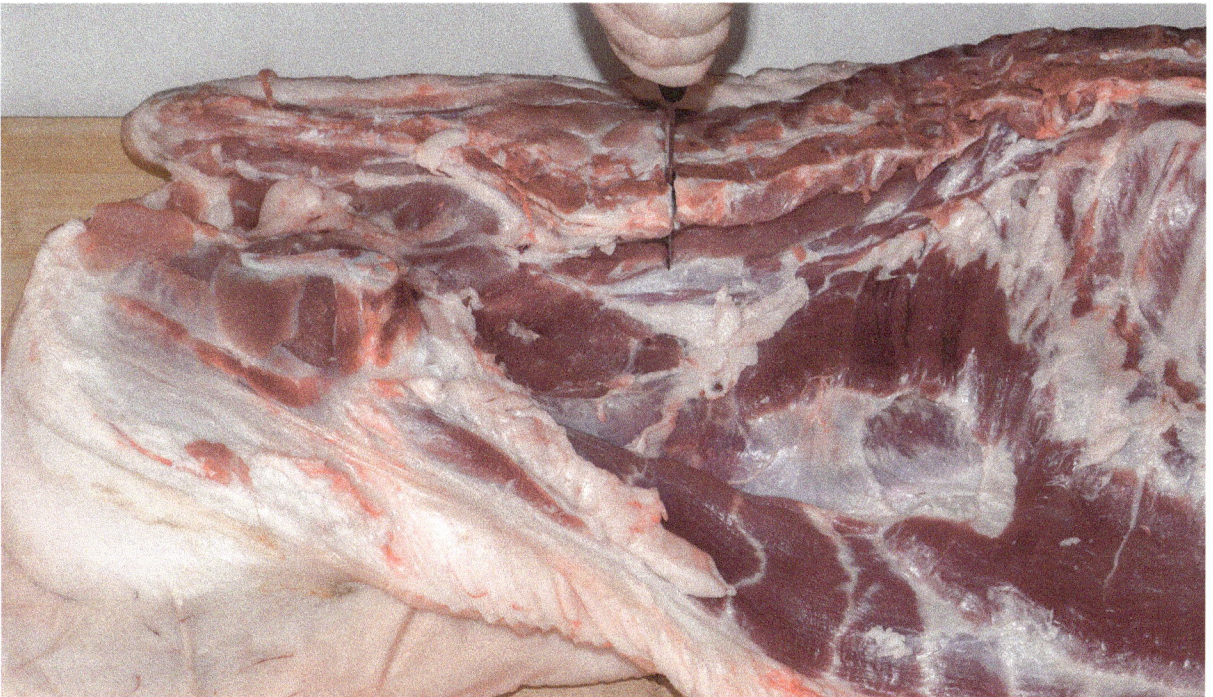

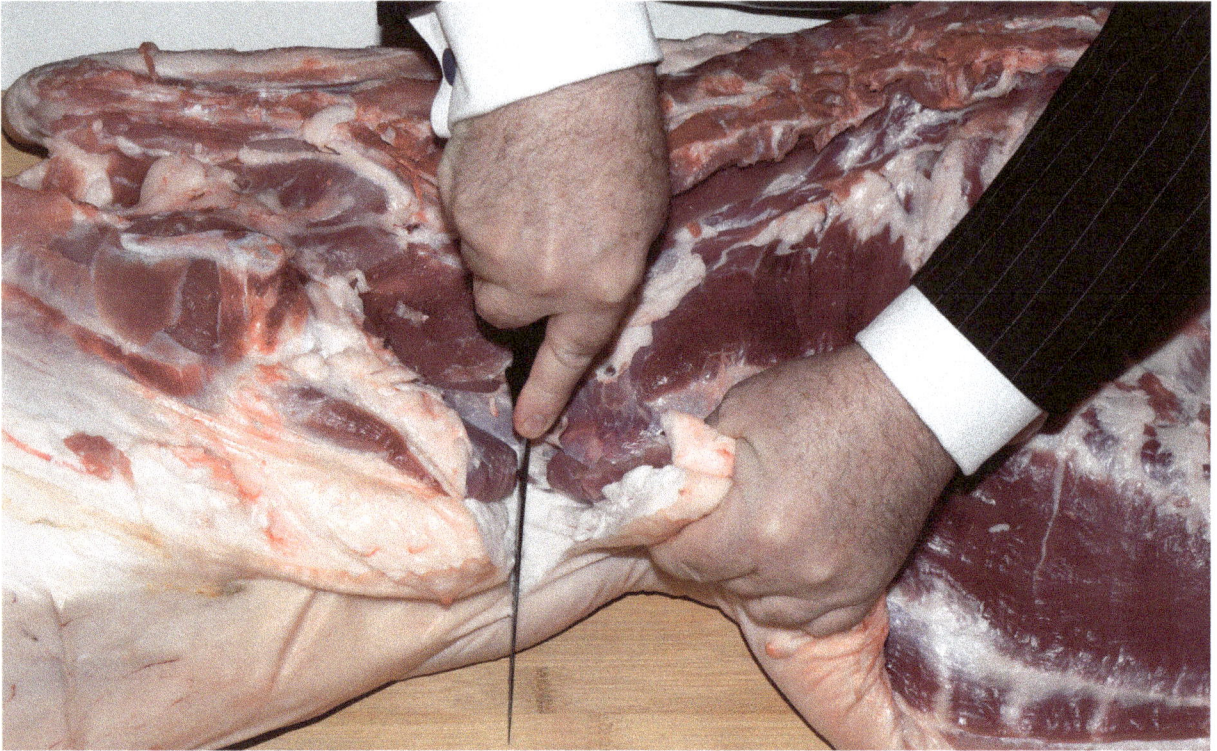

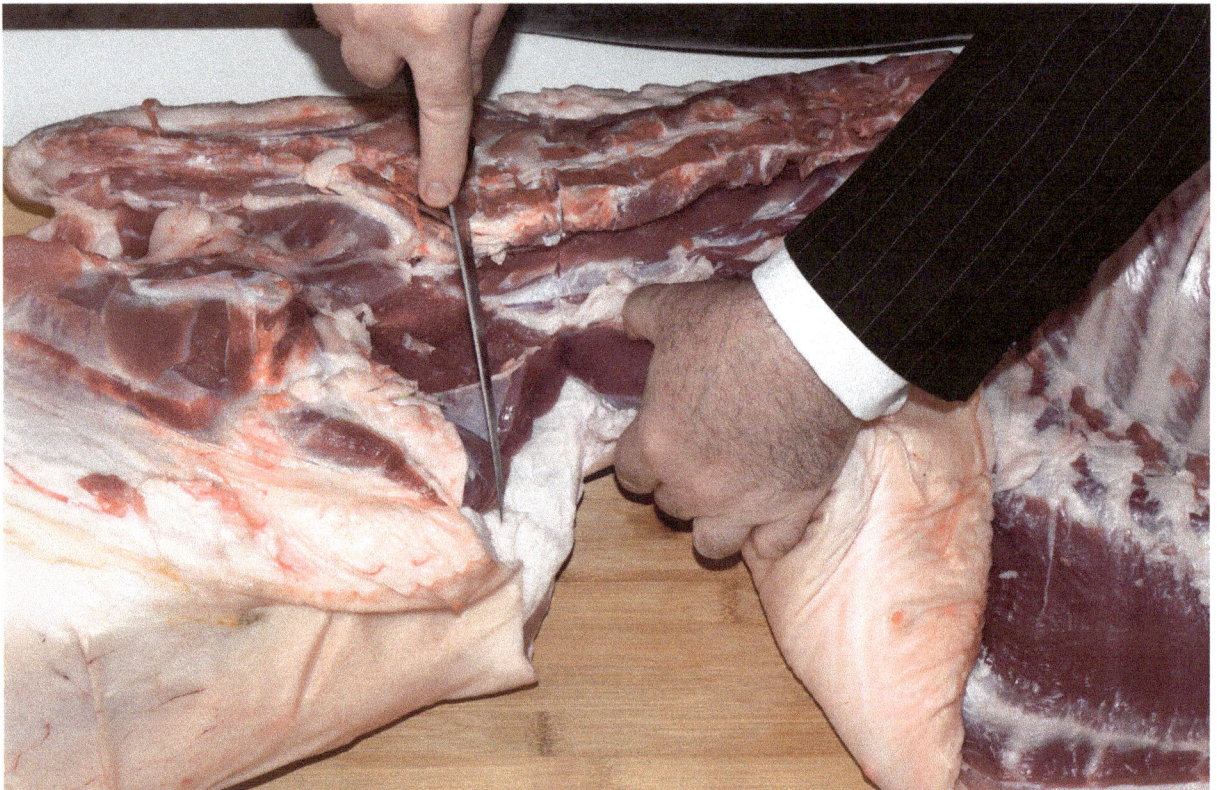

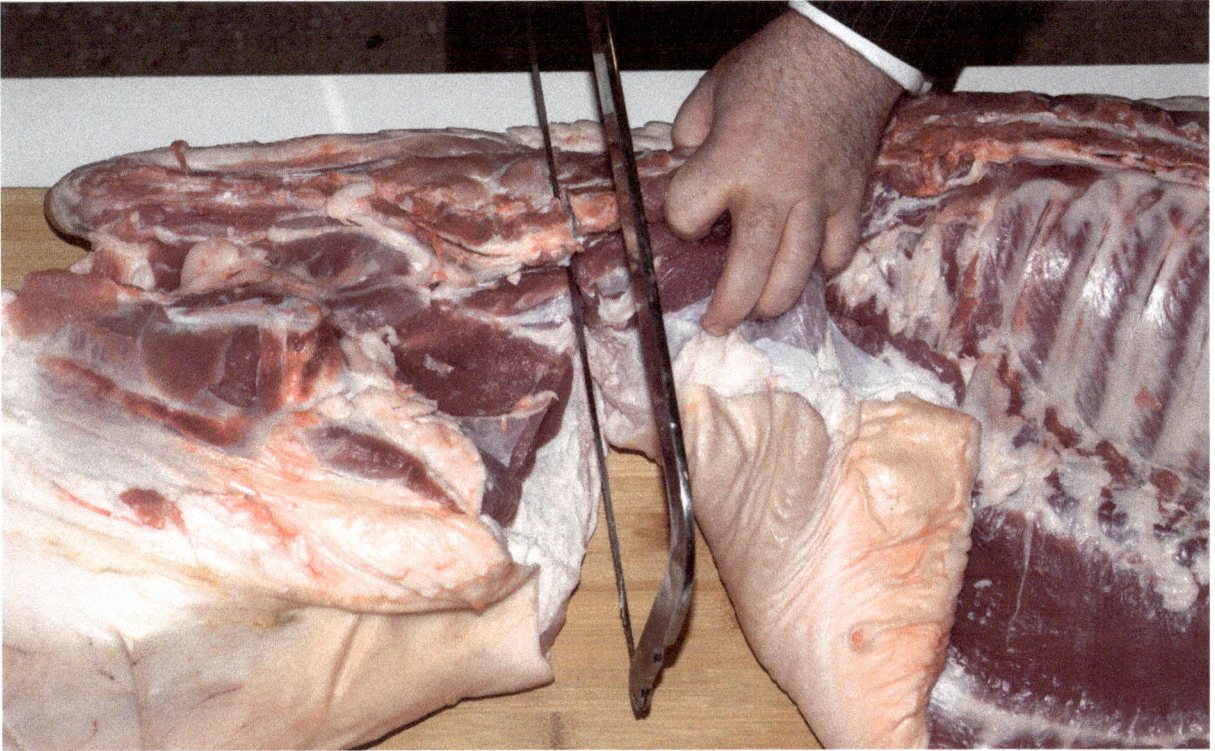

Congratulations, you now have three primal cuts. The next task is to prepare each one for charcuterie production.

THE MIDSECTION

I usually deal with the midsection next. There are several ways that this can be approached. For the purposes of this tutorial, I will separate the belly from the loin section, each will be used separately.

Using a knife mark a line to separate the belly from the spine and most of the ribs. Where the line is placed will depend on how wide you want the belly section to be. In this illustration I will remove the ribs and keep the skin on. Usually when I make this, I will keep the ribs on as well as the skin. There are two reasons for doing this. First, I like the look of the ribs and skin on the final bacon. Secondly before slicing I will remove the ribs and use them as a flavouring or condiment when making soups or casseroles. I always keep the rind on because I like the look of it and afterwards it can be given to the dogs, who appreciate the true value of pork rind.

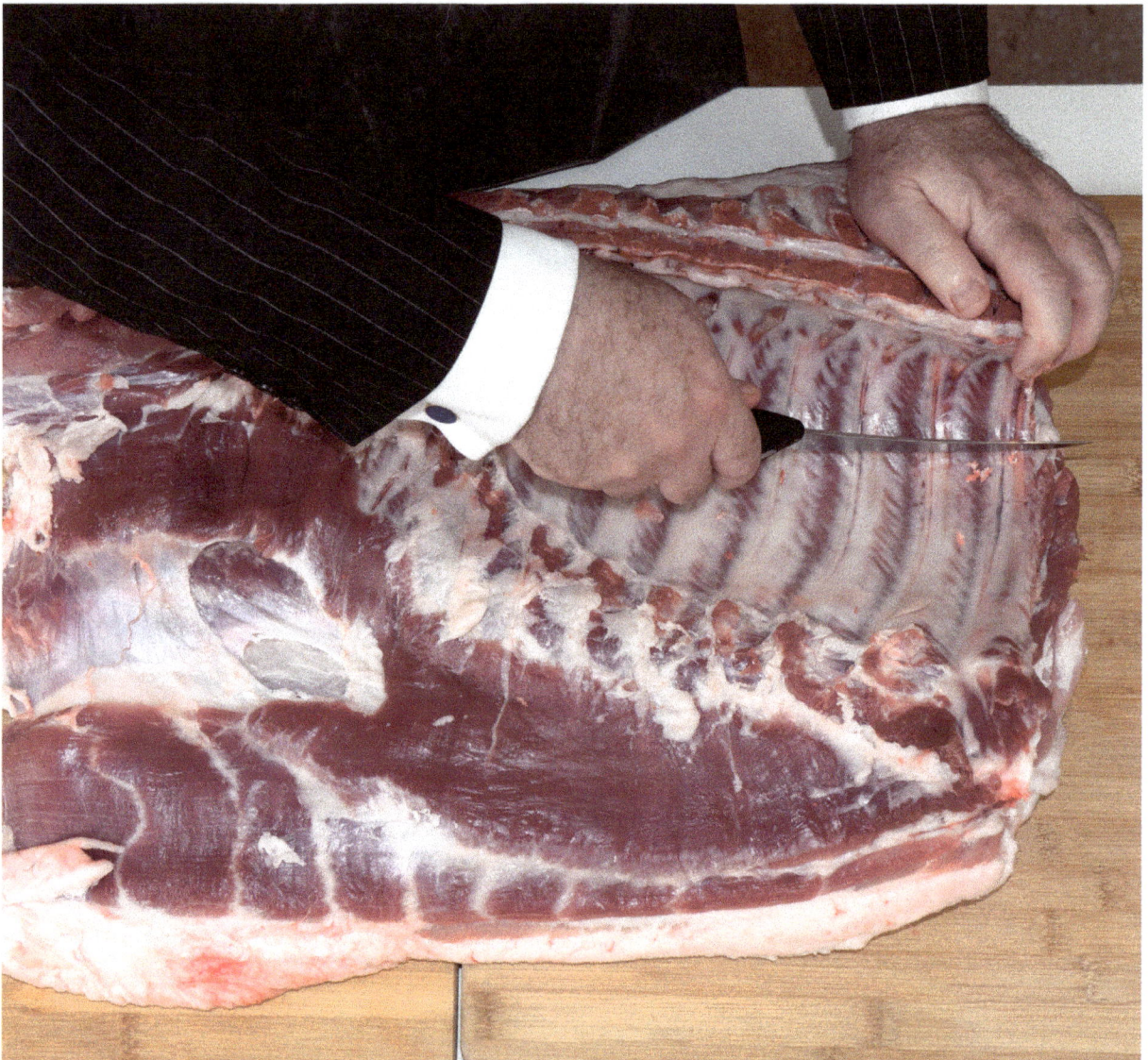

Use a knife to cut the boneless part of the belly along with the line you have chosen.

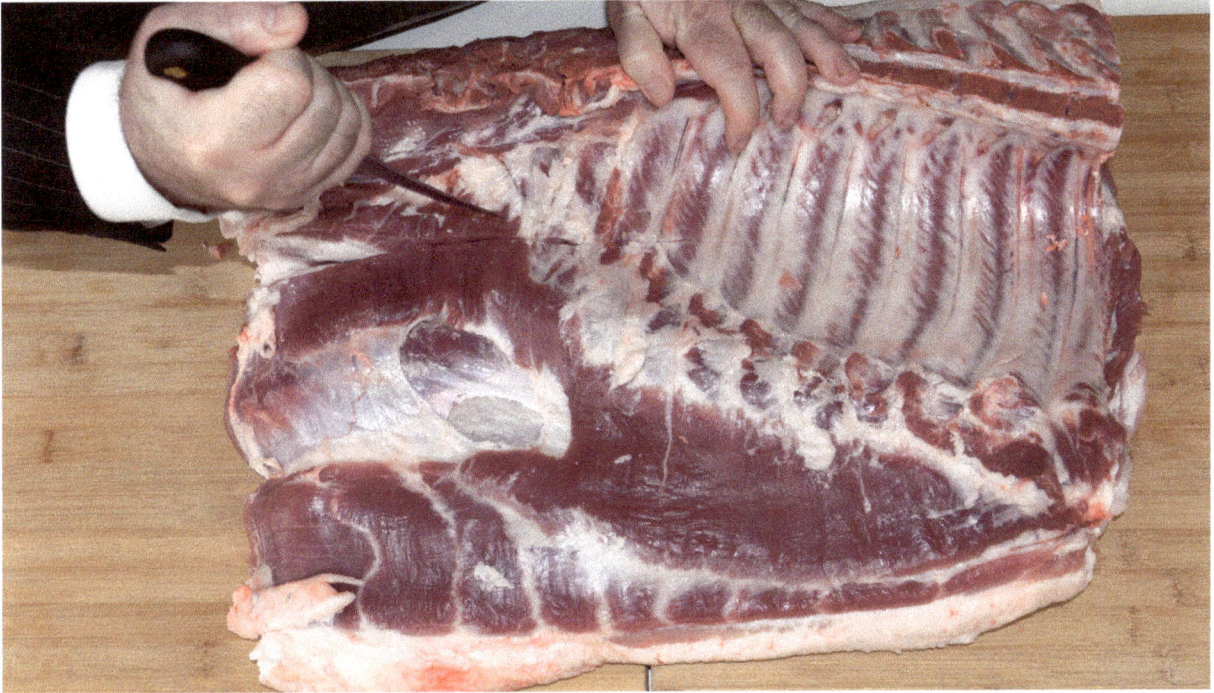

Use a saw to cut the ribs along the scored line.

Use a knife to cut the meat under the ribs along the scored line.

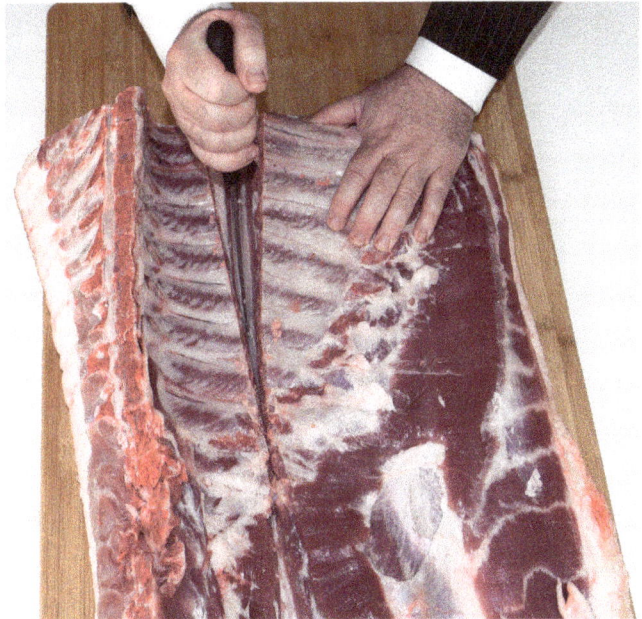

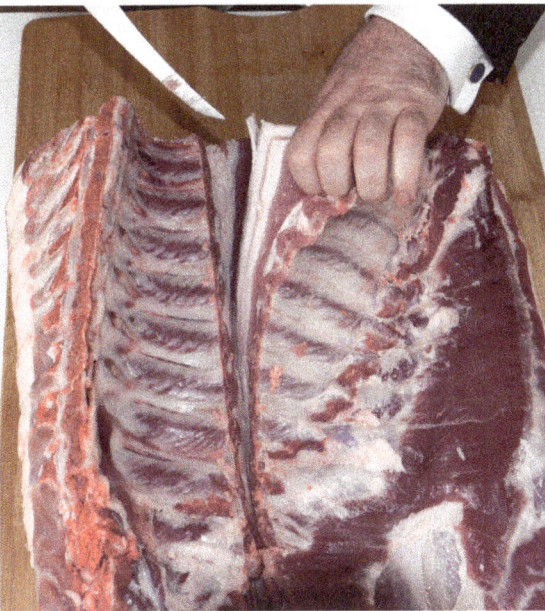

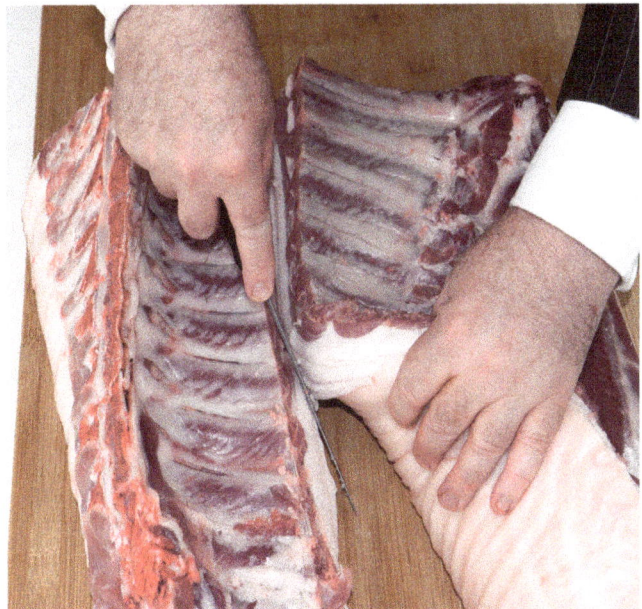

You now have a mostly bone free belly section and a loin section complete with spine and ribs.

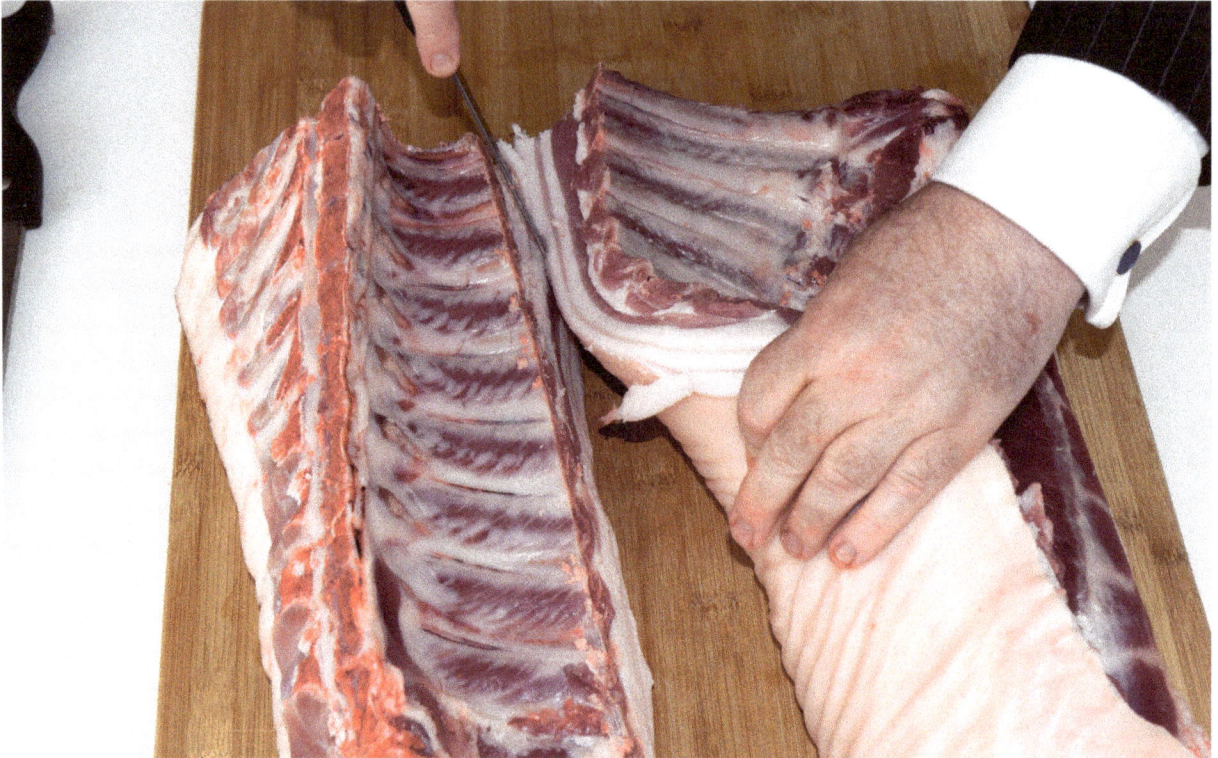

Return to the belly section, squaring off the boneless long edge, retain any trim for mince.

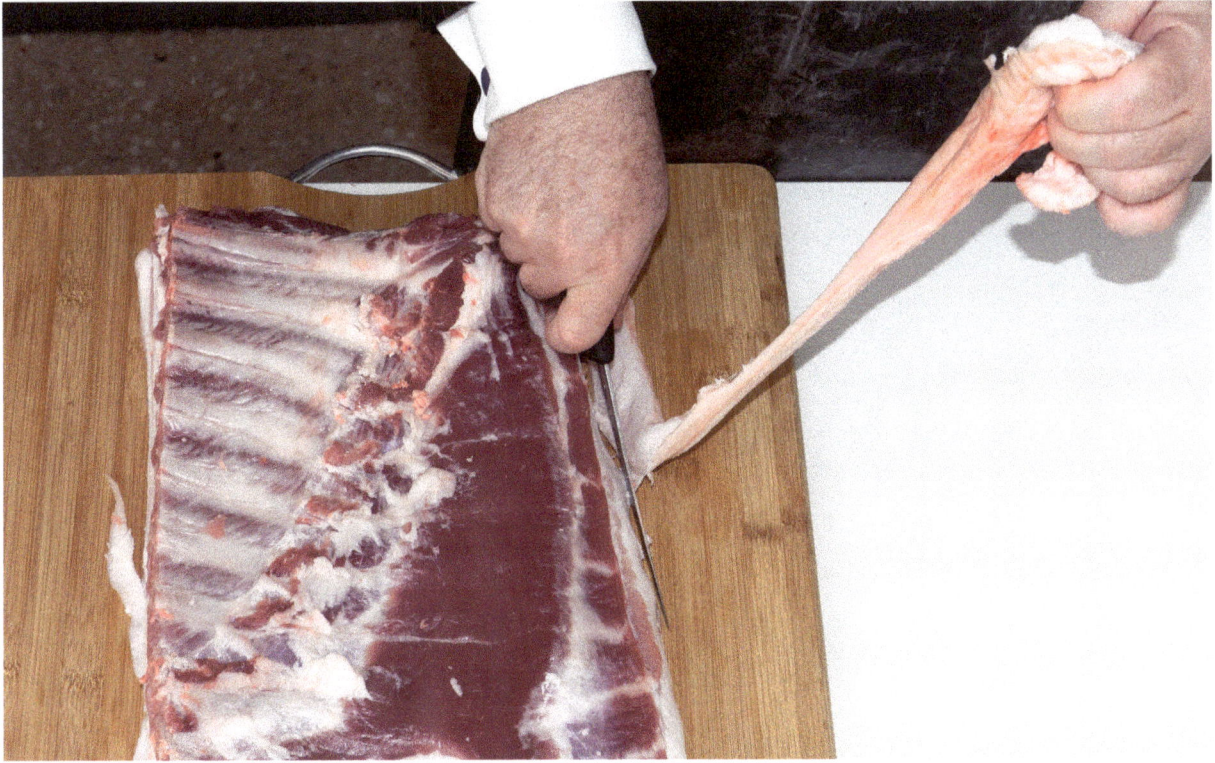

Remove any cartilage

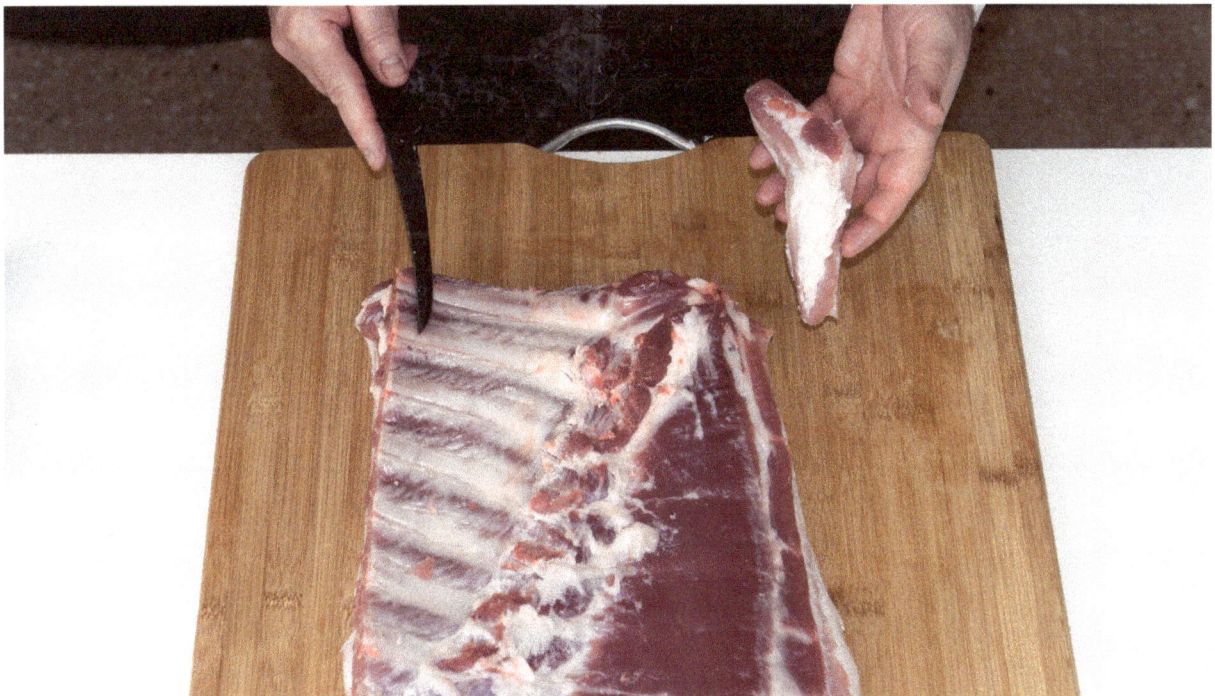

Square off the short ends

Using a sharp knife cut along the lower edge of the ribs, but only to the depth of the ribs.

Separate the ribs from the belly section, making sure to keep as much meat on the belly as possible.

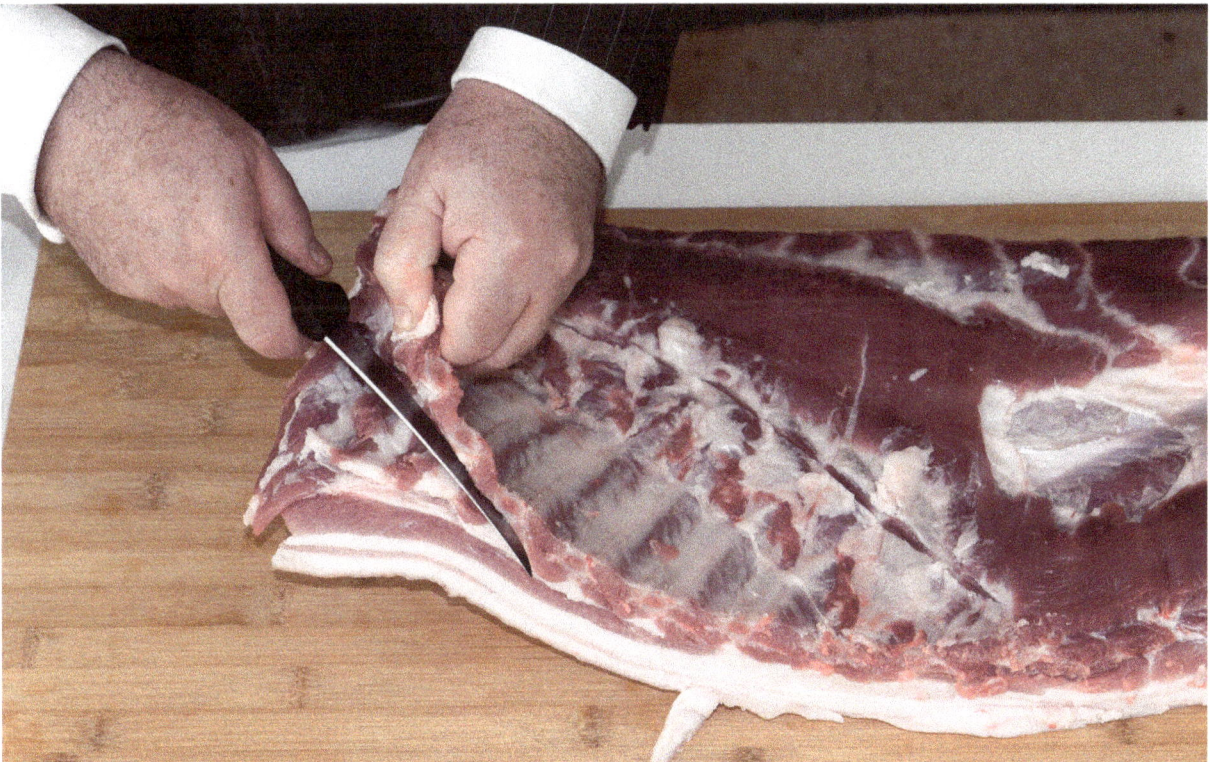

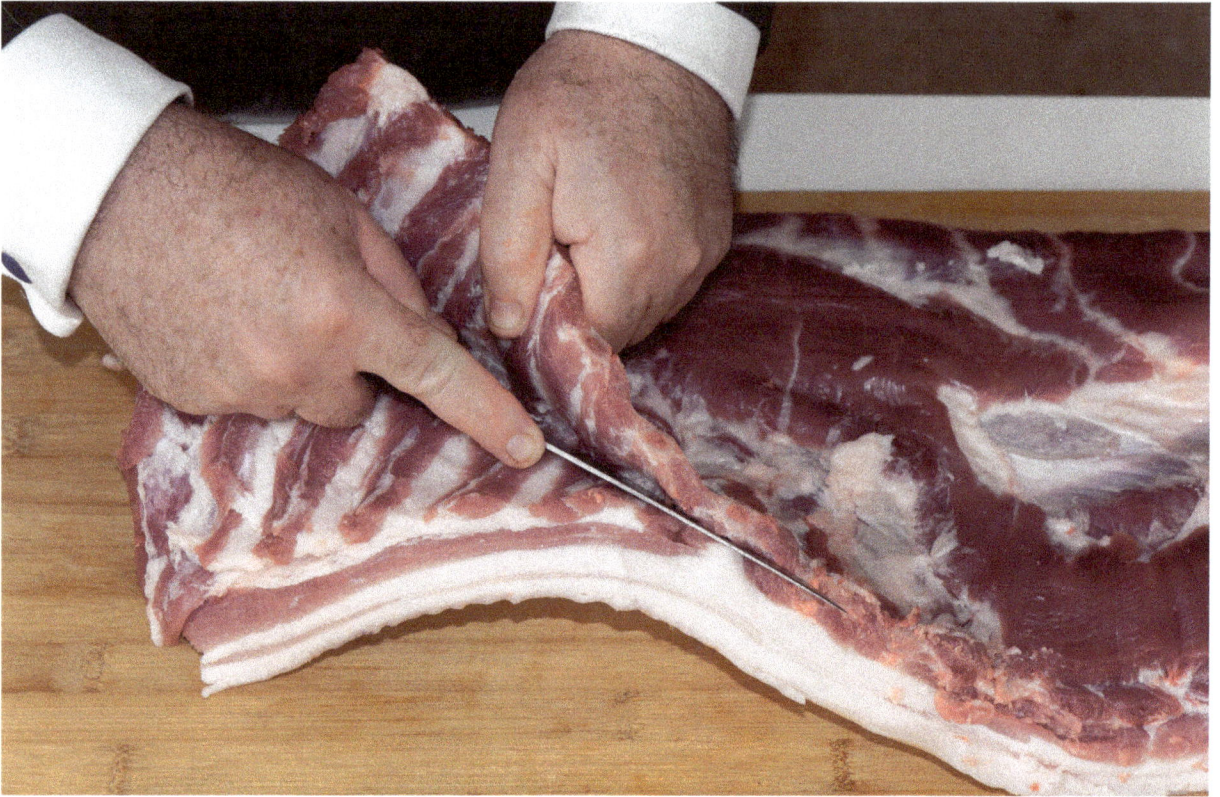

Square off any ragged ends, they do not look good and only give bugs a place to party. Repeatez apres Moi," no bug parties on my watch".

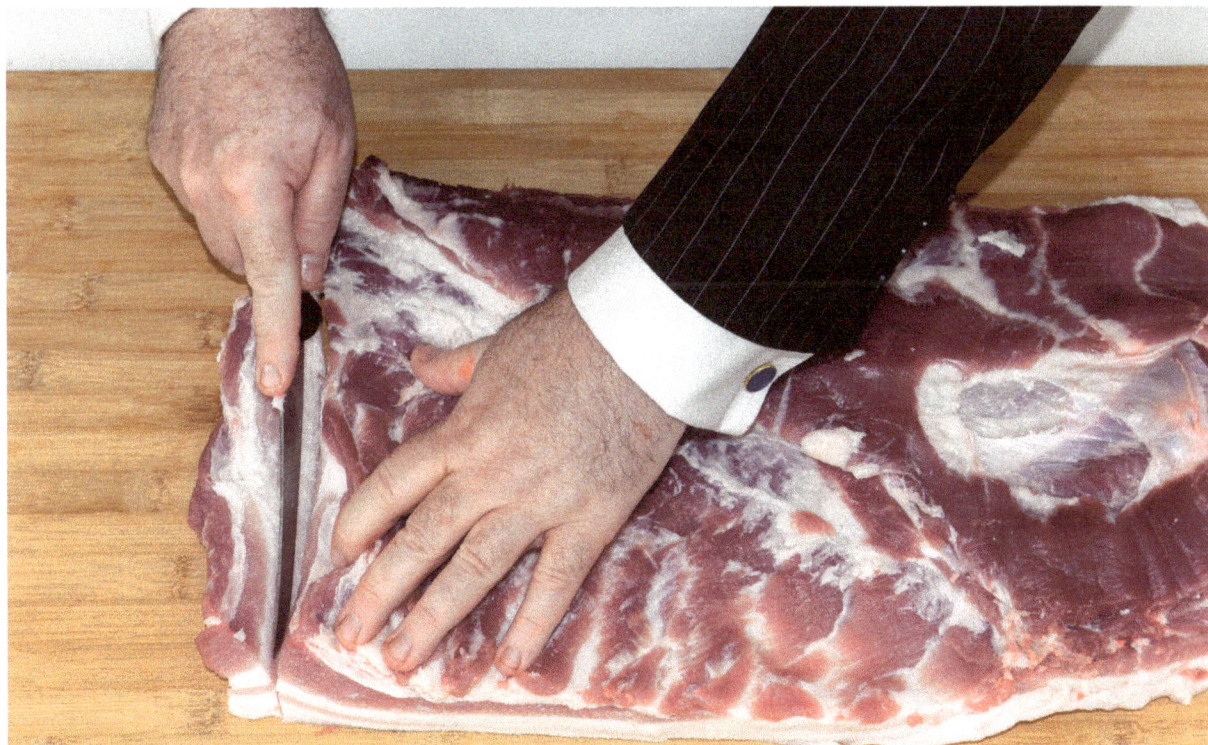

You now have a boneless pork belly which can be used to make bacon or pancetta.

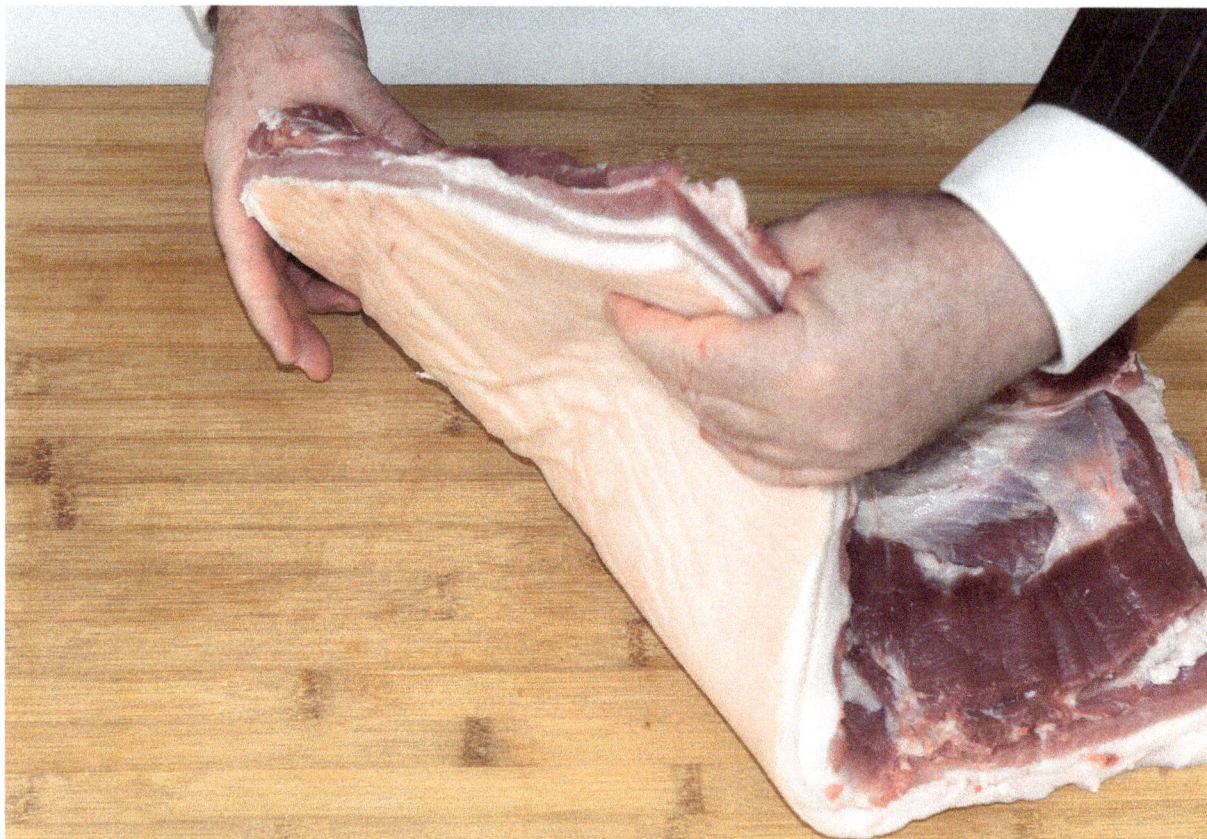

Depending on the size of the animal and the size of your smoker it may be convenient to cut this piece of meat into smaller sections.

Another interesting product is rolled pancetta. I mention this because it does require some particular butchery preparation. Take a piece of the now boneless belly and carefully remove the skin leaving as much meat as possible on the belly. It is necessary to remove the skin because when the meat is rolled you do not want any skin inside the product which would be tough to eat. More of this later.

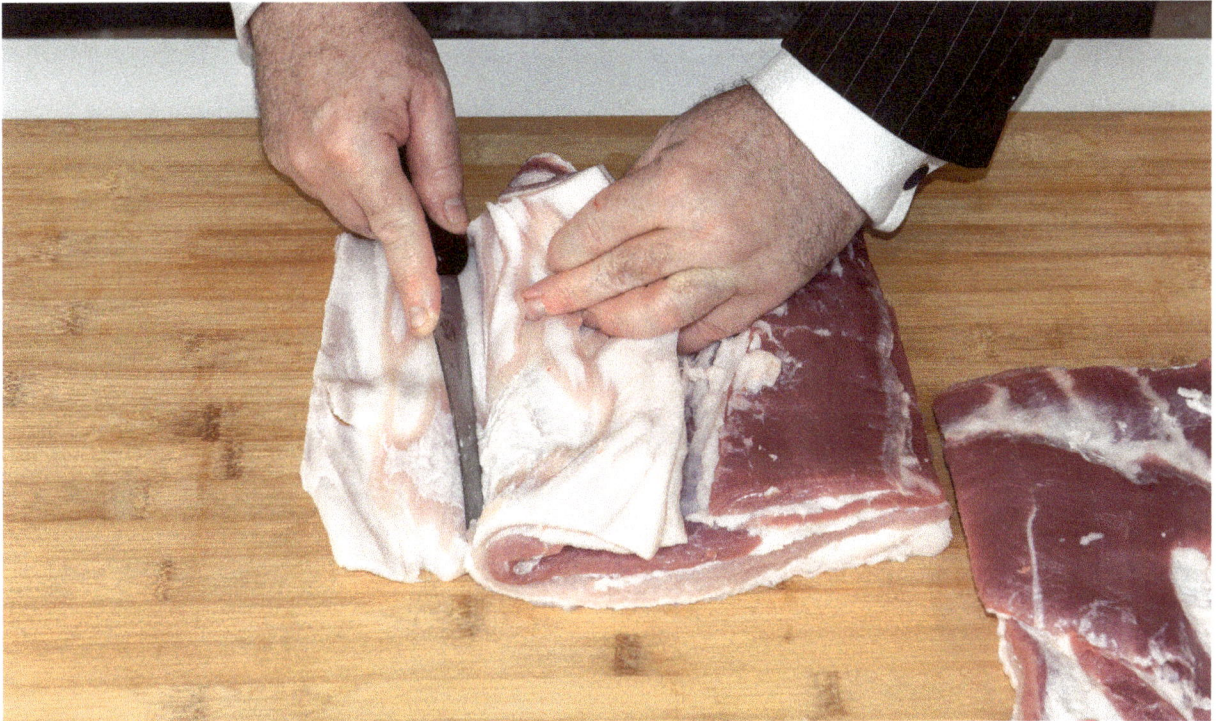

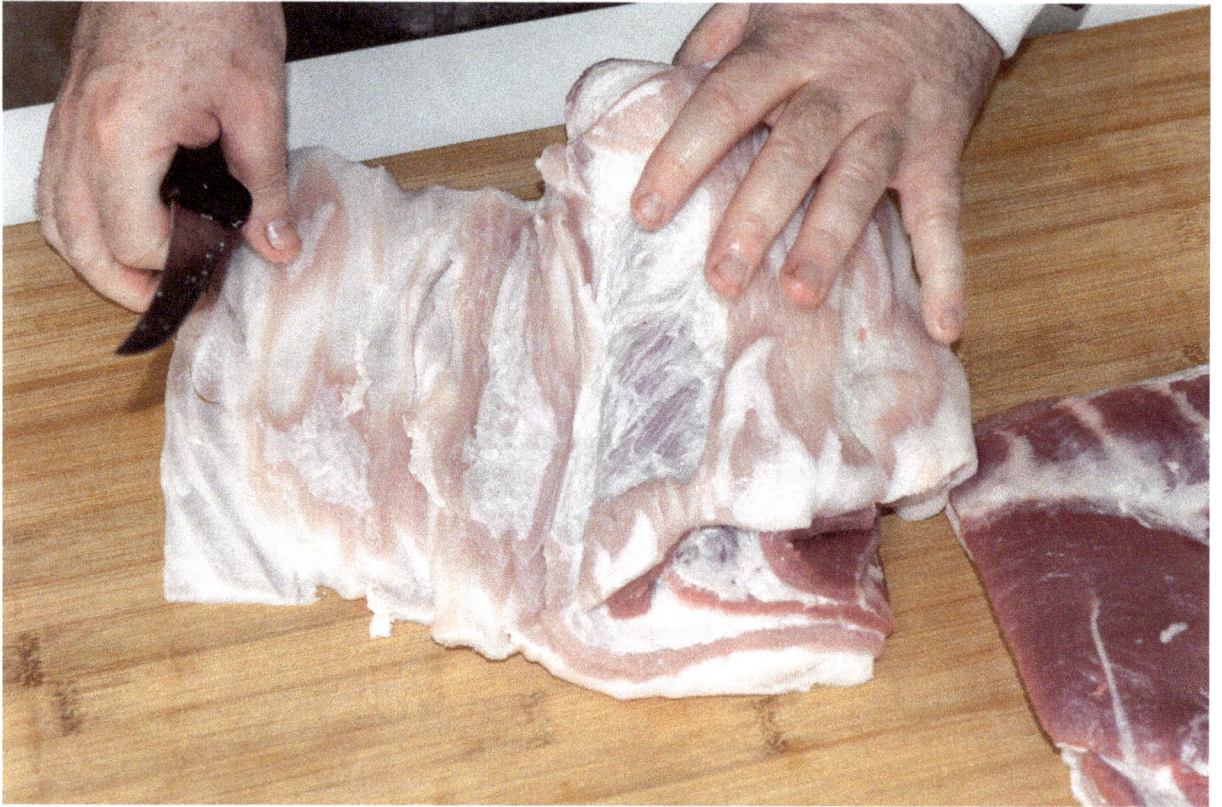

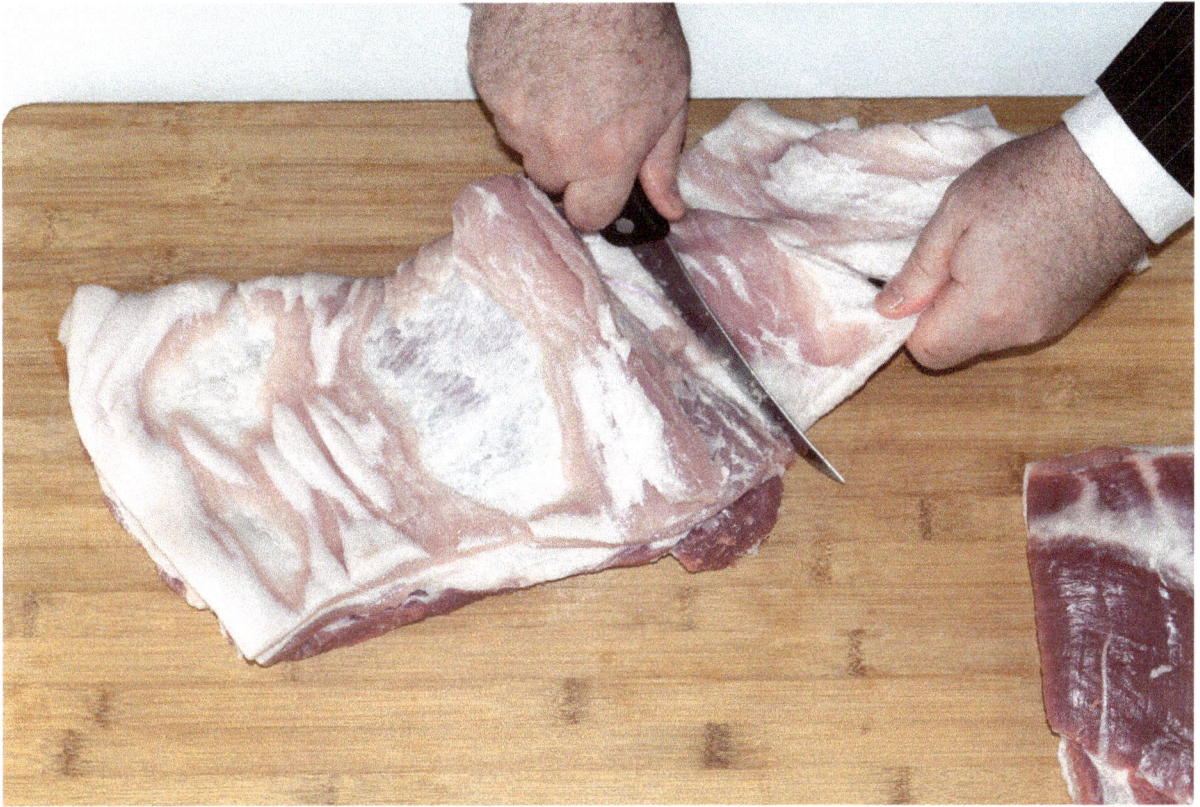

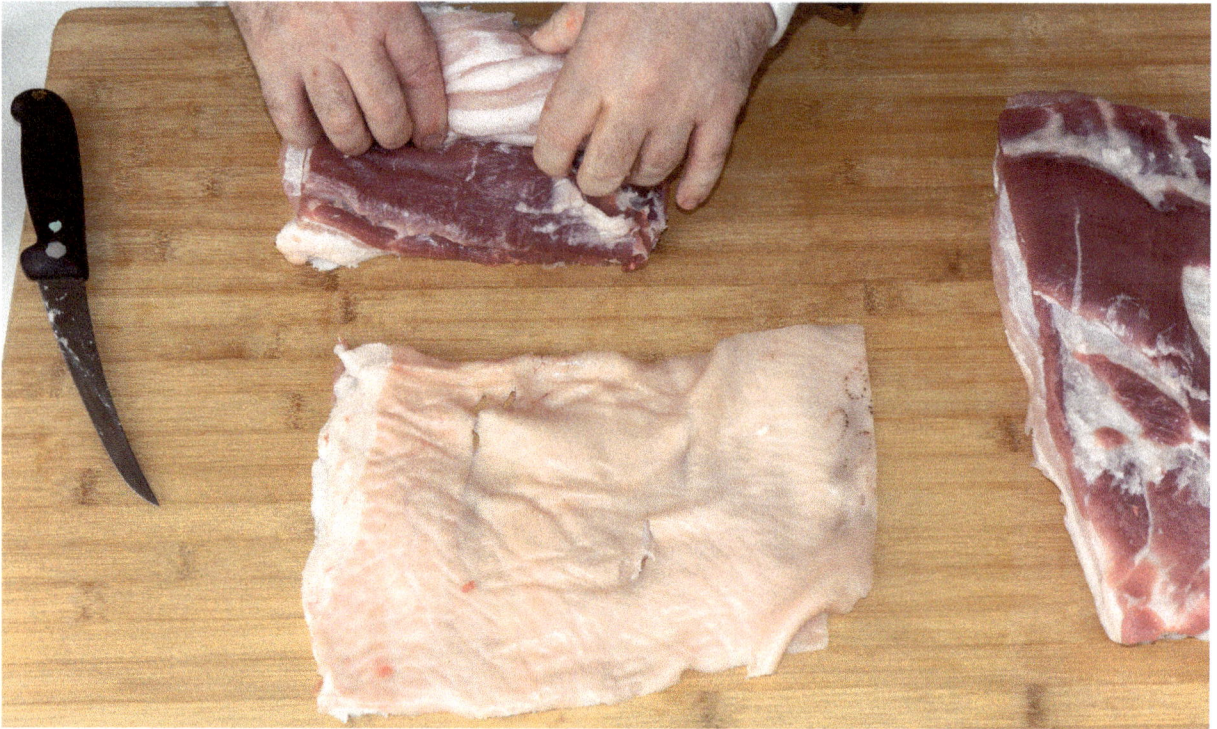

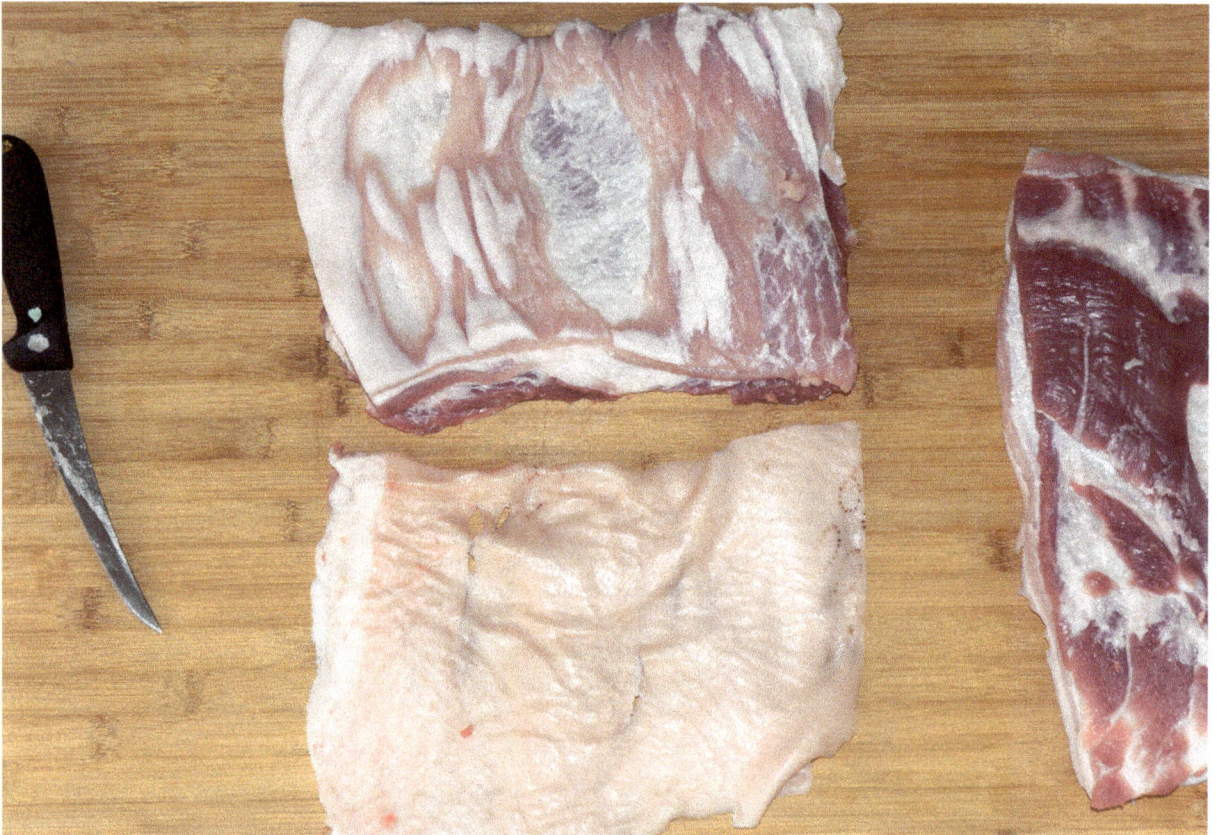

You now return to the loin which is on the bone and on the rind. It can be cured , air dried and or smoked without any further preparation. However, it is difficult to deal with in this form if you do not break it down further. A suggestions is as follows. First remove the part which is without ribs. This can be cured and dried separately.

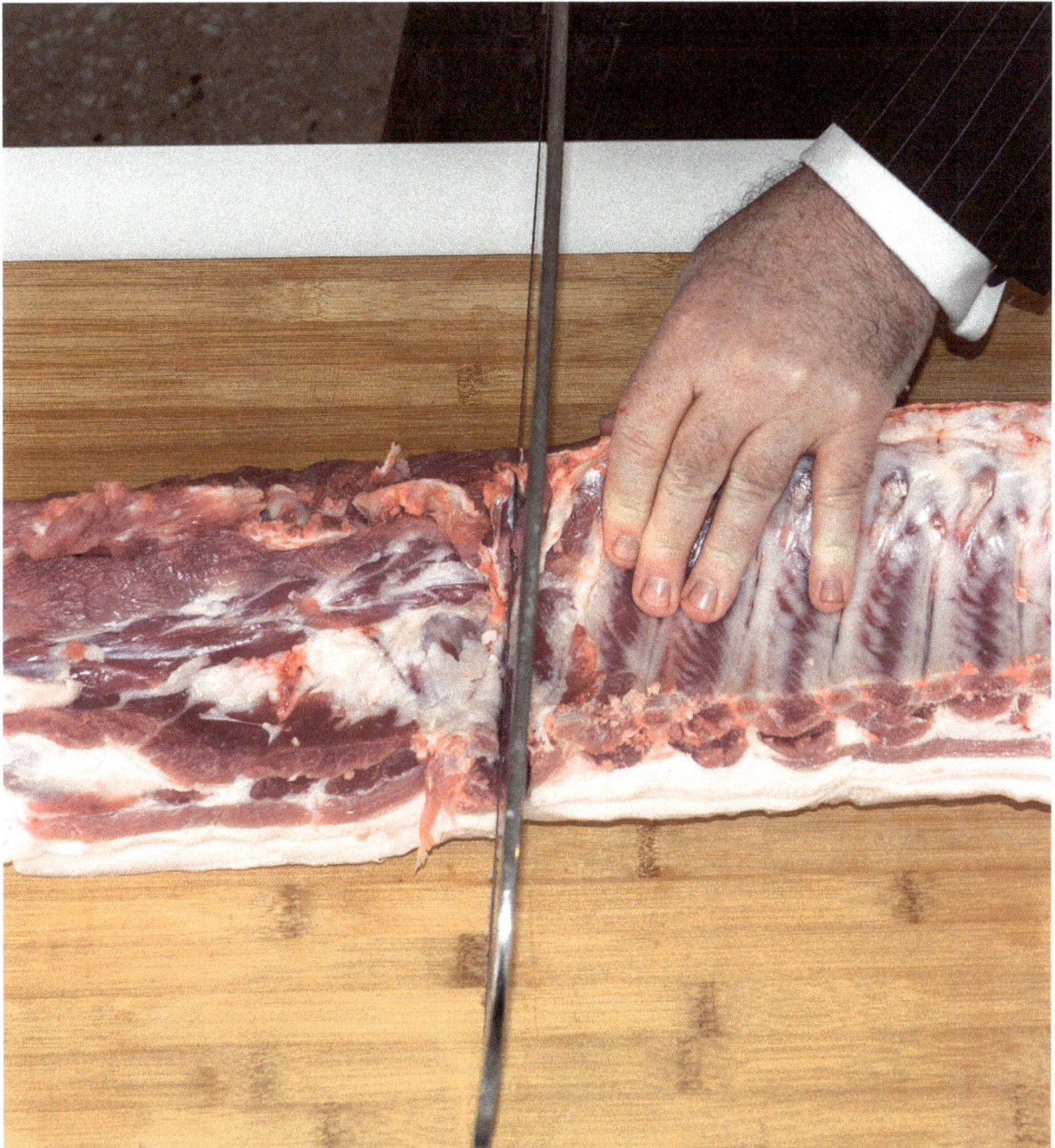

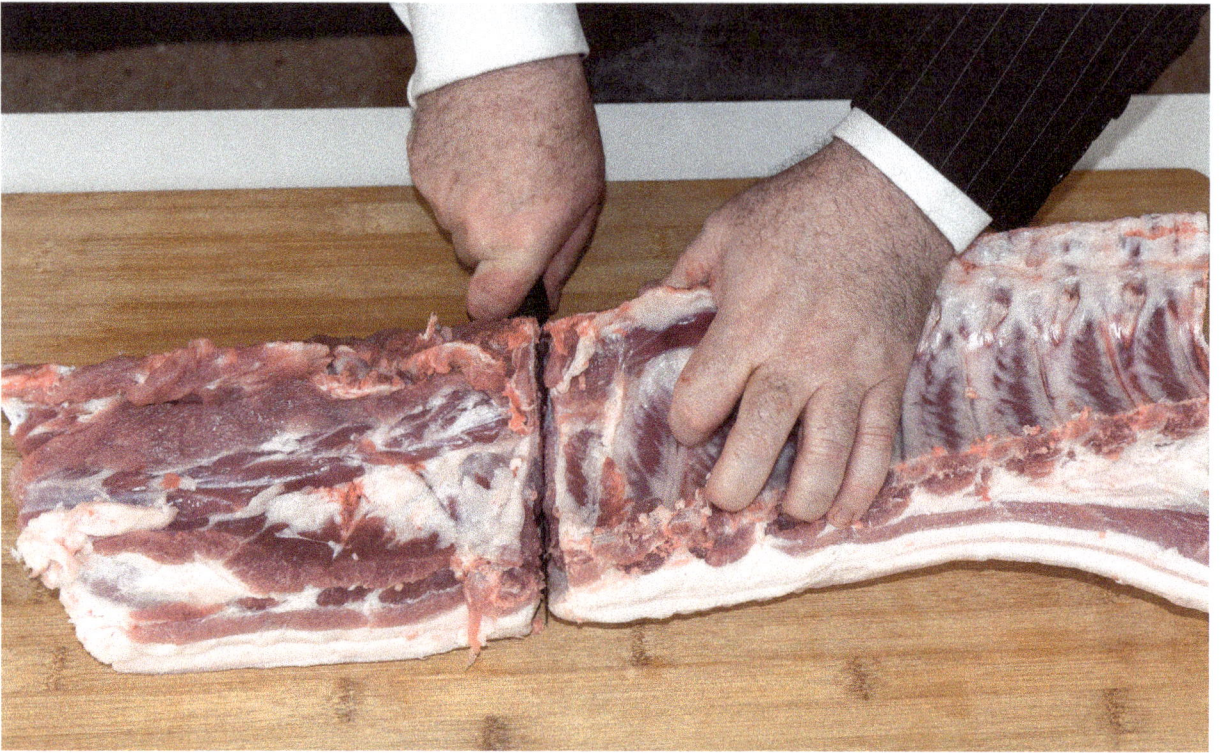
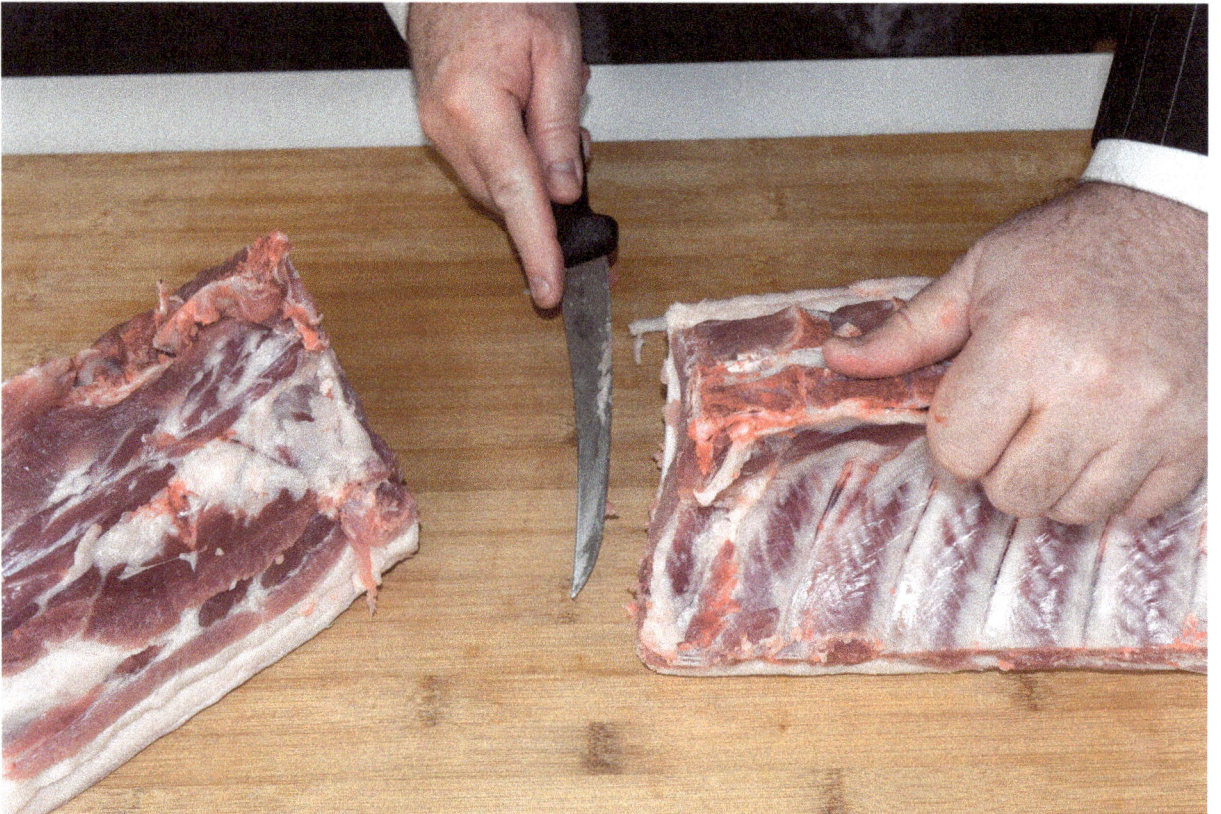

The remaining loin has both spine and ribs attached.

The ribs and spine can be removed, and the resultant cut of meat is a boneless loin with the back fat and rind attached. This can be cured and air dried and becomes the Italian classic, Lonza. I recommend keeping the fat and rind on during this process as it provides some protection against over drying in this leanest cut of the pork. However, what I often do, and is demonstrated in the following images, is to cure and then smoke along without removing the spine and ribs or back fat and rind. This is the Austrian classic, Kassler. The product can be used as it is although it is much more convenient to remove the spine so that individual chops can be cut whilst leaving the rib bones intact for aesthetic purposes if nothing else. To do so, first release the meat from the feather bones on one side and then, using a saw remove the spine such that the loin can be cut through between the ribs into individual chops once it has been cured and smoked.

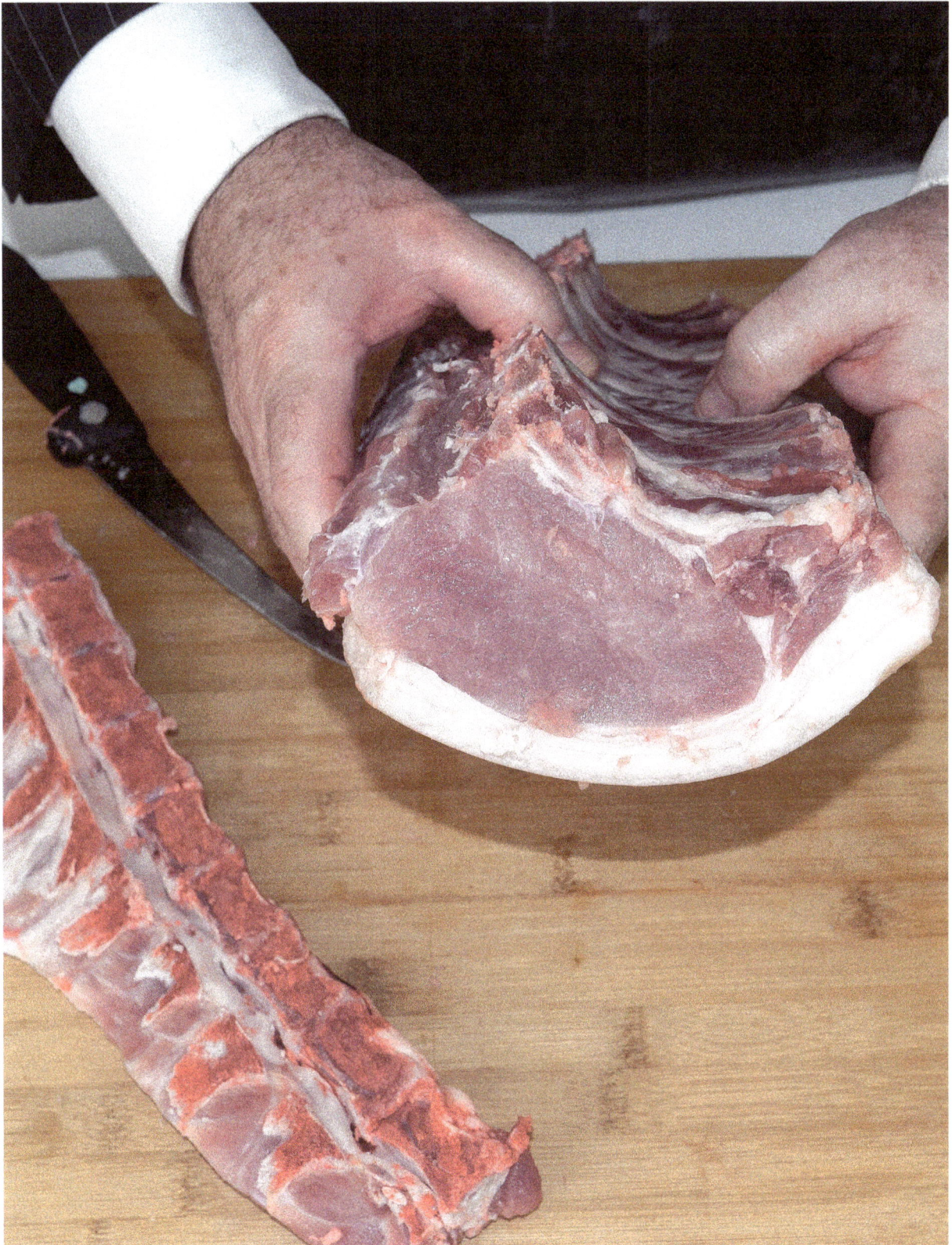

THE LEG

The half pig carcass is split down the spine. Therefore the leg will have the pelvis (and perhaps the tail) attached. This will need to be removed. If you do not remove the residual pelvis then the exposed bone will attract bugs who will then proceed to have a party and destroy all your hard work. First task is to remove the pelvis. There is no easy way to describe this. It is a very weirdly shaped bone and includes the socket part of the ball and socket joint which articulates the leg from the pelvis. Use a sharp knife to trace around the outside of the pelvic bone and try to loosen it by cutting underneath. Try not to cut too deeply as you will only make places for the bugs to enter the meat. Remember also that the ball part of the ball and socket joint is attached to the socket by a short tendon. This prevents the leg from being dislocated but also means that until that tendon is severed the leg cannot be dissociated from the residual pelvis

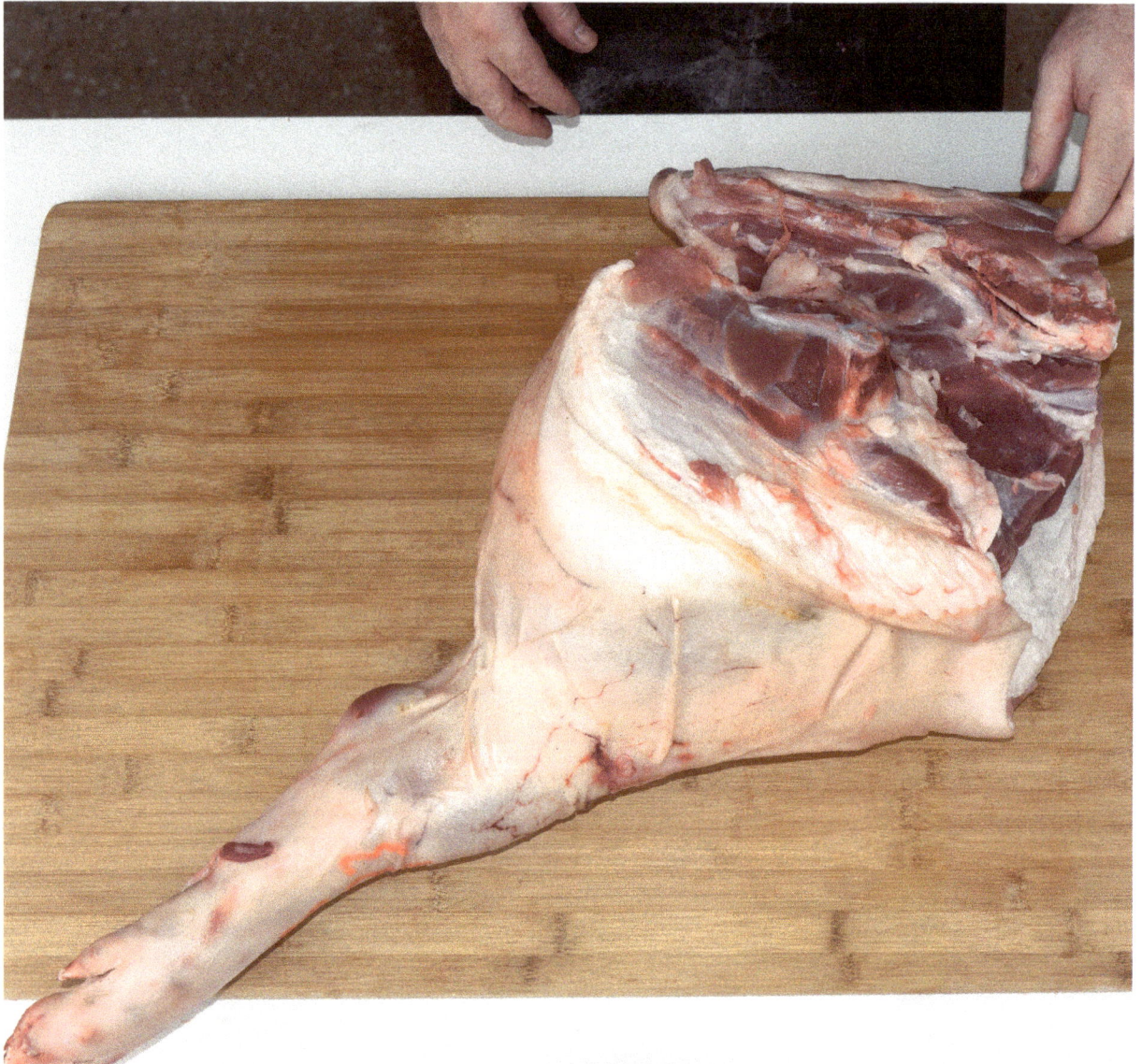

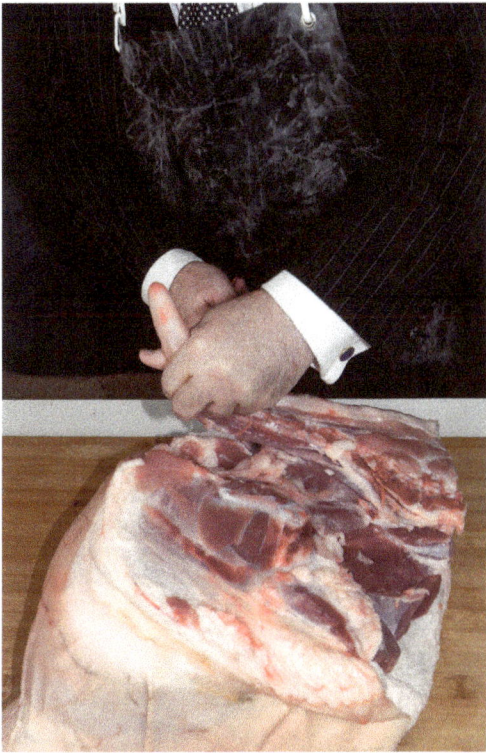

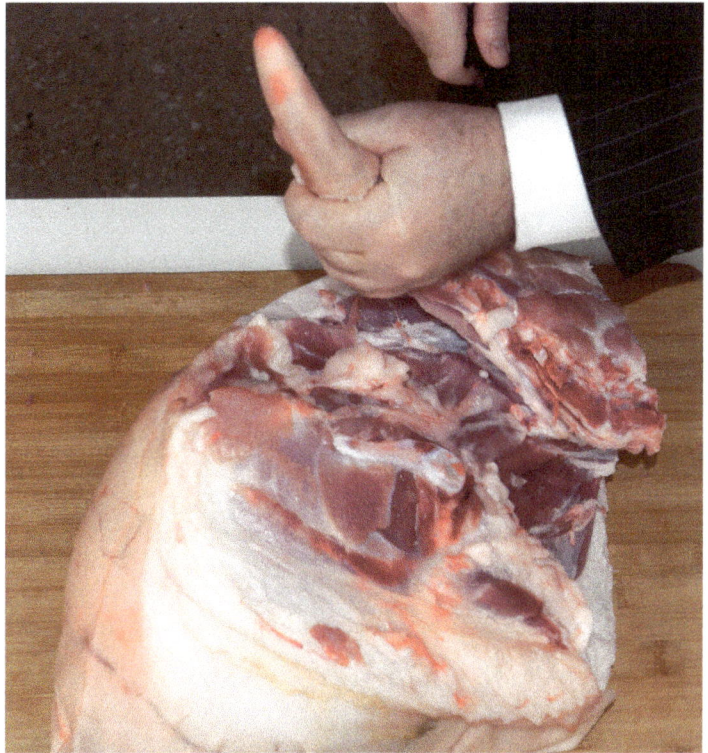

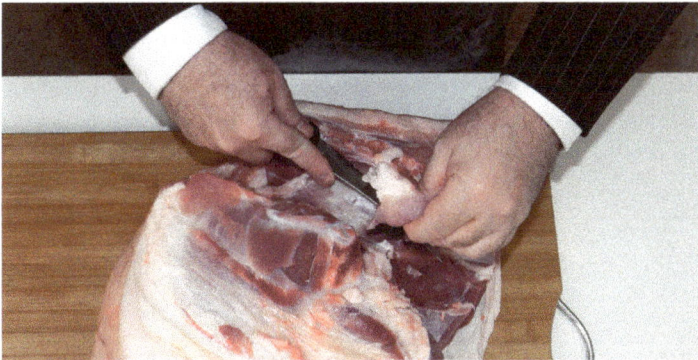

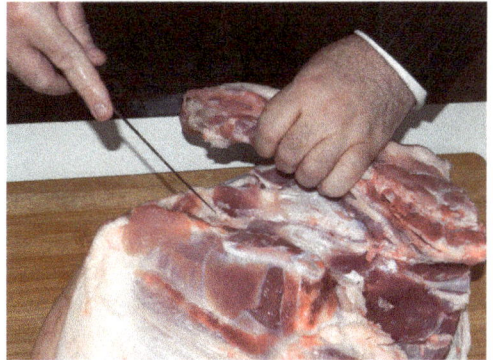

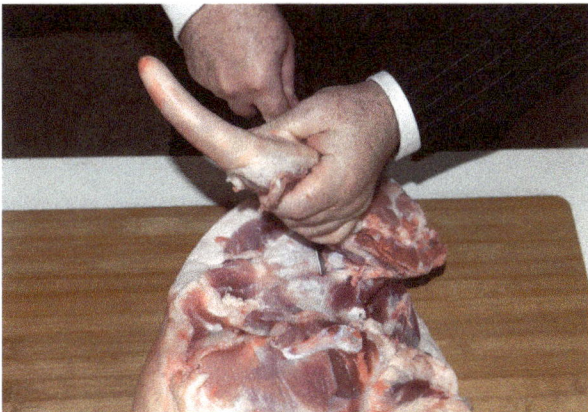

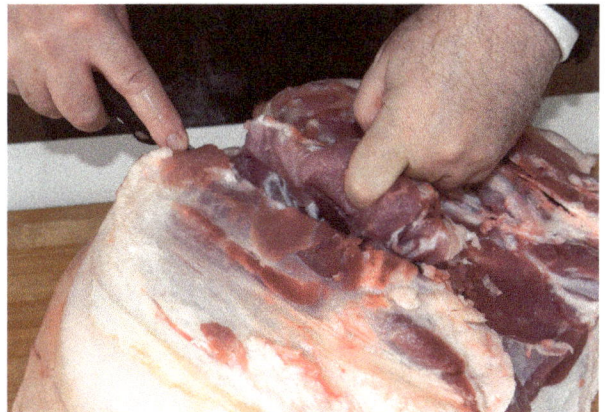

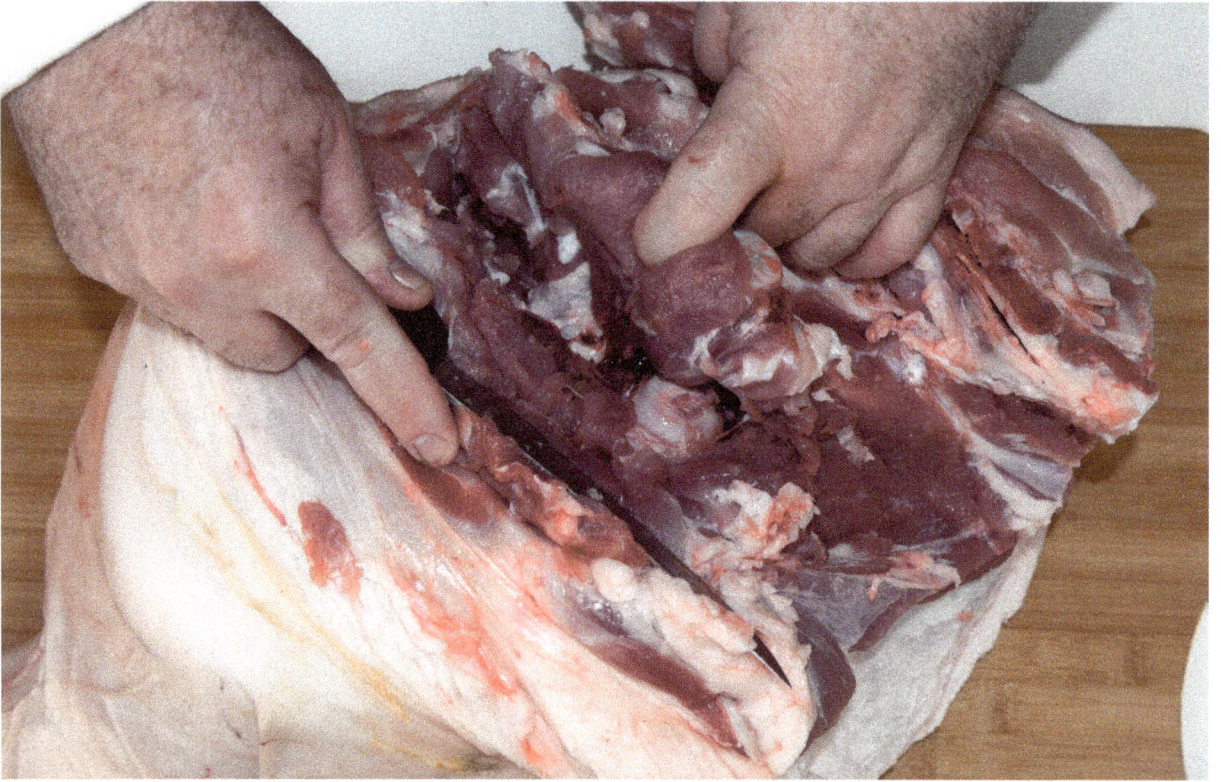
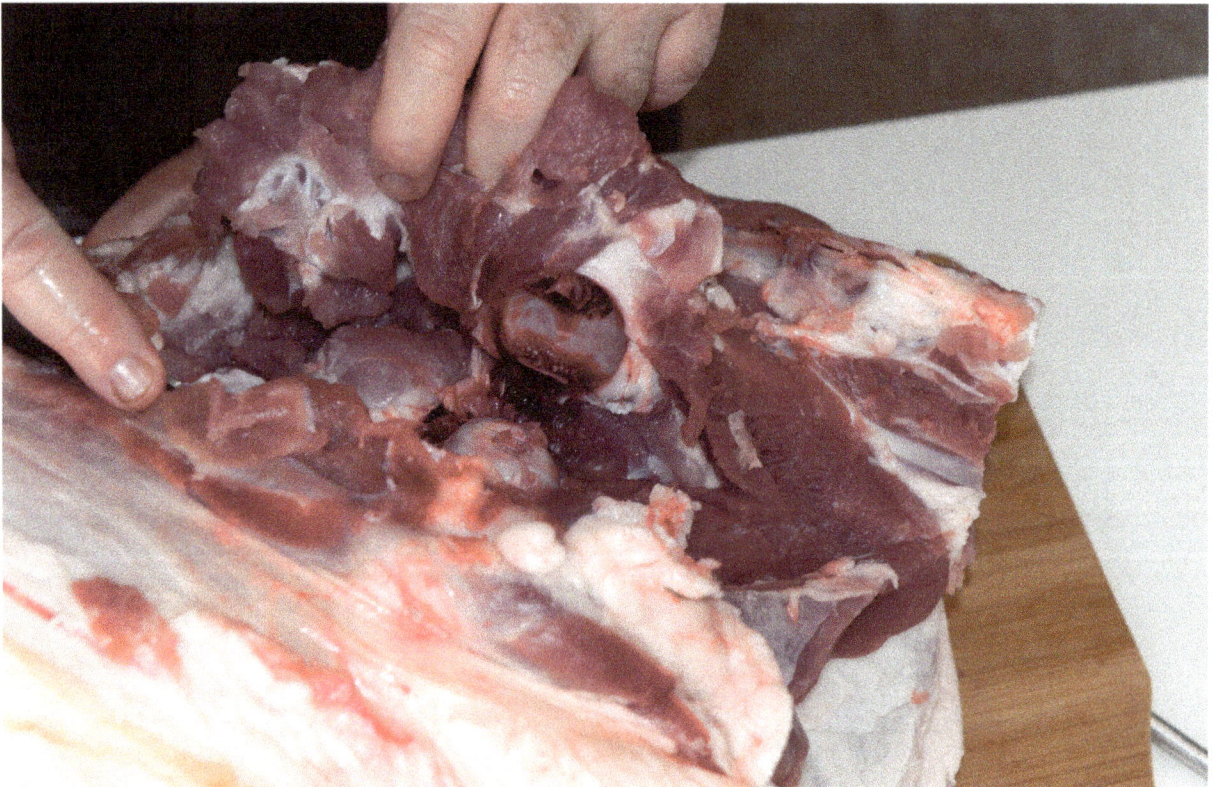

Once the residual pelvis has been removed you will see the ball part of the joint which is the head of the femur bone, the main bone in the leg.

You can now clearly see the point where the tendon is connected the ball to the socket joint.

There are three main arteries in the leg which all descend from around the top of the femur into the muscles in the leg. The femoral artery is the main one, I forget the names of the other two. Once you have removed the residual pelvis these three arteries are accessible but not easily visible. However, you will usually see some blood in the tissue closest to the head of the femur, this is the femoral artery. The other two are respectively to the left and to the right of the femoral artery. The point of this anatomical dissertation is that there can be some blood retained in these arteries especially the femoral artery even in well hung and bled commercial pork. Retained blood in these vessels is even more like the in the case of home killed pork. You must ensure that the blood is removed from these vessels so that does not spoil the meat from within during the curing process.

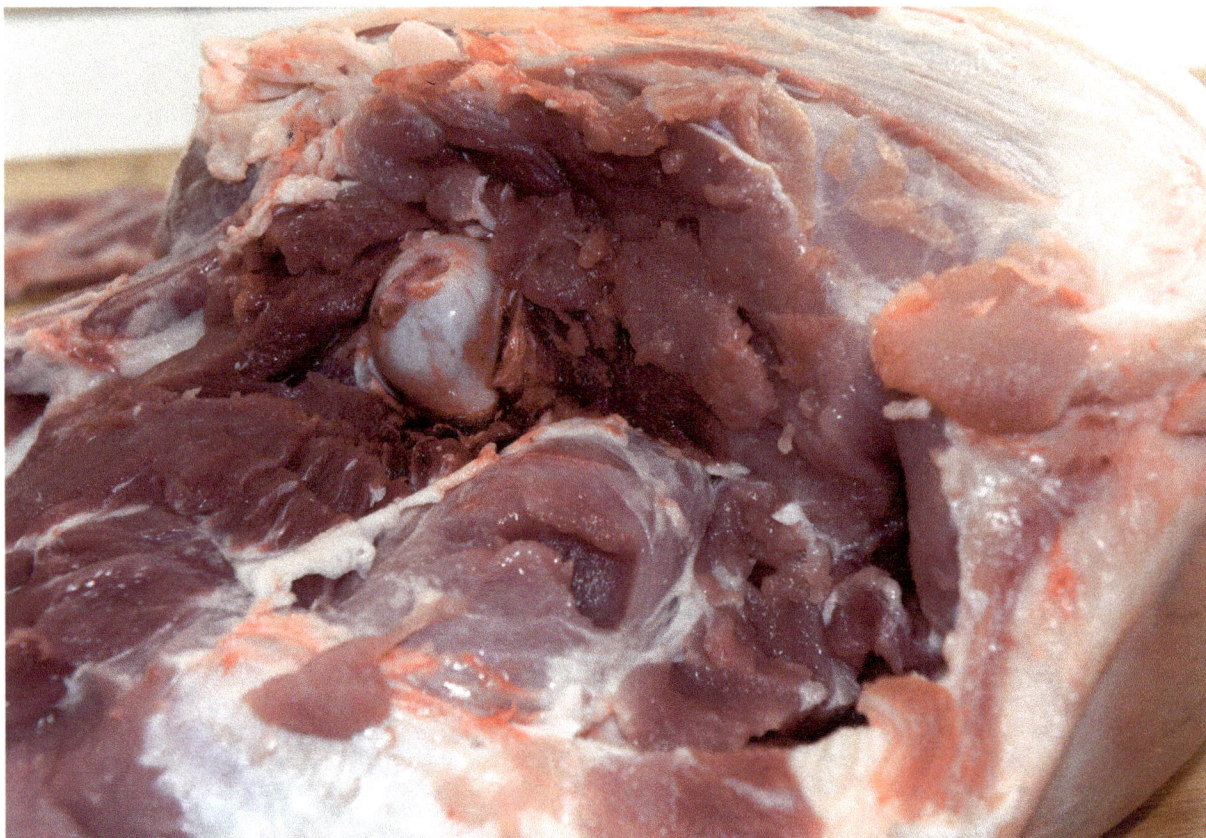

The way to remove any residual blood is to massage or push the leg from below the cut surface, thereby forcing any blood in the arteries out. Do not expect to see a great deal of blood, perhaps one third of a teaspoon. Wipe any blood away with some kitchen paper and repeat the process until there is no more blood appearing. This may take five minutes or more. Resist the temptation to attack the leg with a rolling pin unless it is in a smooth rolling motion. Simply whacking the meat will not achieve the purpose but will break down the muscle fibres of the leg resulting in a mushy product at the end.

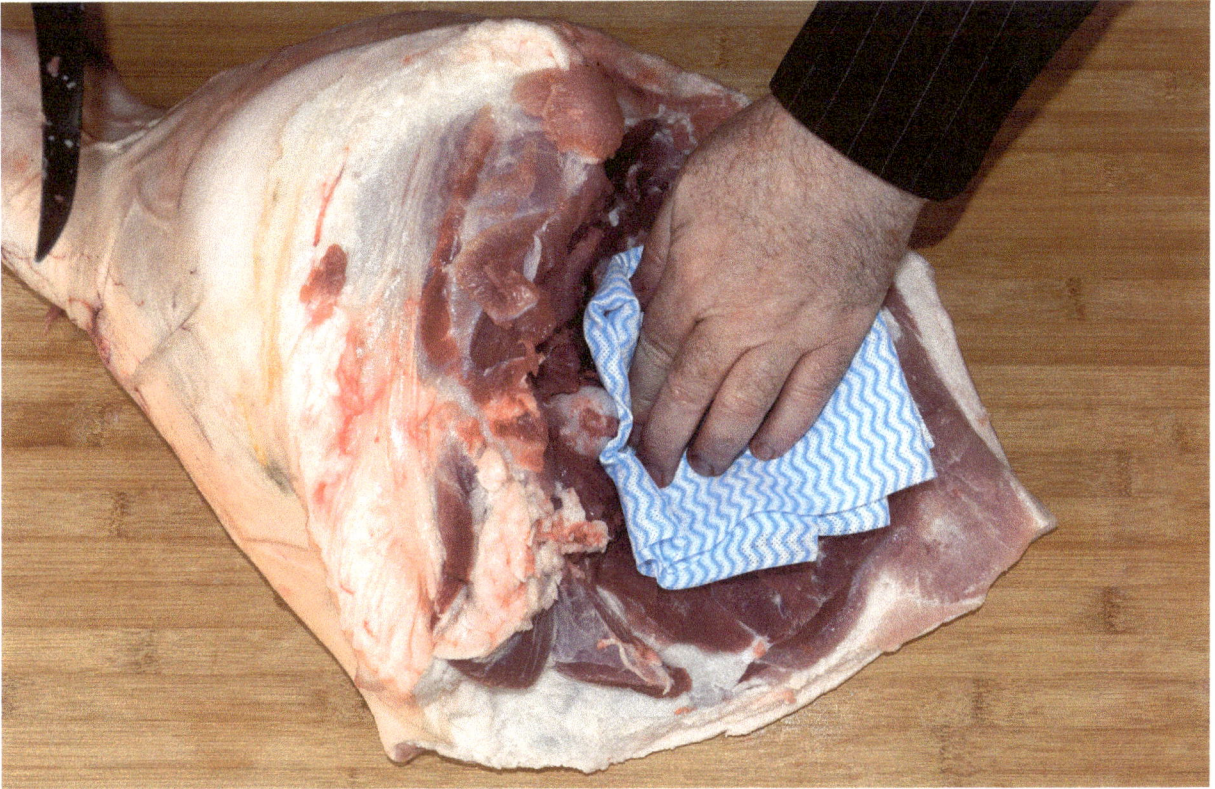
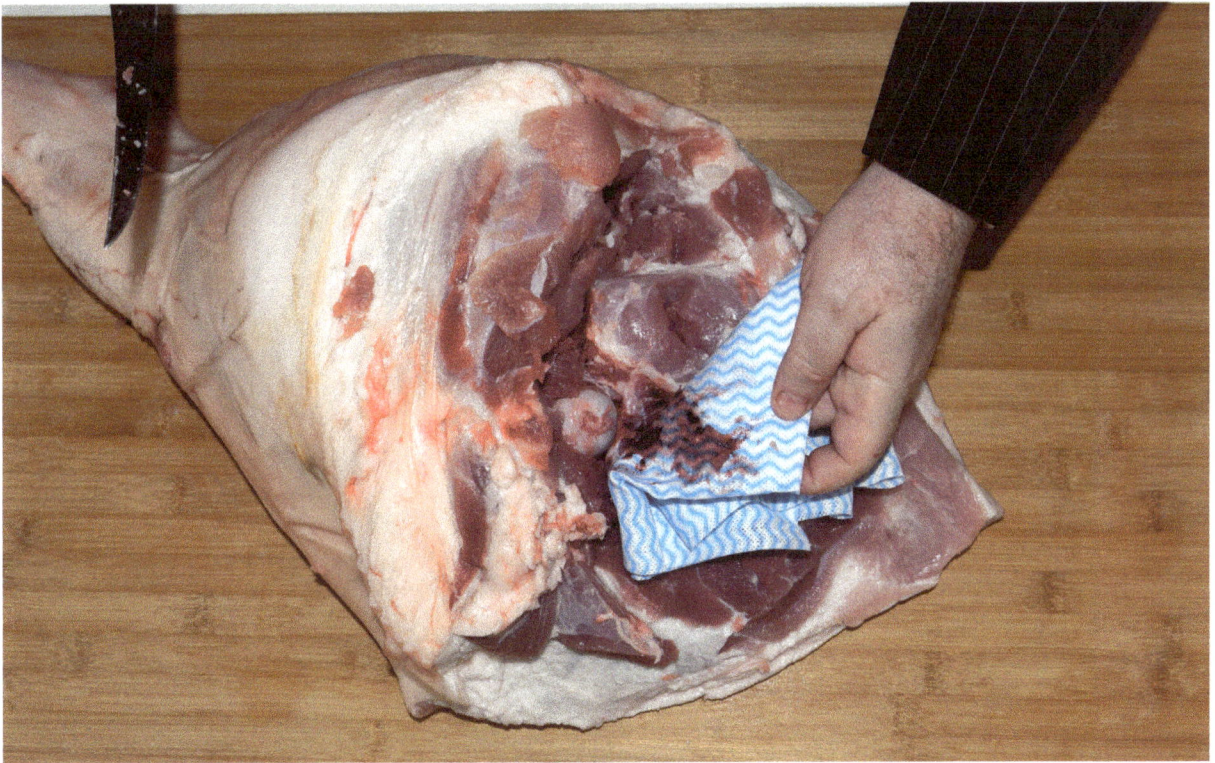

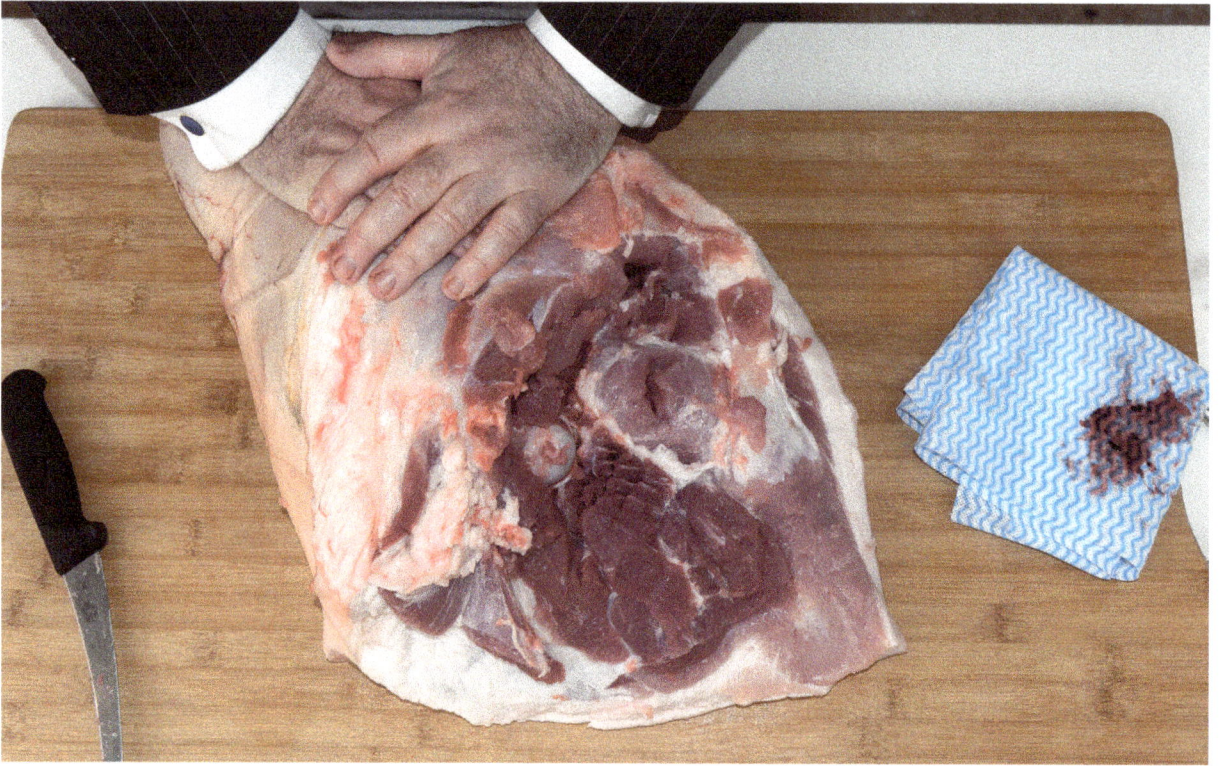

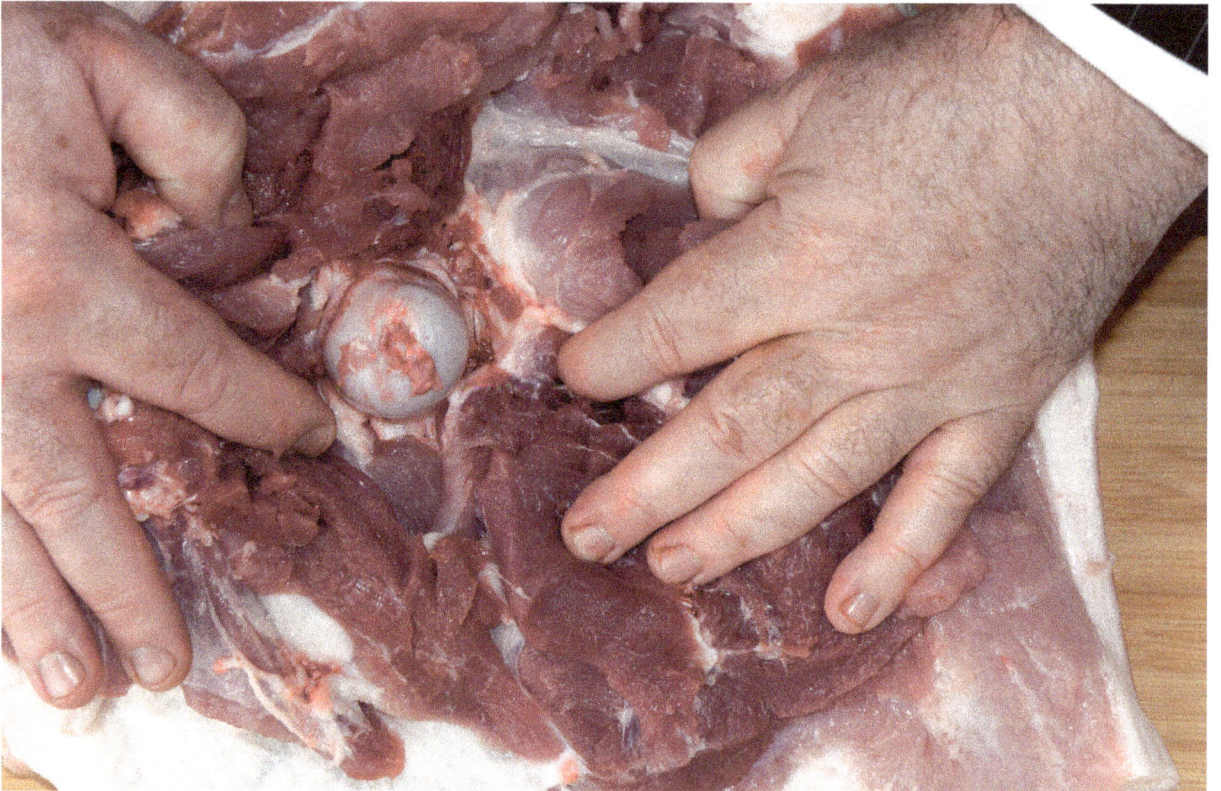

The next task is to trim the meat to expose the head of the femur, trim the leg into a familiar prosciutto shape and to remove any ragged surfaces which can only be conducive to bug entertainment and socialisation.

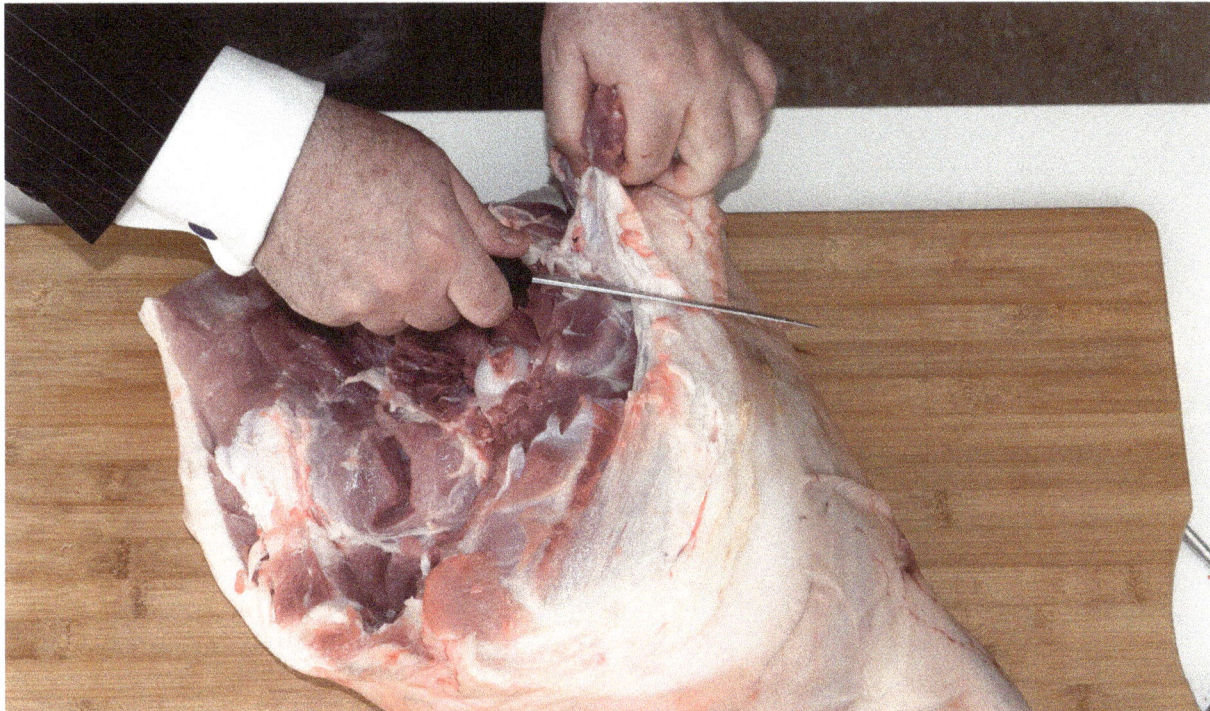

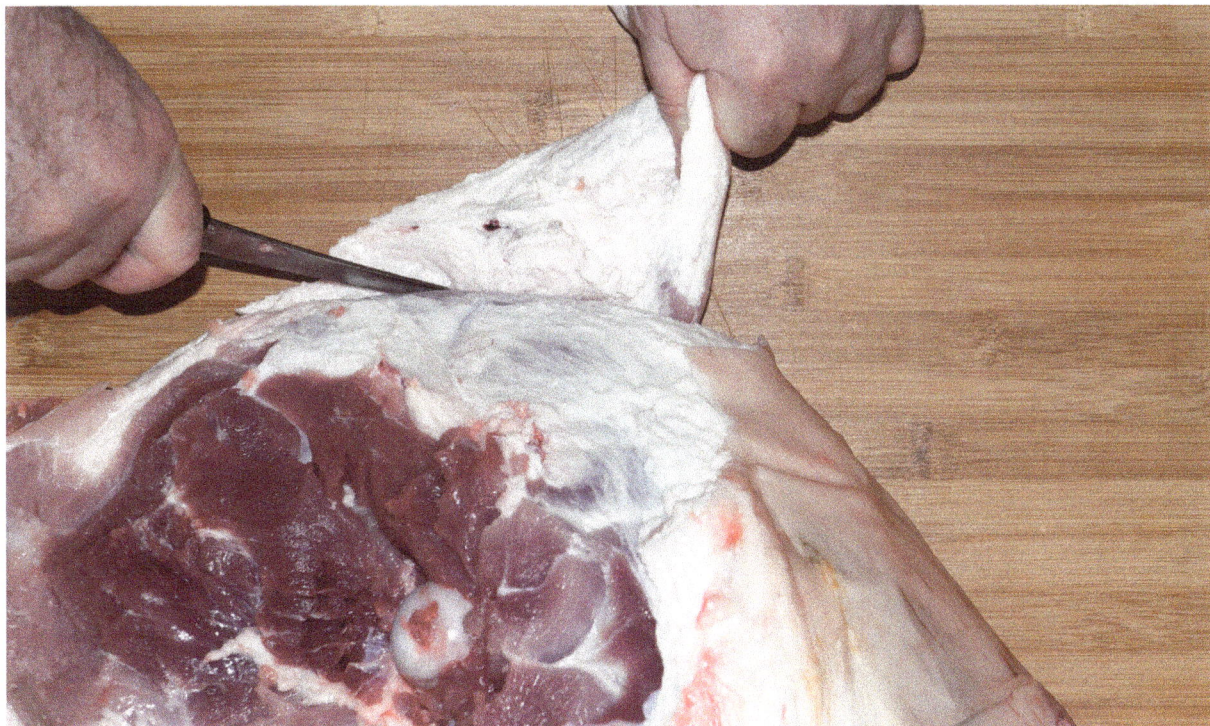

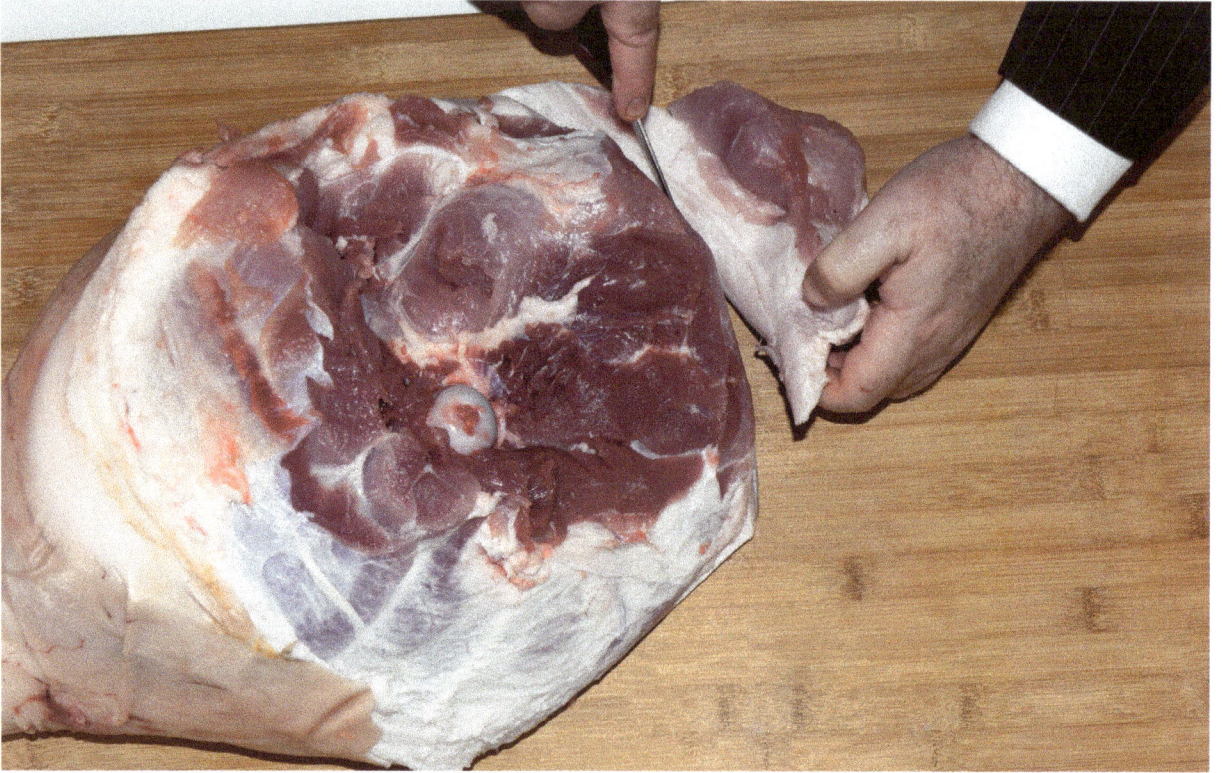
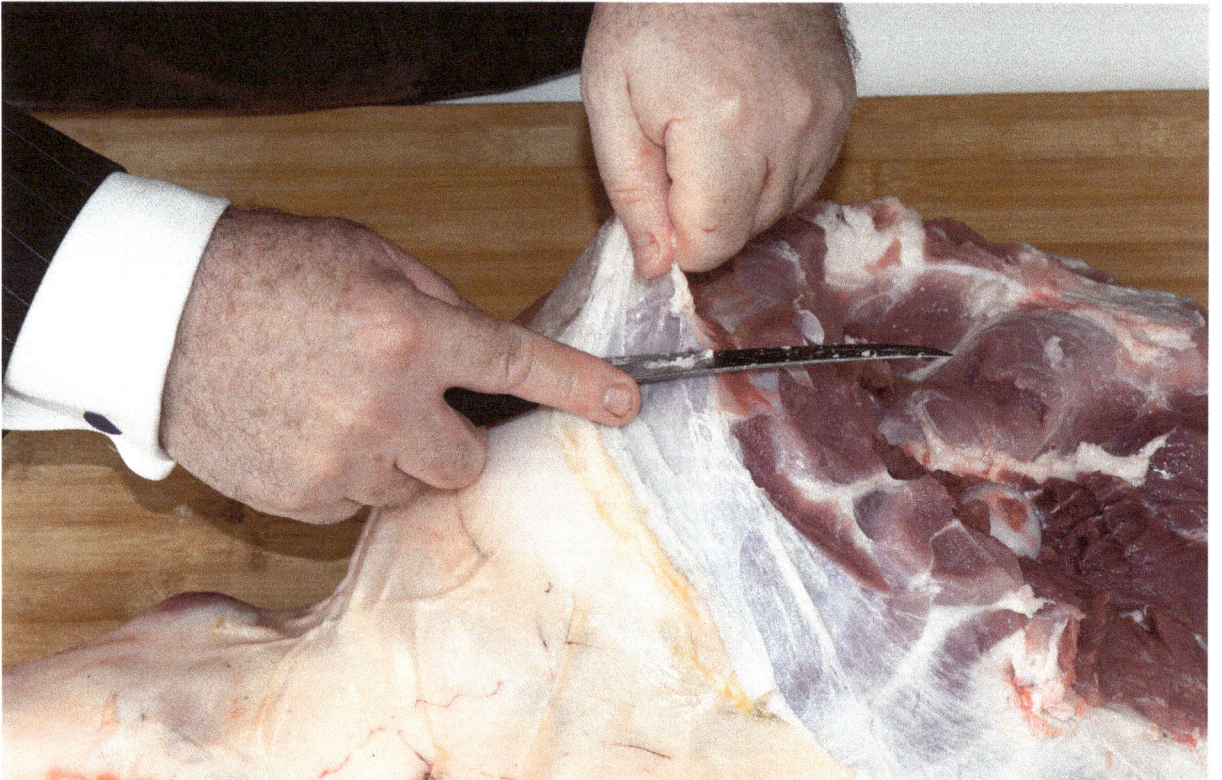

You now have a leg of pork which has been transformed into a classic shape for the purposes of prosciutto production.

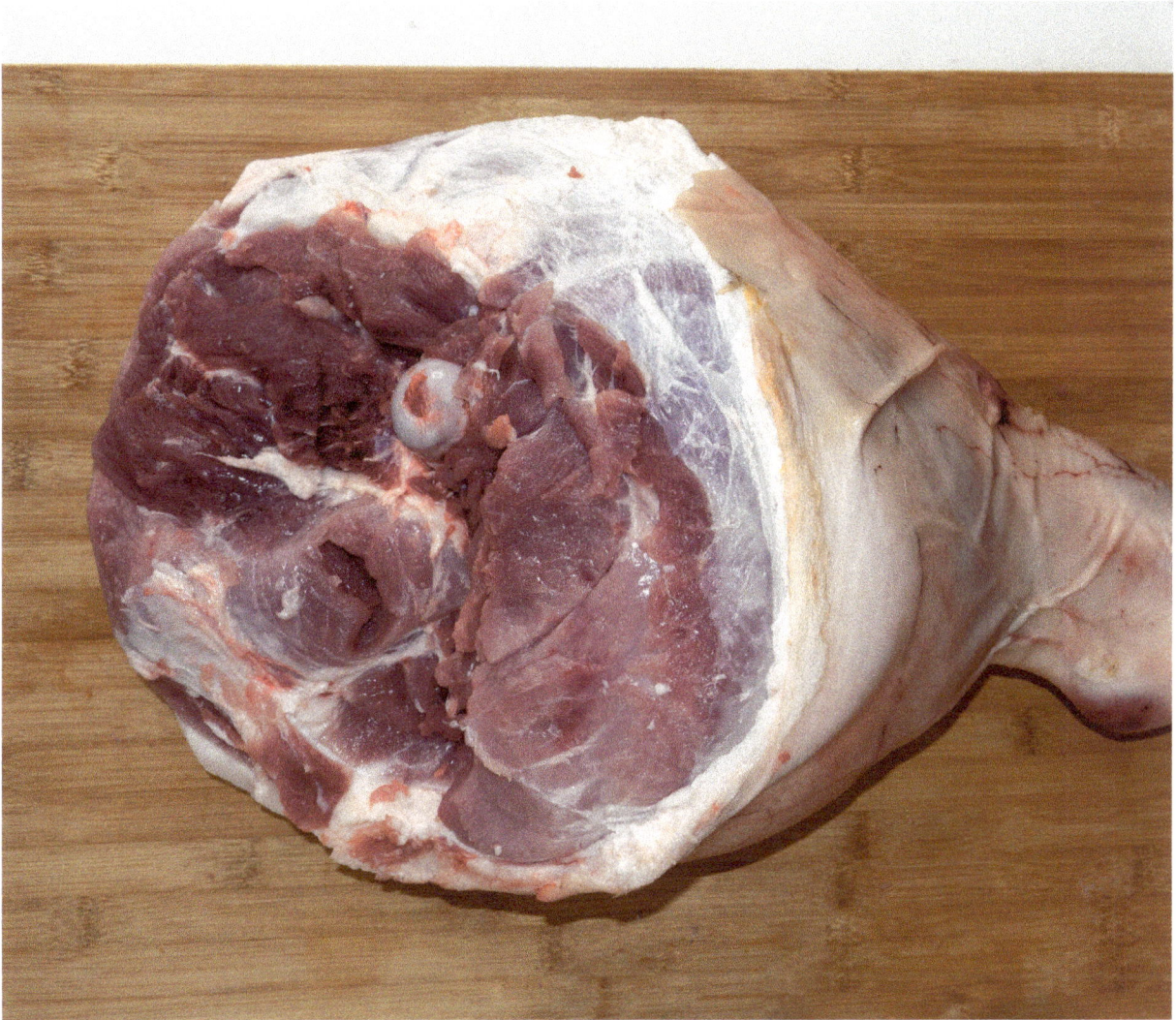

The final decision is whether to remove the hock and trotter. This is a decision in relation to which minds may reasonably differ. On the one hand retaining the leg in its complete glory is not only the classic way to present a prosciutto but is also extremely impressive. It is my preferred course of action. On the other hand, removal of the hock and trotter saves space when salt curing and then in drying the product, which can be extremely important. However, removing the hock and trotter does create a backdoor which provide access to bugs for the purposes of large-scale entertainment. If you choose to remove the hock and trotter you should ensure that the back door is rendered uninviting to bugs. This is done by forcing away the skin and meat from the bone as much as possible and packing the cut surface with salt. If you do not do this it is extremely likely that bugs will gain ingress and spoil meat from inside which will not be visible until it is all too late.

To separate the hock from the leg, first mark the cut with a knife at the desired point. This will usually be dictated by the size of your salt curing container or the height of the space in your drying location. Cut to the bone and then finish the task with a bone saw. Make sure to wipe away the bone dust from the cut surface with a damp cloth. Make sure to pack the cut end with salt and cure.

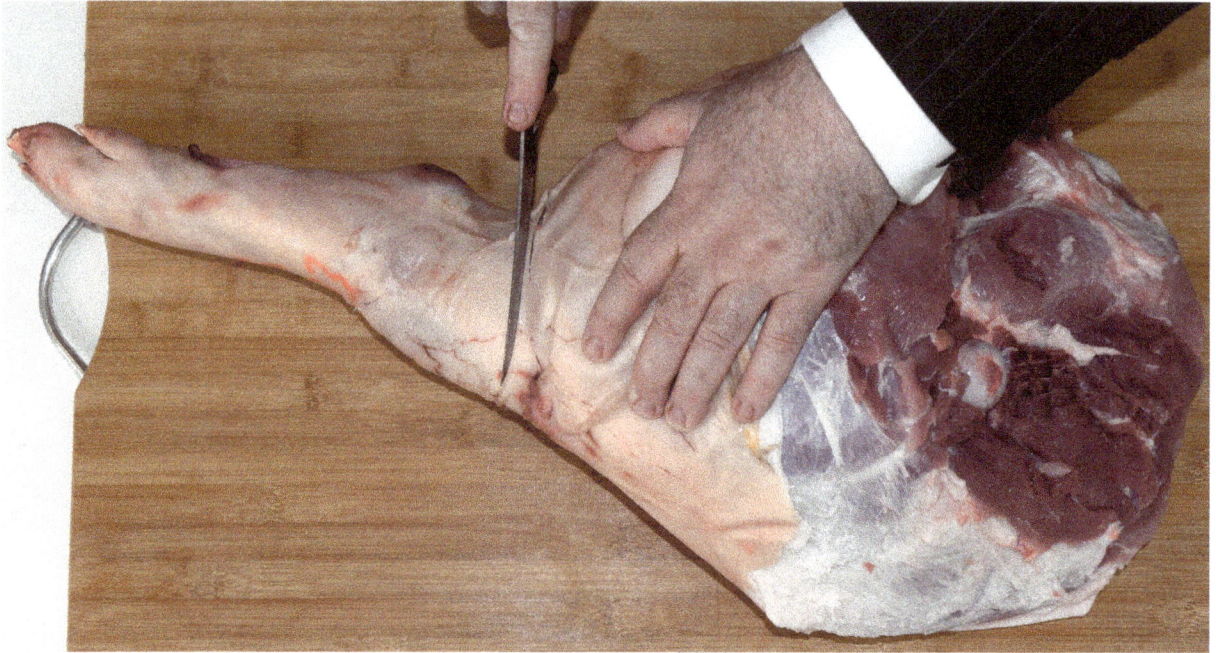

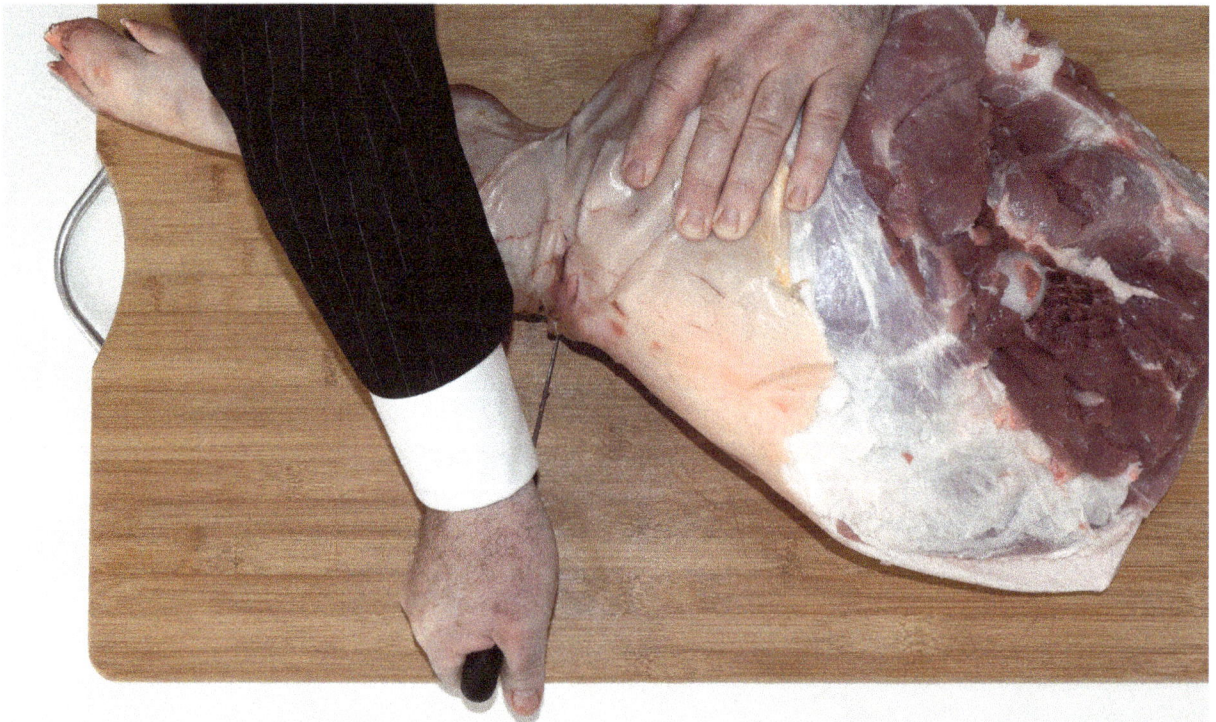

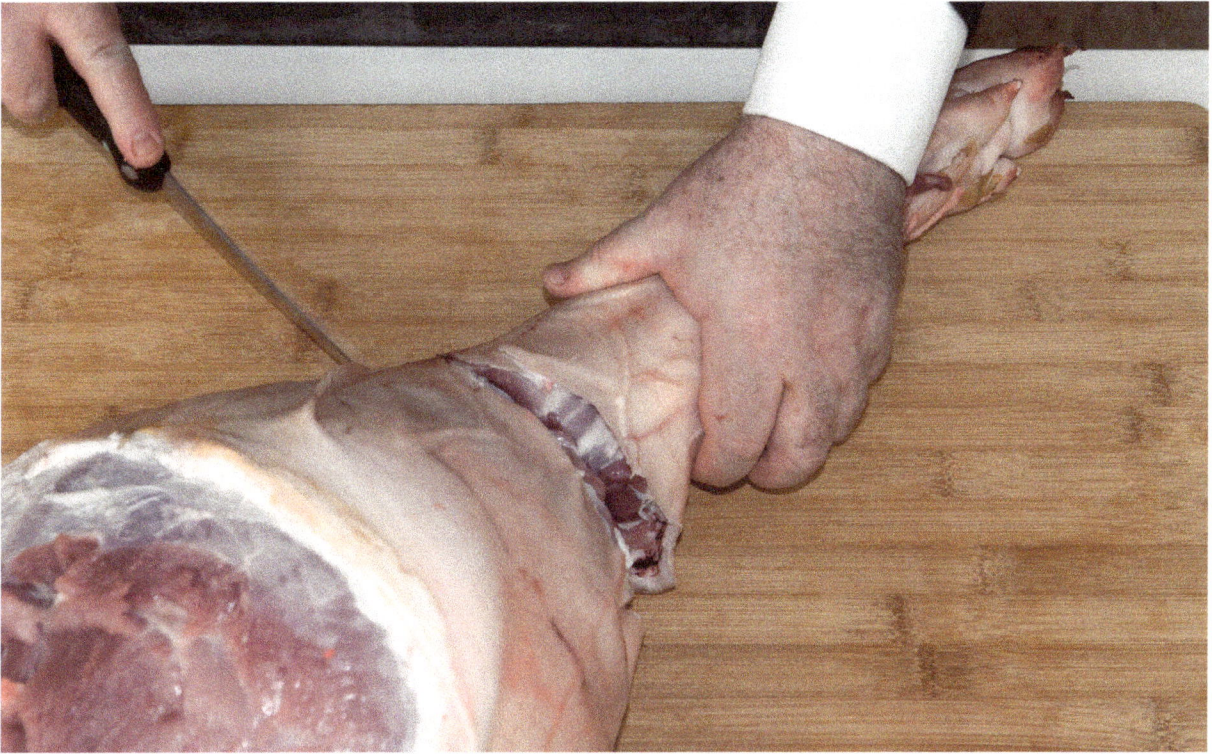

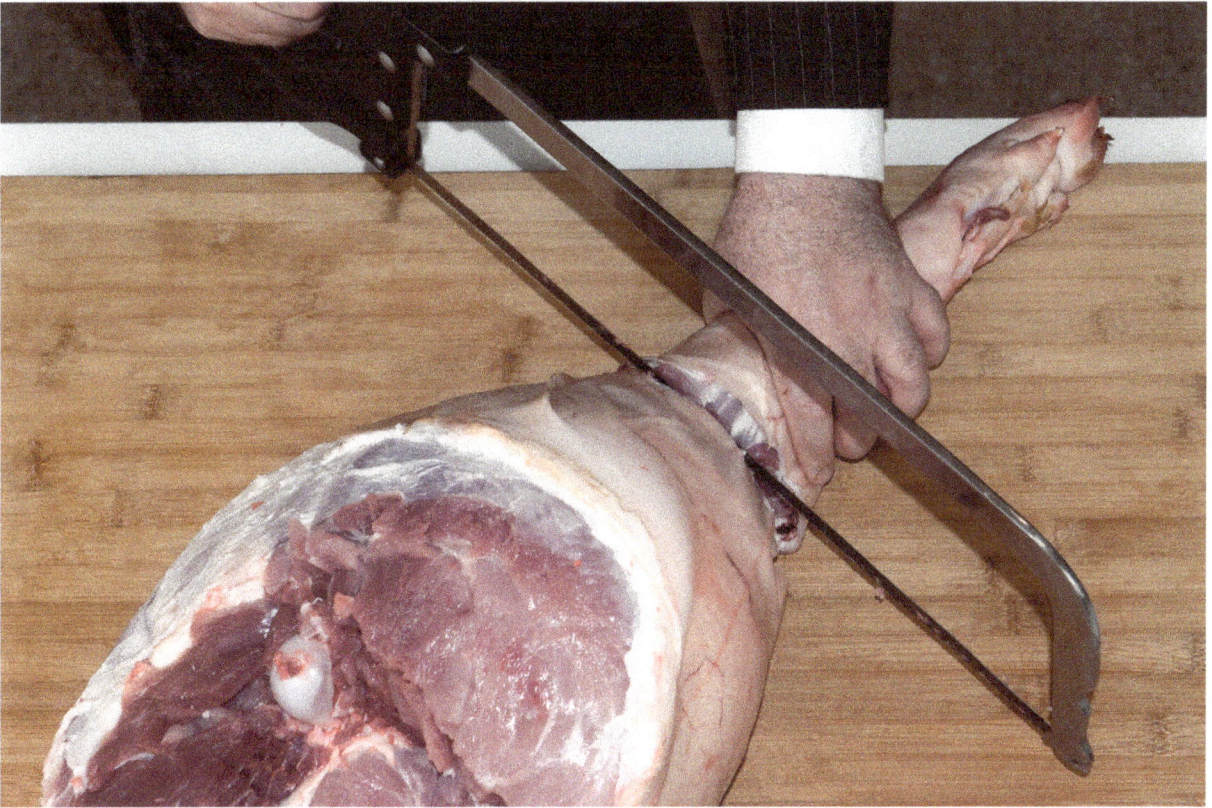

The leg can now be processed for prosciutto without any further butchery steps. Alternatively, the bone can be removed so a boneless prosciutto is achieved. This has benefits when it comes to slicing the prosciutto, but it does create a greater surface area which will provide opportunities for bug festivities. Another option is to compress the leg in a steel mesh press. These devices give a nice flat profile to the prosciutto and may accelerate the air-drying process. However, neither is necessary.

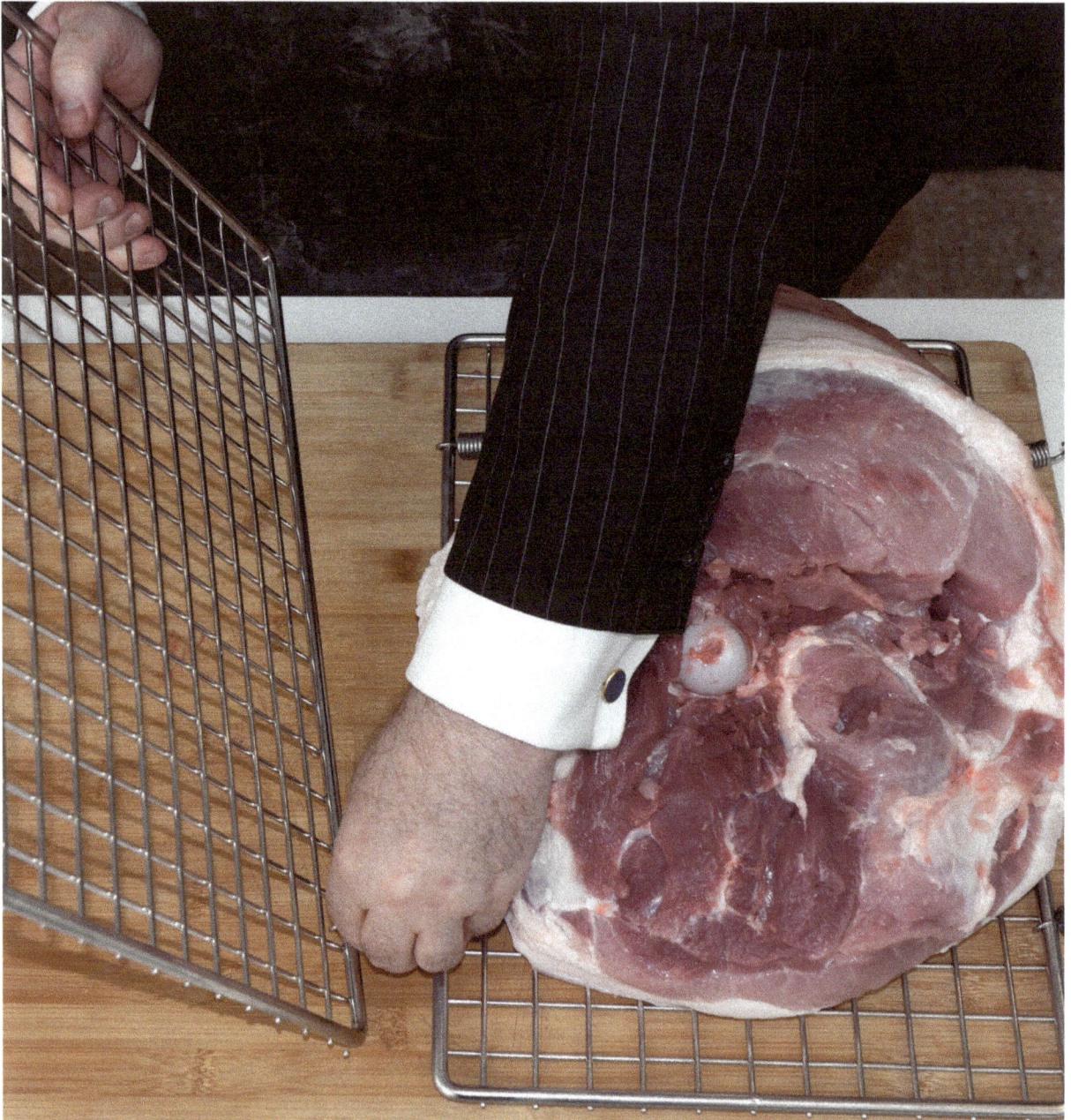

Lastly do not discard the hock and trotter. They have multiple uses. The hock can be separated from the trotter, cured and smoked. Think pea and ham soup or braised with lentils or sauerkraut. The trotter can be braised if you like that sort of thing. A more challenging use is to keep the hock and trotter intact, tunnel bone out the bones and meat without piercing the skin. Using a bone saw cut through the bone but leave the trotter attached to the skin. The now empty hock is a vessel to be stuffed but with the trotter attached. It can be filled with minced meat and skin, and then poached. This is the Italian classic, zampone. A lesser-known use is to fill the empty hock and trotter with hand cut meat and fat which is then air dried. This is a high-risk product, but I have made it with some success. It is a variation on ventrecina, made in a pig's stomach. (see Squeal for details).

THE SHOULDER

It is now time to deal with the shoulder. The shoulder is an extremely complex primal, it has lots of bones, a prized section of meat for charcuterie and a difficult foreleg joint to remove. Much of the shoulder will be used for trim, the hock can be cured and smoked, or the hock and trotter boned out and used for a zampone. However, the real purpose of the shoulder from a charcuterie perspective is the muscle known as the scotch fillet or the Boston butt or the coppa. It is a large complex muscle buried deep in the shoulder between the spine and ribs and the foreleg joint. Because it is largely invisible until the whole spine and ribs are removed special care must be taken not to destroy it during the process.

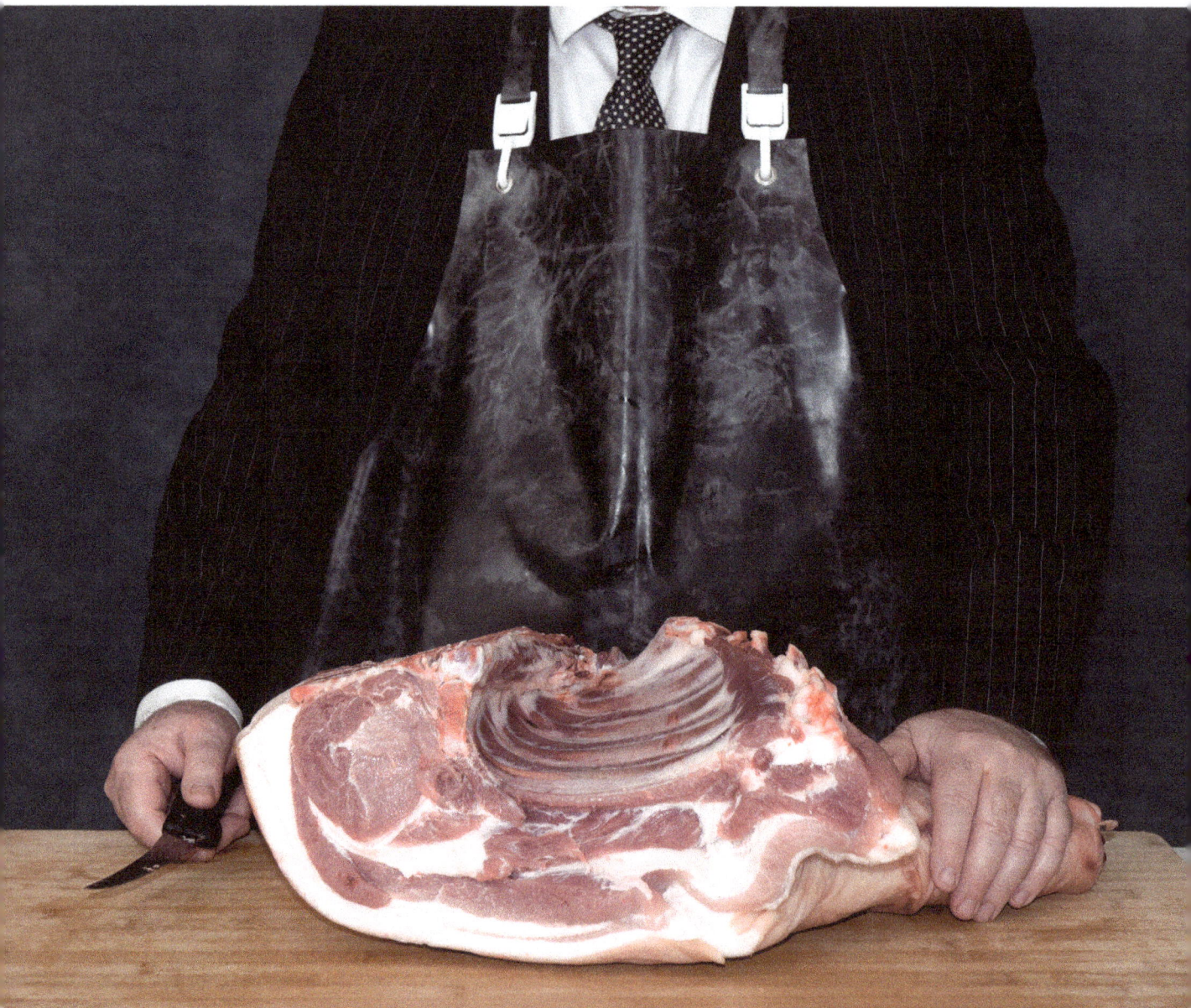

In the images above the end of the coppa where it overlaps with the beginning of the loin can be seen approximately below the knife. The loin is the paler section of meat, the coppa is the darker meat. You will recall that the reason to separate the shoulder from the mid-section at the point of the fifth and sixth ribs is to maximise the length of the coppa.

Using a knife mark a line along ribs approximately in the middle of the widest part, then cut through the ribs using a saw taking care not to damage the meat below.

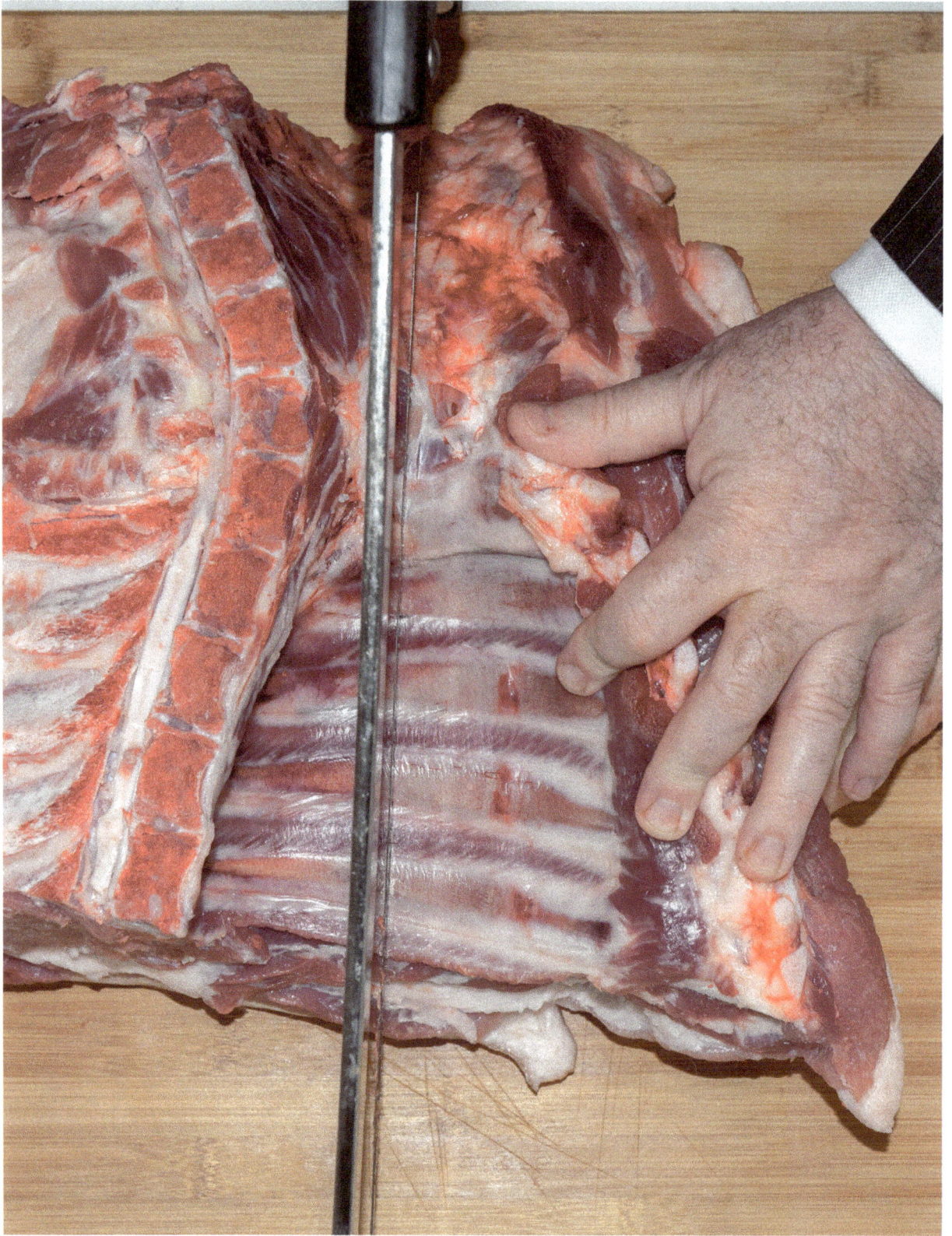

Next carefully separate the bones from the meat below, again taking care not to damage the coppa.

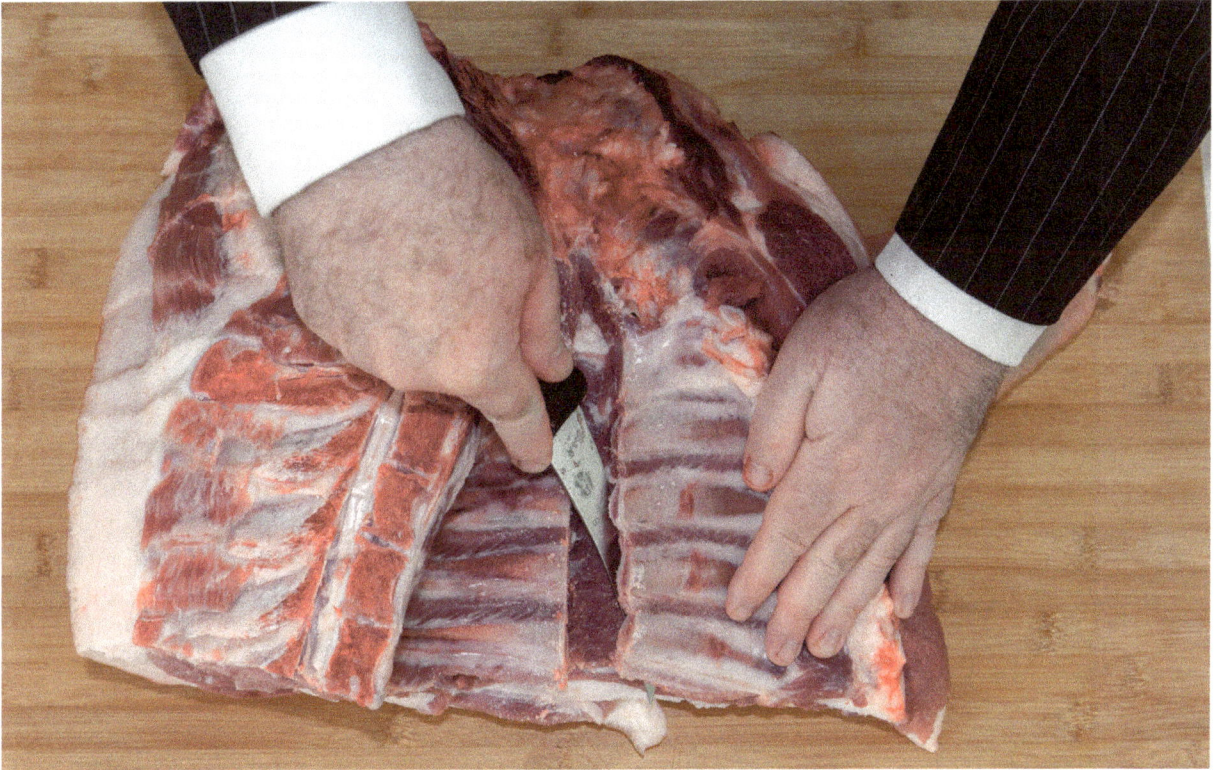

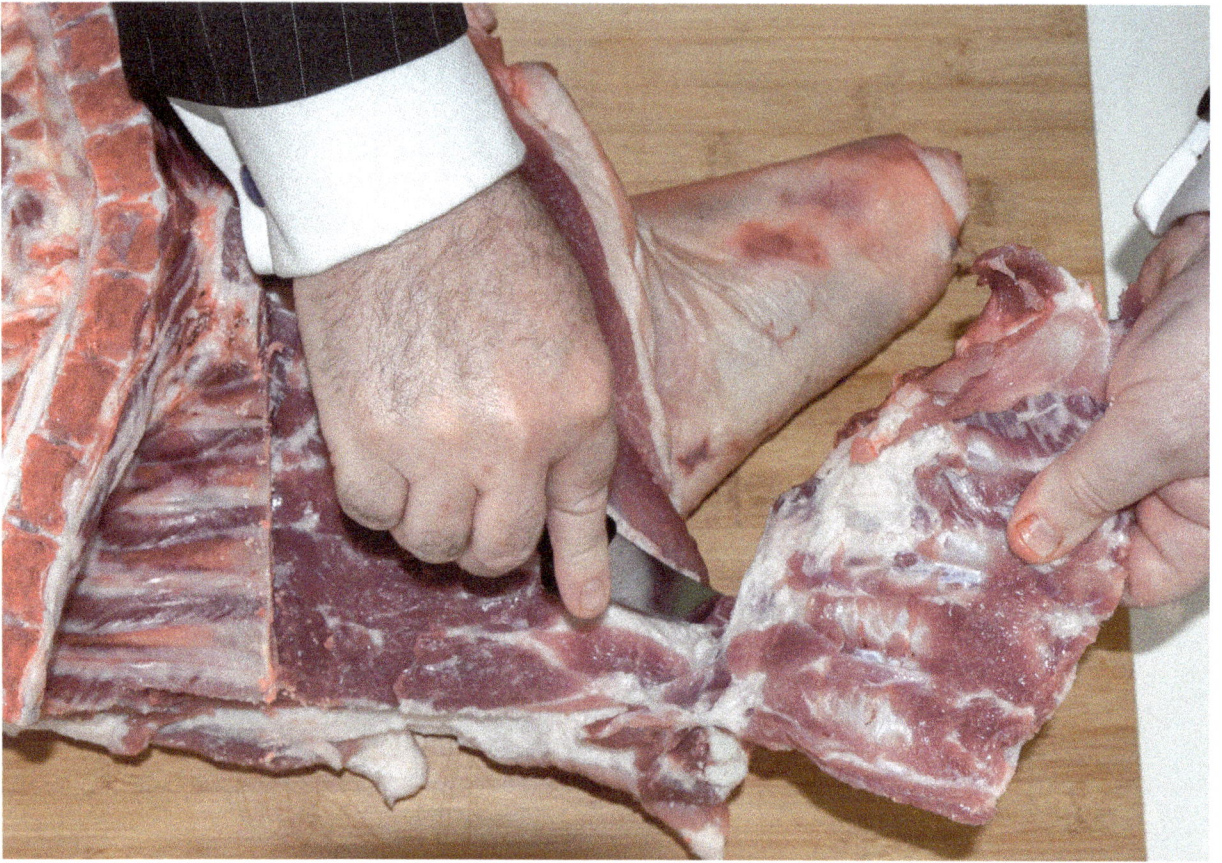

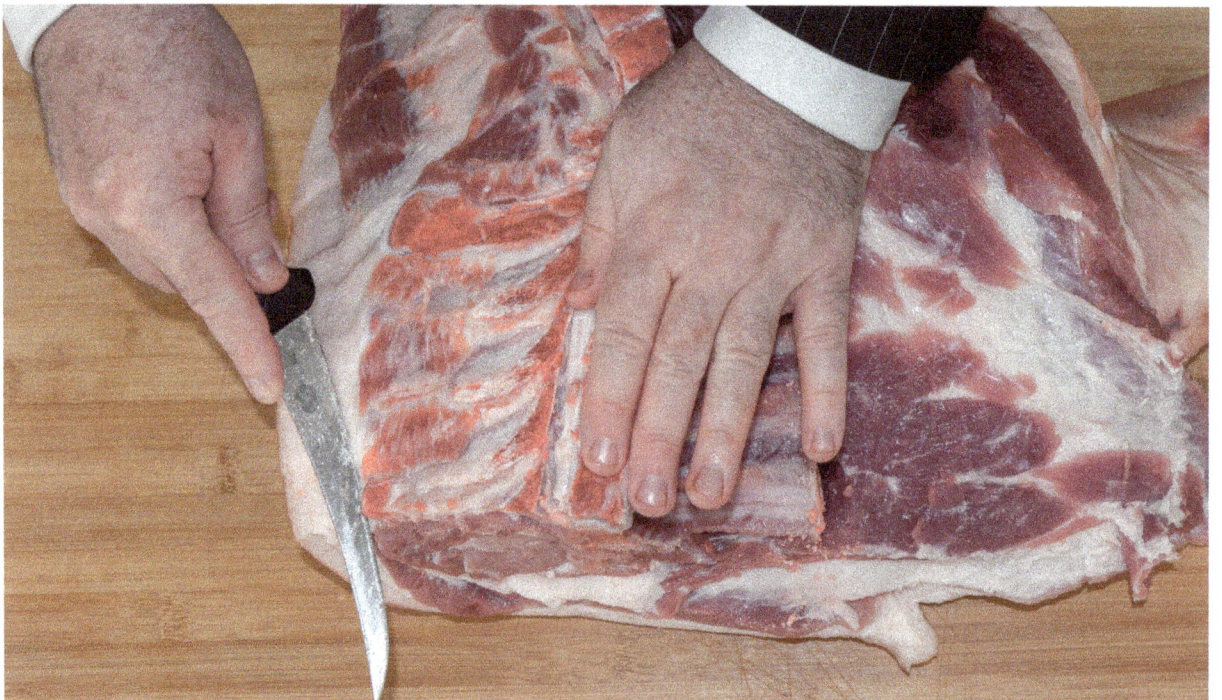

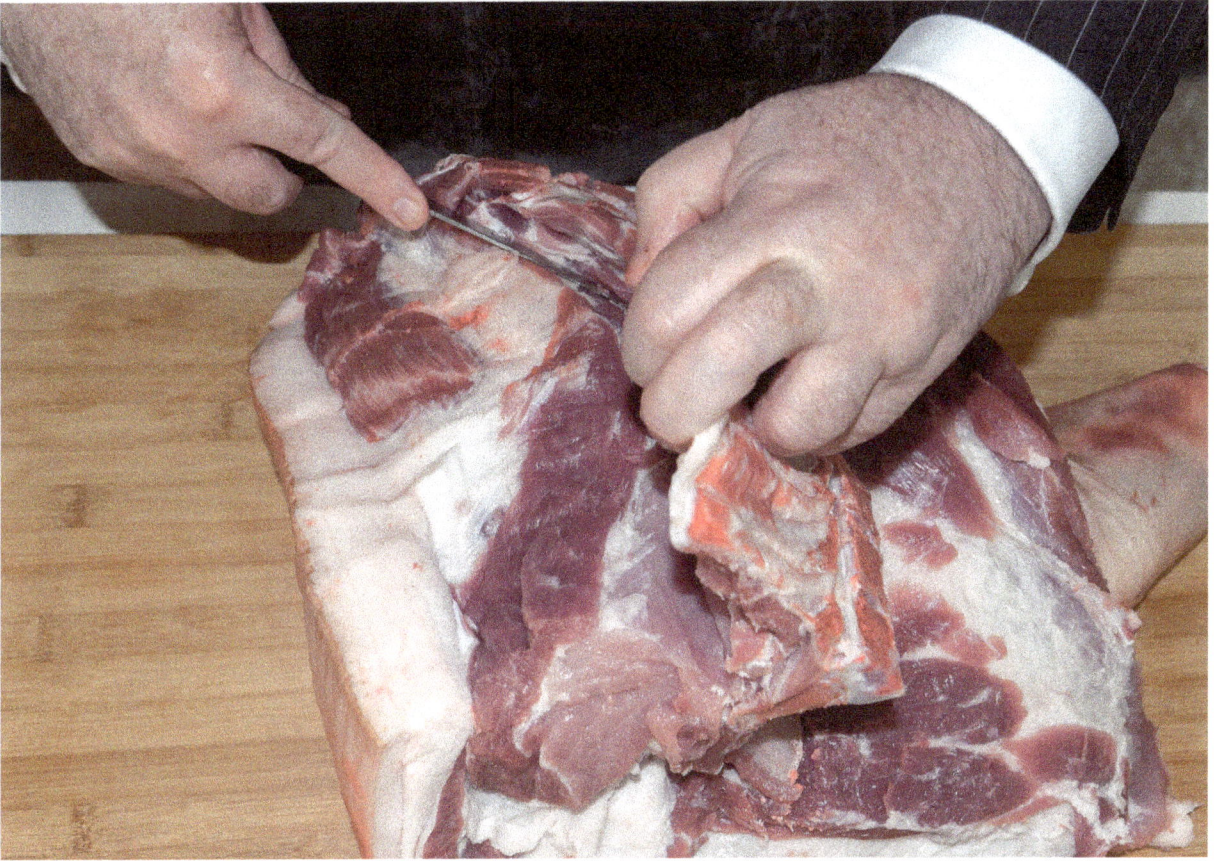

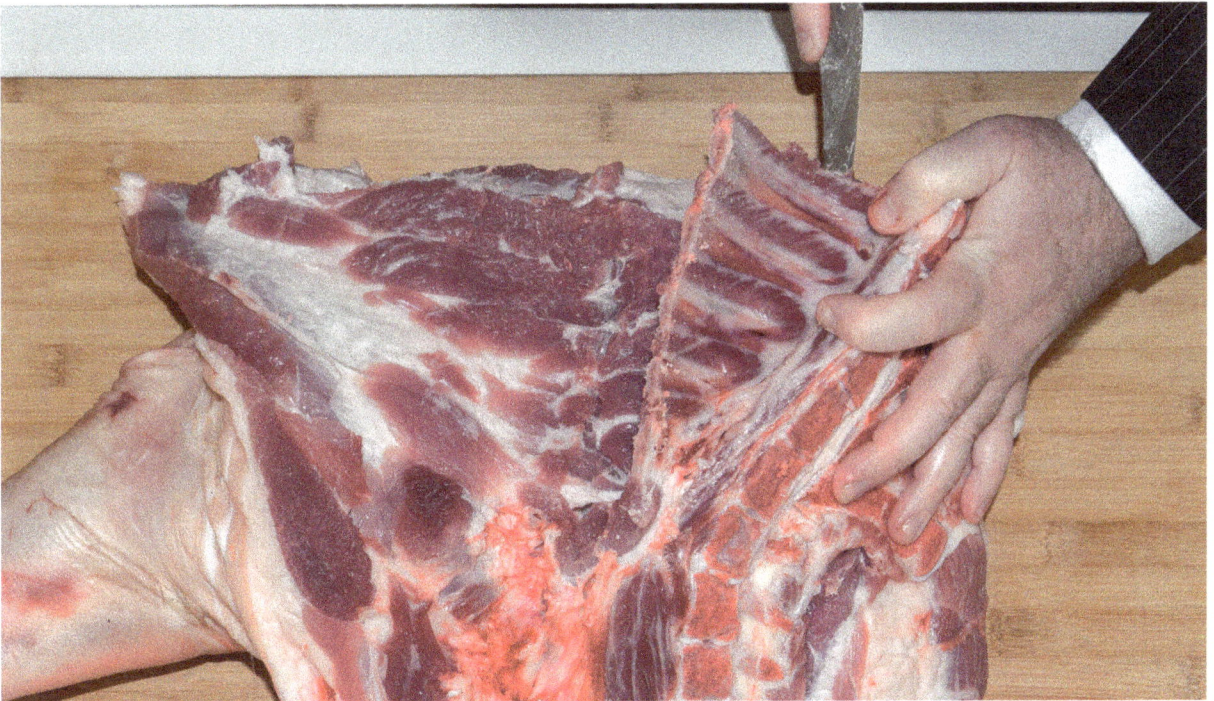

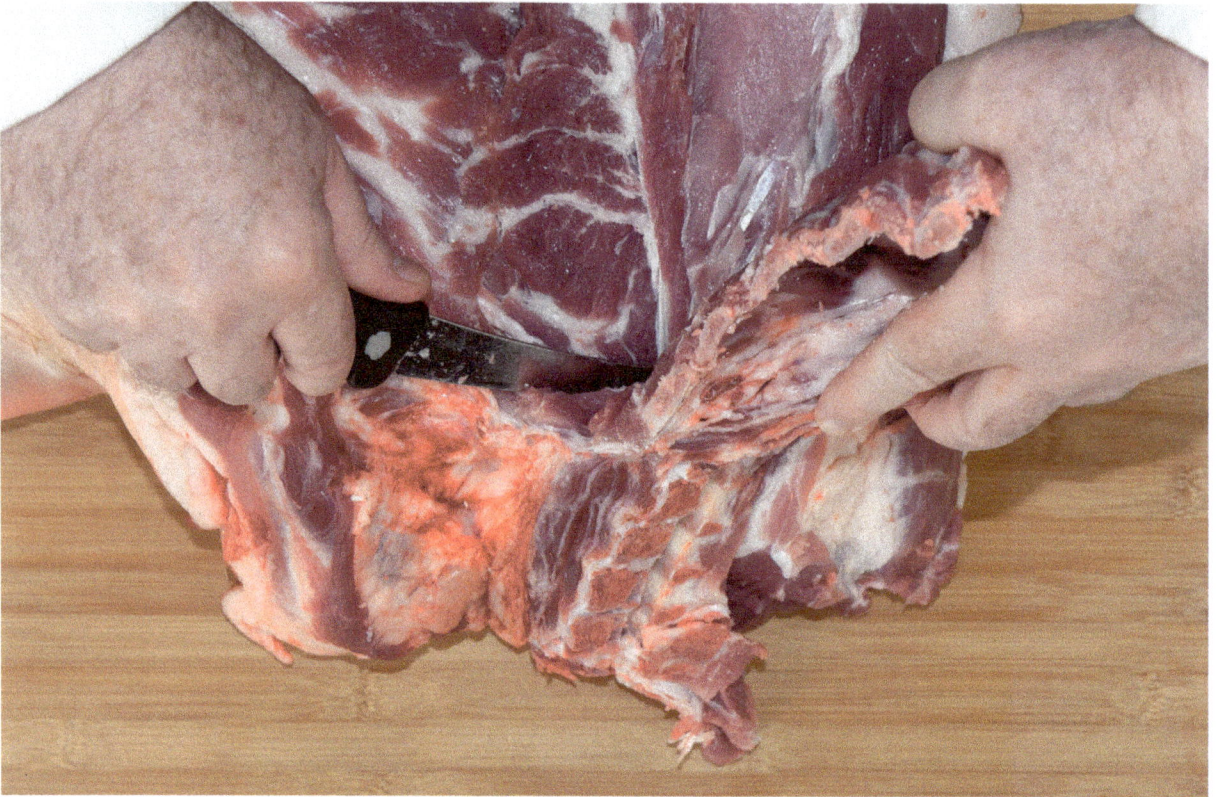
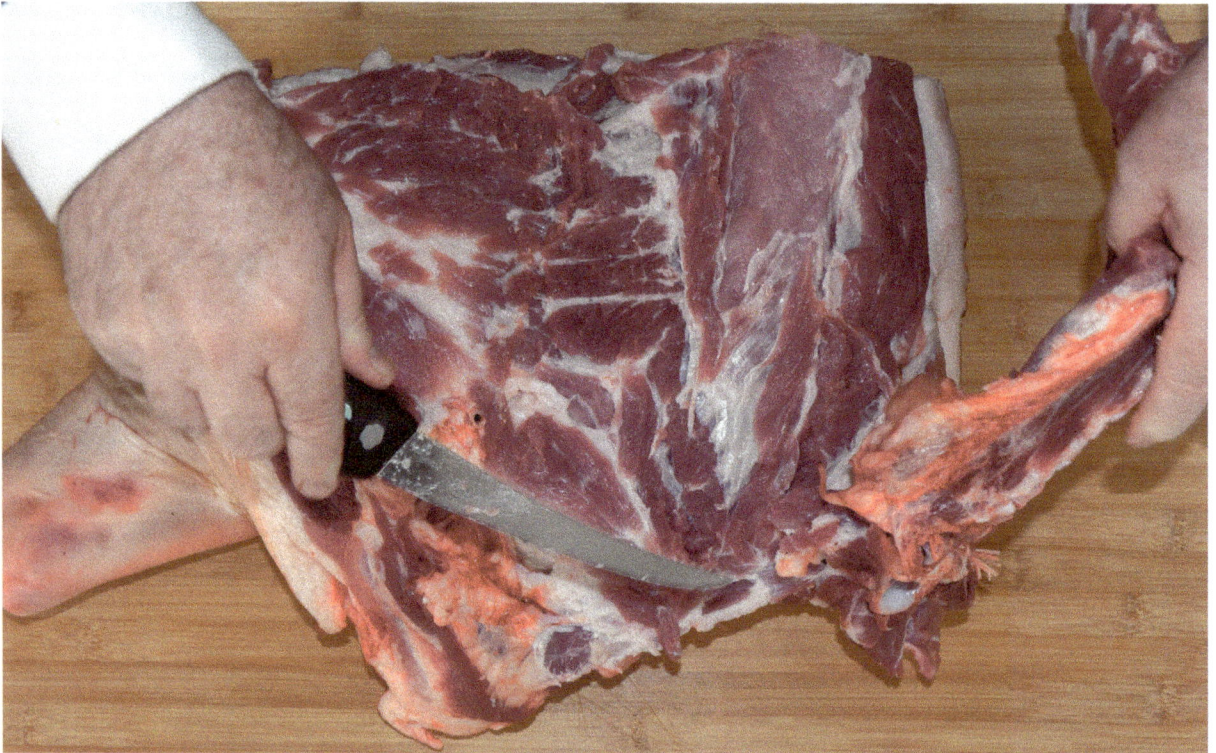

Now start separating the coppa from the remainder of the shoulder by first making an incision along the inside edge and then carefully cutting beneath by using the muscle seams as a guide. The full coppa is not a single muscle but rather a complex group of muscles with several large seams of fat running along the length. It is, depending upon the size of the animal, between 2 and 3 kg in weight and roughly oval or nearly cylindrical in shape. However, it is not as well-defined as the fillet and certainly not a single muscle as in the case of the fillet.

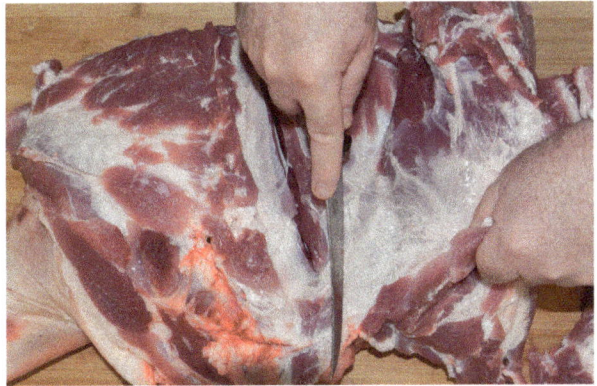

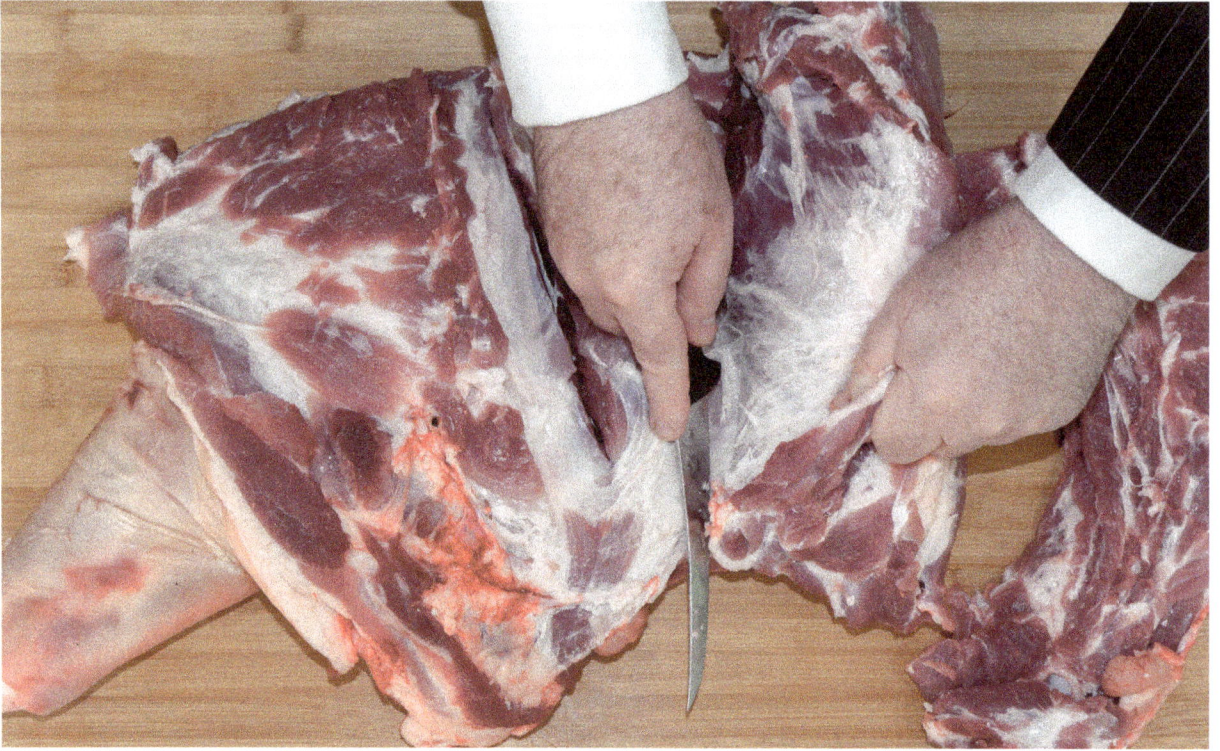
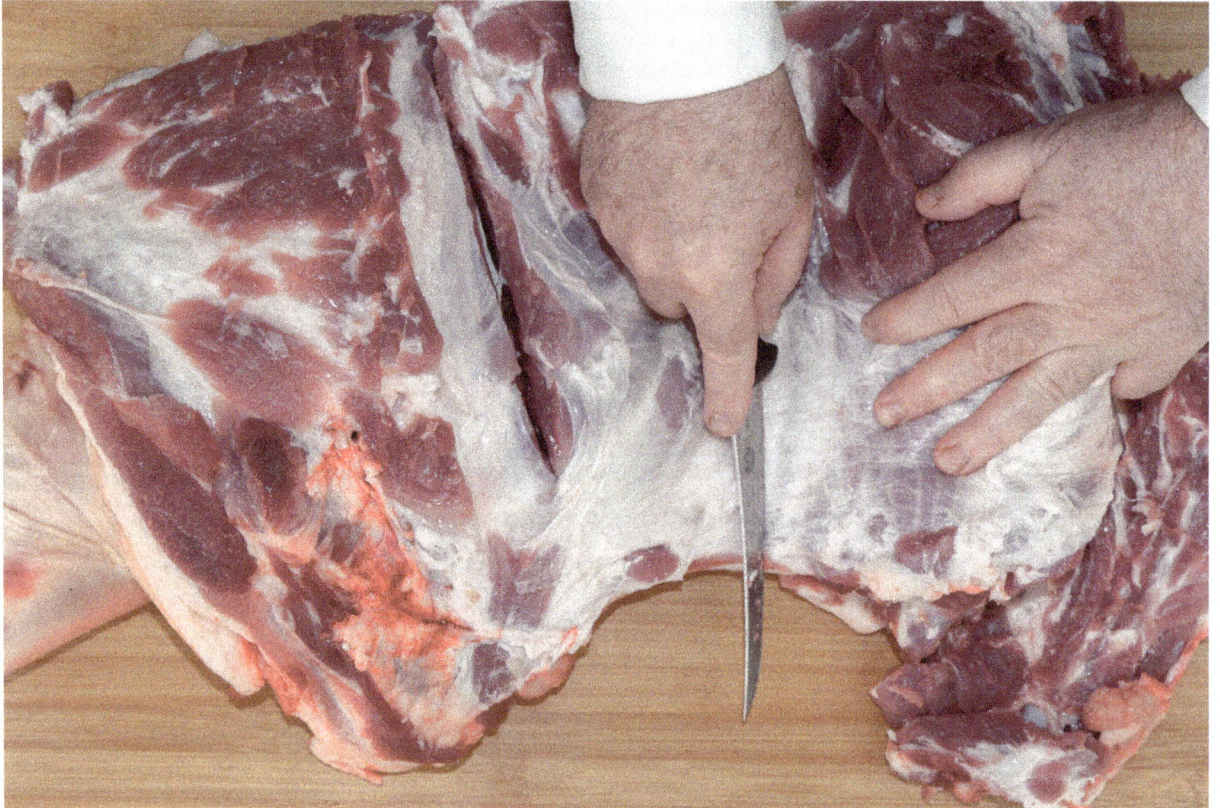

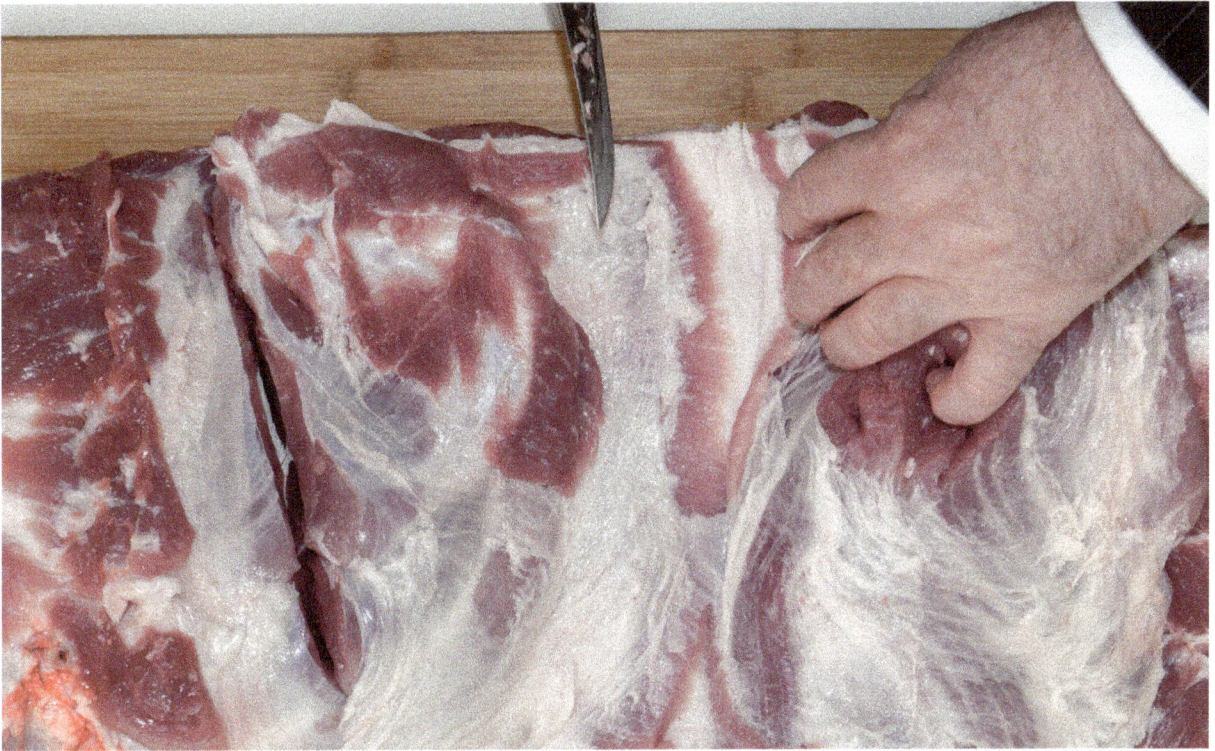
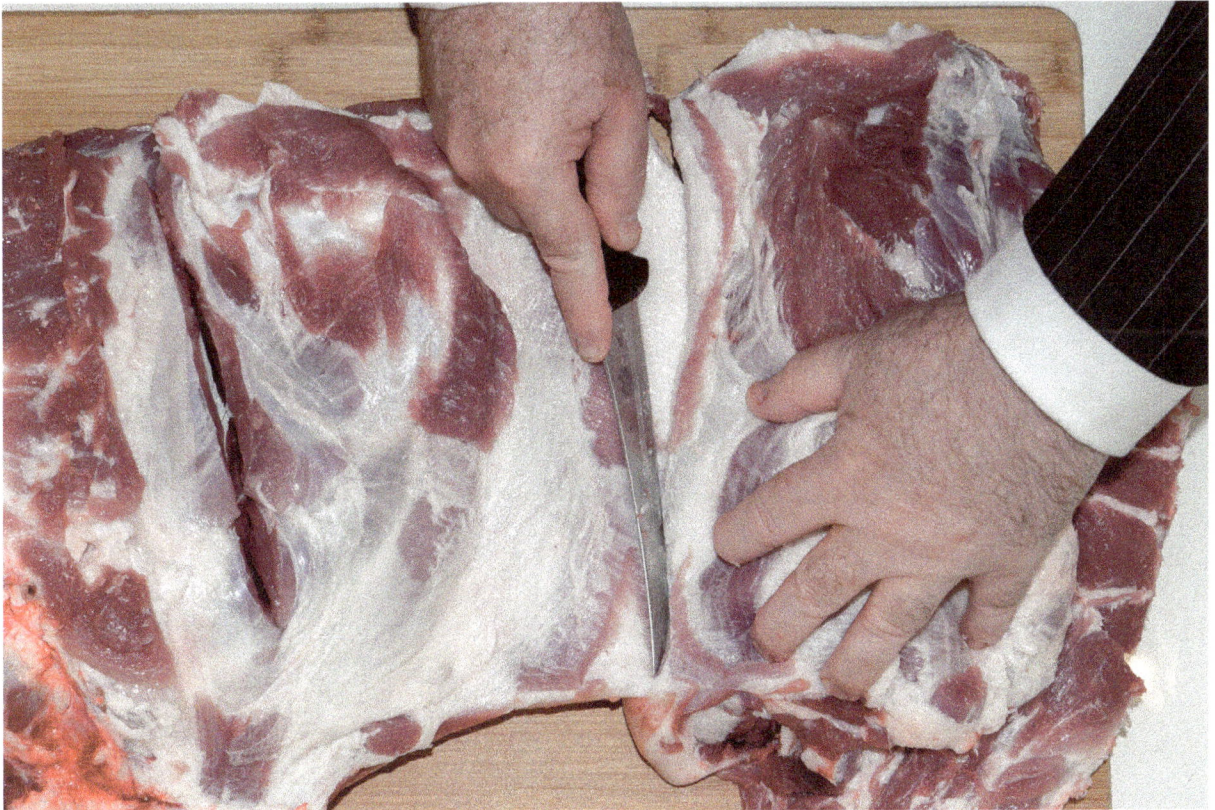

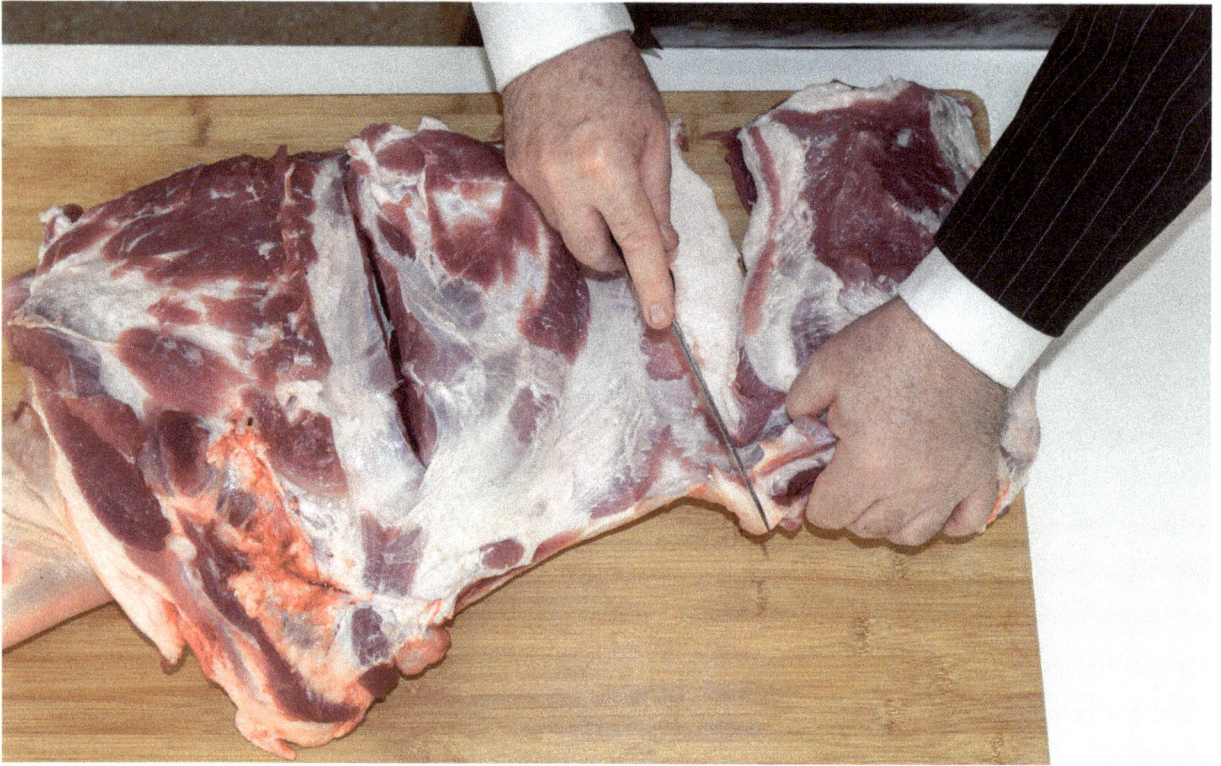

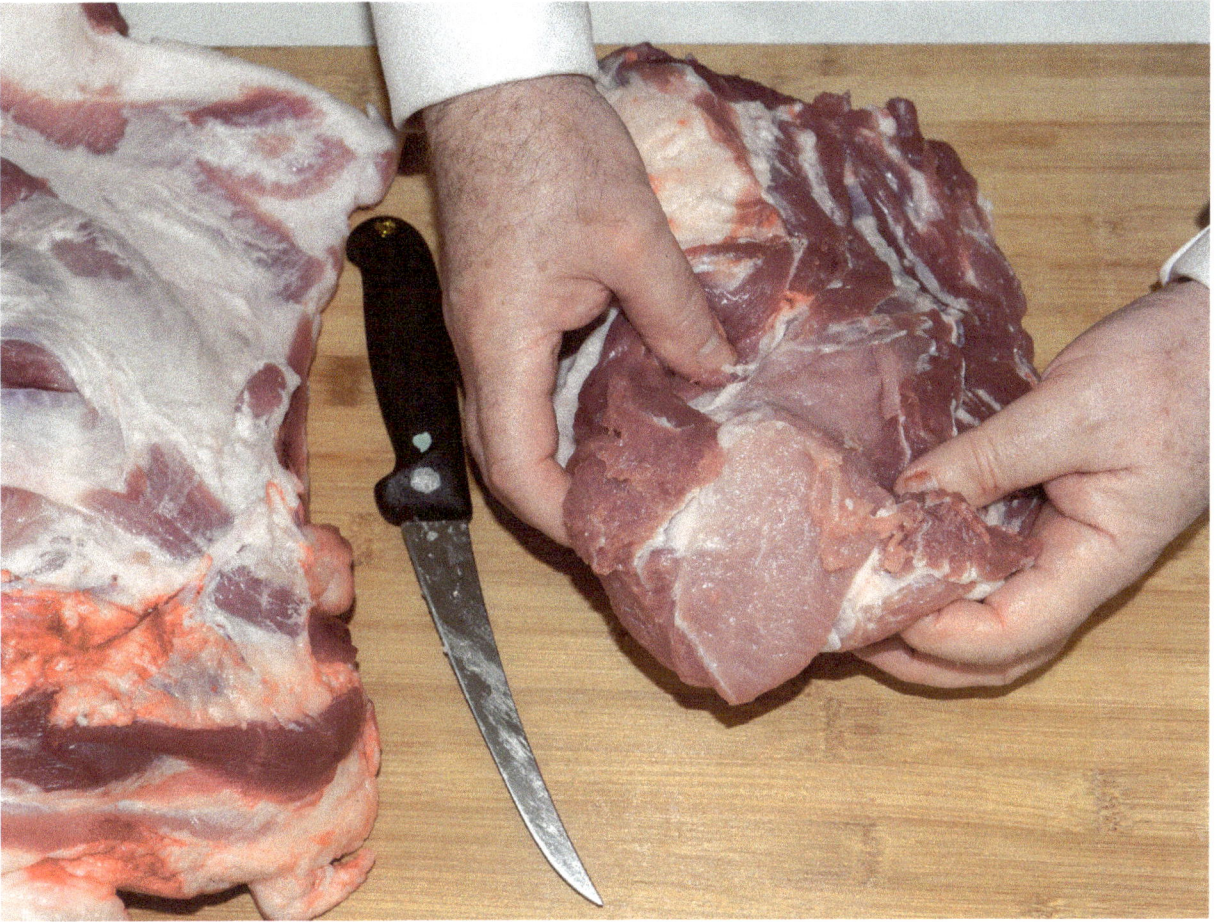

Once the coppa has been separated then trim or square off the ends and remove any ragged surfaces. The classic profile of the coppa can be seen once the end is squared off, a complex pattern of meat and internal fat.

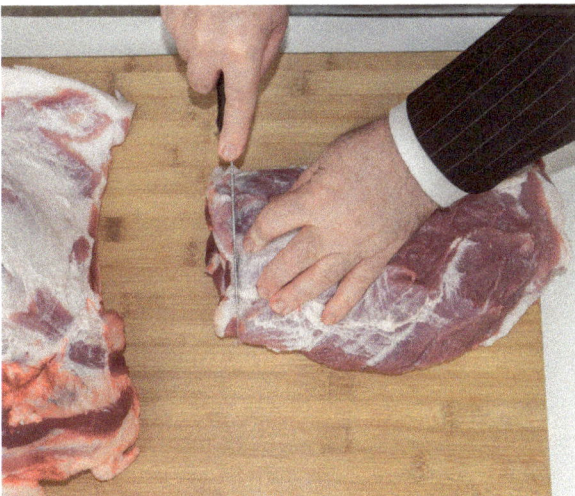

The remainder of the shoulder has no particular value in charcuterie as individual muscle cuts but is highly desirable for the purposes of mince. The mince is used to produce air-dried sausages and is highly prized because of its ratio of meat to fat which is about 70:30 or 80:20, ideal for air dried sausage production. In this example I use the remaining shoulder meat to prepare meat for that purpose. In so doing I separated meat, fat, and skin. Remember that even the skin is useful. It can be minced and added to products such as cottechino or used to wrap around lean meat for roasting.

THE END

At the end after a lot of hard work you have reduced a 30 kg or 40 kg half pig carcass to a series of products which are used in the production of charcuterie. You should be rightly proud of your work. You can now prceed to create artisan charcuterie.

You will also have a lot of trim, go through this and separate skin, sinew and connective tissue from anything that is useful.

Congratulations you are now an artisan butcher of the charcuterie persuasion.

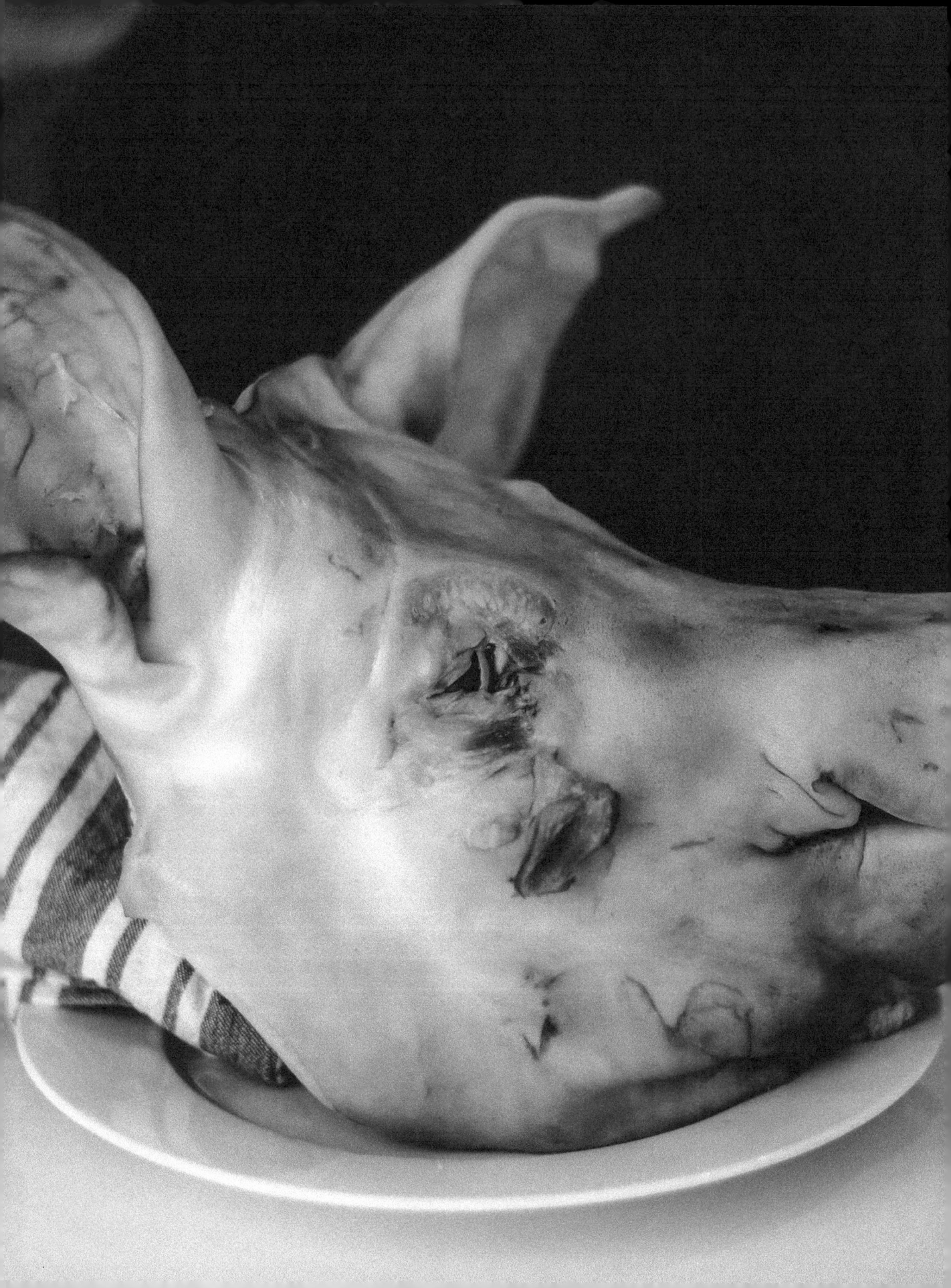

THE HEAD

The fourth primal, the bit that no one wants except the charcutier (that is you by the way). The head of a commercial pig is quite substantial. It will weigh more than 5 kg with a yield, after boning, of approximately 2.5 kg - 3.5 kg. Deboning a pig head sounds quite daunting but it is not difficult, just take your time.

Make sure the head is clean, particularly the inside of the ears and that it has no hair. Commercial pig is usually very well cleaned and devoid of hairs. Make sure that you select a pigs head which has the ears intact and, if possible, also the tongue.

Place the hand on a board with the cut side up and the snout facing you. Strategically placed rolled up damp tea towels will help balance the head. Do not remove the ears at this stage, they help balance the head. You could start from the opposite side, that is to say the face of the head but I think the end result is neater if you start from the rear.

Start peeling the tissue away from the head on one side, trying to keep as much meat and fat on the meat side as possible. Also try not to pierce the flesh and the skin. This part takes some time and it will be necessary to rotate the head and reposition it from time to time.

Try and remove the snout intact and attached to the rest of the meat fat and skin. It looks quite good in the finished product.

Take particular care when both sides are off and you are attempting to remove the final part being the centre of the "face". There is very little fat, virtually no meat and the bone is really just overlaid by the skin. This is where you are most likely to pierce the skin . If do it is not the end of the world as we know it.

Now that you have removed the flesh and skin from the skull you can discard the skull but not before you dig inside and remove the tongue.

The quite significant piece of meat you have now it is often referred to by butchers as the mask.

There will be two large holes where the eyes were positioned and perhaps some slight open parts on the jawline.

Now remove the ears as close to the point where they join the head as possible.

You will observe that the mask has little meat, quite a lot of fat and obviously is still attached to the skin.

Remove any obvious blood vessels or bruised meat. Next look for any glandular tissue, in takes the form of small jellybean like shapes of slightly different colour to the rest of the meat. They are not good to eat. You will find small clumps of glands on inside where the corner of the jaw was and also higher up near where the ears joined. Remove any glands and discard them.

Trim the tongue and remove any obvious blood vessels from the base of the tongue. The tongue does not need to be skinned, the skin is quite thin unlike a beef tongue.

The deboned head has many uses. It can be stuffed with pork mince, rolled and cooked, the classic French dish porc de tete farci or a favourite, rolled and cooked to make the Italian porchetta de testa. In the case of porchetta de testa the mask (together with ears and tongue) is cured in a brine for several days. Once it is removed the tongue is replaced roughly in its original position, the ears are placed, on the cut surface to cover the holes with the eyes used to be . It is seasoned rolled tightly and then cooked in the sous vide. (see Squeal for details)

SOME TECHNIQUES

Having gone this far it would be remiss of me not to include some charcuterie techniques which are beneficial if not essential to preparation of the products once they have been butchered and prior to final steps in the production towards artisan charcuterie.

You have come a long way, do not give up on me now.

Hanging strings

Once the meat has been prepared it will then be cured and either smoked or air dried. In either of the two latter possibilities, it is usually convenient to hang the meat such that it is not touching other surfaces. The reason for this is perhaps obvious but let me explain, nonetheless. Once the meat has been salt cured it then needs to air dry to complete the preservation process. However, if the raw, albeit salt cured meat, is not fully exposed to air but touching another surface, then it will not air dry evenly. More importantly the surface of the raw meat which is touching another surface will be prone to bug infestation. In other words, notwithstanding the raw meat has been salt cured if it is not completely exposed to air those parts of it which are not will spoil. They will spoil very quickly indeed. It follows that if the meat is placed on a rack, then it will not air dry properly, if it is placed on a flat surface that it will not air dry properly, if it is touching even a small part surface area on another surface then it will not air dry properly. All these surfaces which are not exposed to the air will be prone to bug festivities and spoilage. There is a simple solution. Hang the meat from strings so that it is not touching any other surface including other pieces of meat.

This is an easy thing to achieve I hear you say. Maybe, maybe not. I started this journey by making a hole in the piece of meat, usually belly bacon, with a knife. Sometimes a metal skewer was deployed. The intention was that once the hole was made that a string would somehow be passed through it. Numerous close calls and self-inflicted mutilations ensued. Some involved alcohol, some did not. I make no admissions. In any event none of these attempts were very effective.

Years passed and ultimately I used a woodworking or leather crafting tool called an awl. This is a type of skewer with an arrow type blade at the end with a hole in the centre, the skewer has a wooden handle at the other end. It worked quite well. But was limited by its lack of length in terms of the skewer.

Years passed again and I came across butchery tool which is used to pass string through various thicknesses of meat for the purposes of tying the meat. This is essentially a much larger version of a awl and is variously described as a butchers needle or a larding needle. This tool makes it safe, quick and easy to put string through a piece of meat for the purposes of either tying the meat or making loops from which to hang the meat. The needle is pushed through the meat, then the string is placed through the hole in the end of the needle, the needle is brought back through the meat carrying the string with it. The two ends of the string of joint and miraculously, a loop is created from which to hang the meat. The same methodology creates a starting point from which to securely trust a piece of meat which, for example, needs to be rolled very tightly.

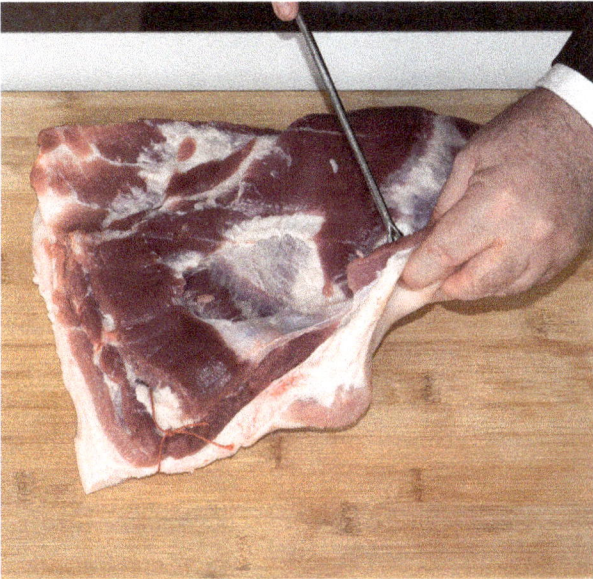

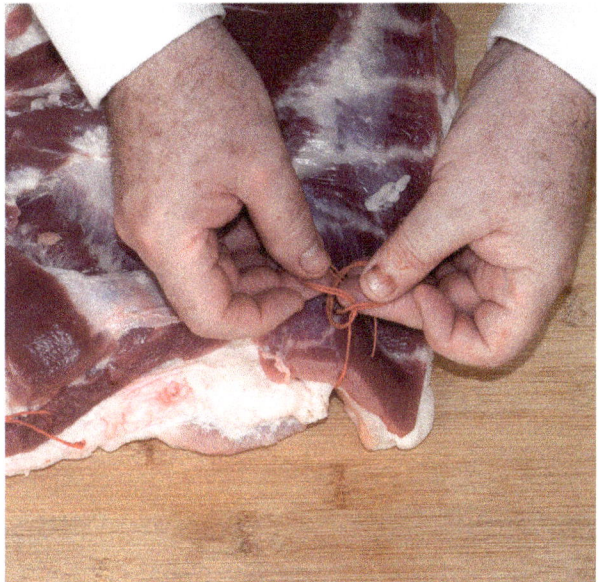

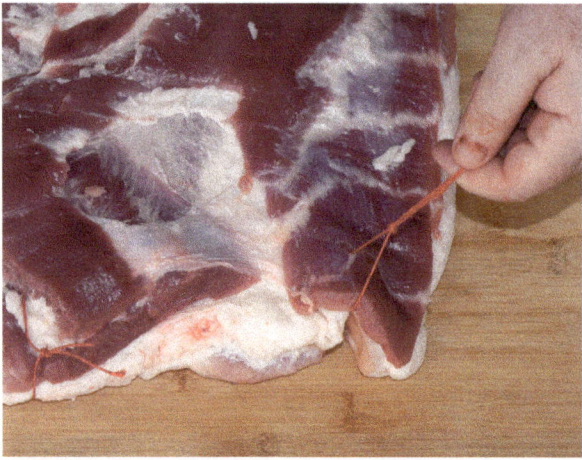
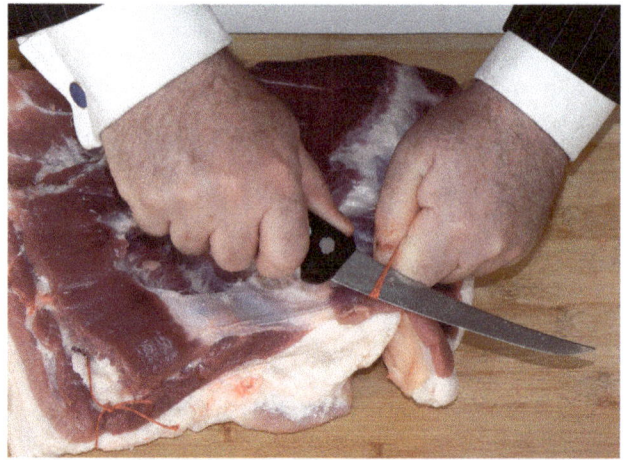

Rolling and tying meat

Often the product will need to be rolled either before or after curing. This helps even curing and prevents spoilage from inside. This is a simple technique but does require some explanation if not some finesse. The example below is for the purposes of preparing a rolled pancetta. As discussed above this utilises a piece of belly pork which is boneless and skinless. Having removed the bone and the rind the belly needs to be tightly rolled usually from the smaller section to the wider part. Then it needs to be held tightly with strings. Start in the middle using a piece of string secured with a butcher's knot. Then proceed to place strings evenly other side of the central string. All strings are secured with a butcher's knot and then a locking knot. Depending on the size of the piece of meat you may need to proceed to add further strings, in each case placed in the centre of the available space between two existing strings.

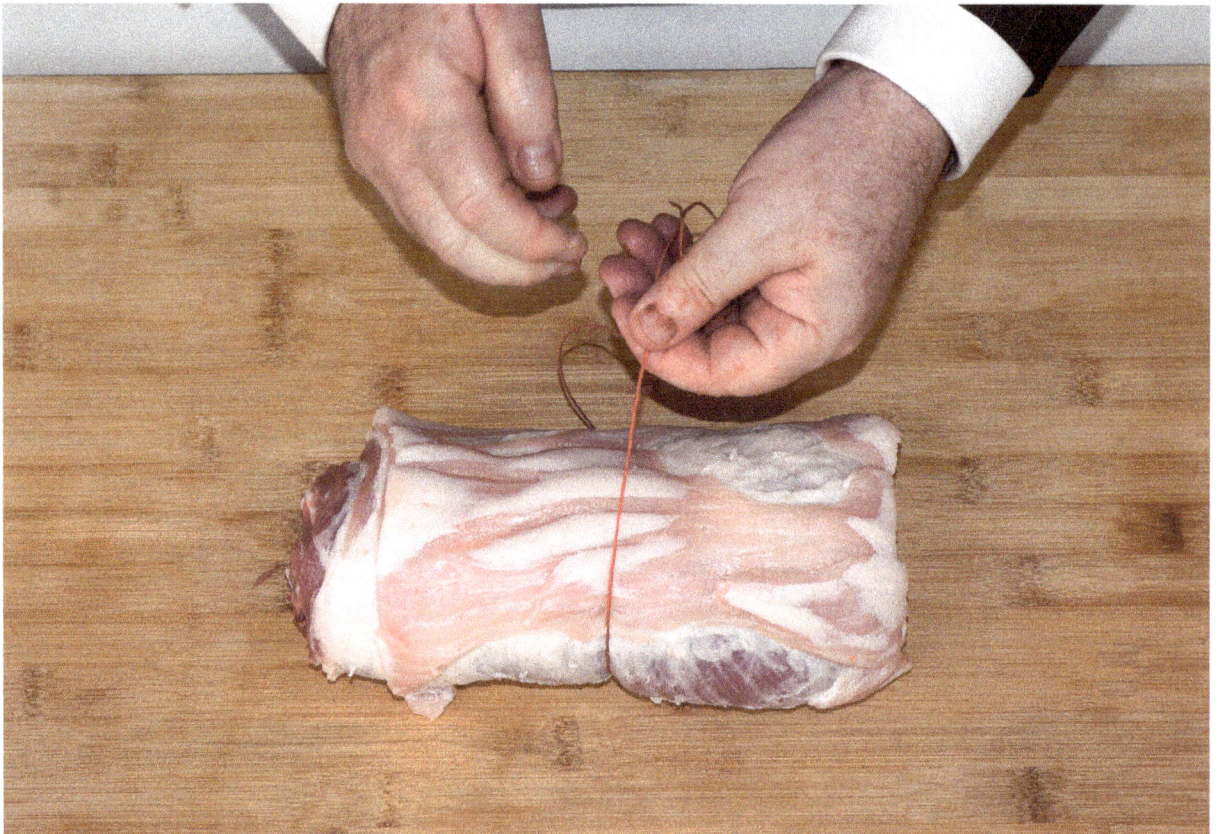

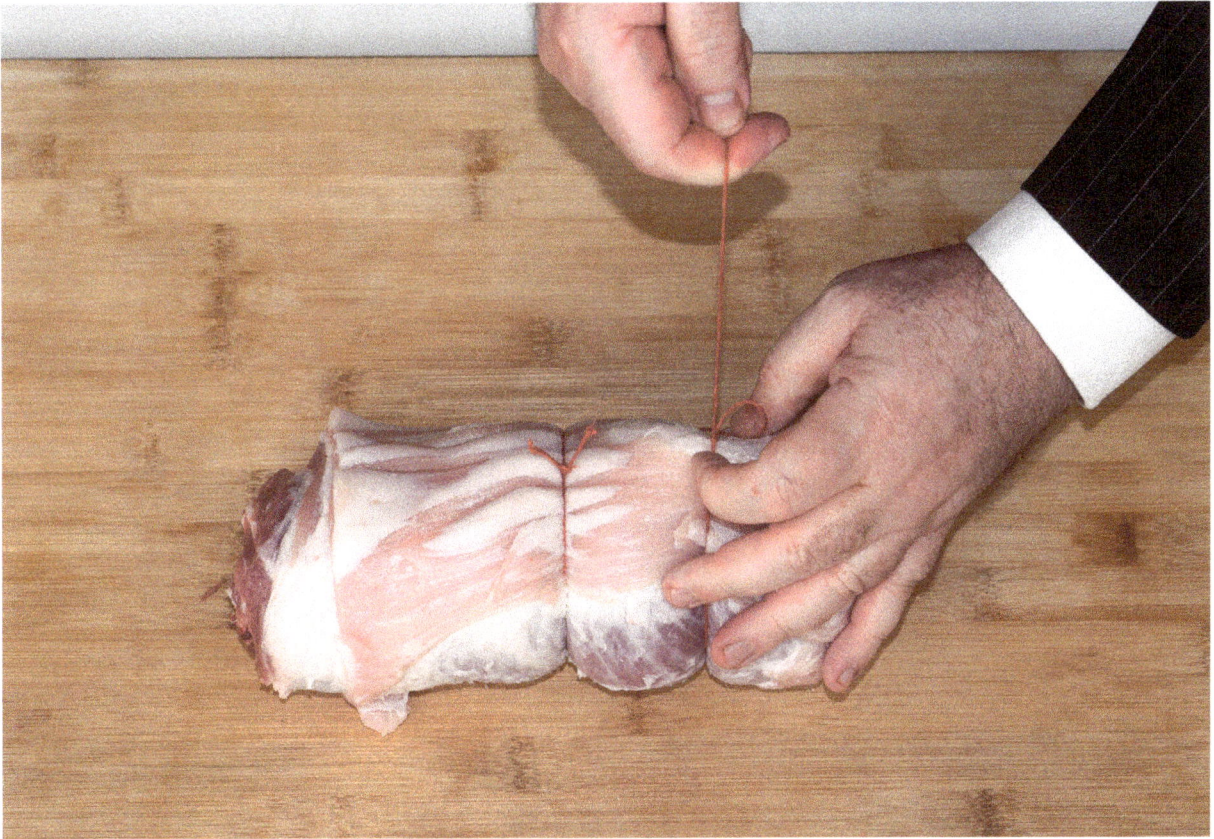

The netting

Many charcuterie products whether whole muscle or salami type air dried products benefit from netting in much the same way as they benefit from tying. Elasticised netting is particularly useful because it exerts a constant pressure on the product as it shrinks during the air-drying processes and helps to avoid internal air gaps and accordingly bug festivities. There is another reason for netting a product that is simply because they look really good and authentic. The trick is to use the diameter netting which is only just big enough for the product and therefore as the product shrinks during the air-drying process, as it inevitably will, the netting continues to compress the product. Unfortunately, the netting is really strong, and it is practically impossible to place the netting over raw meat without the aid of a very specific tool. This is the netting tube. Netting tubes come in various diameters and have a particularly useful wide base which sits flat on the bench top so that they do not move about and a cone on the top which is removable. Having chosen the netting tube of the appropriate diameter to allow one's meat to pass through it then, with the cone in place, the netting is stretched over the tube in sufficient quantity so that the meat will be totally encased. The purpose of the removable cone becomes obvious. It facilitates the stretching of the net and therefore its placement over the netting tube, a cylinder. Without which it would be extremely difficult to place the very strong netting in the correct position.

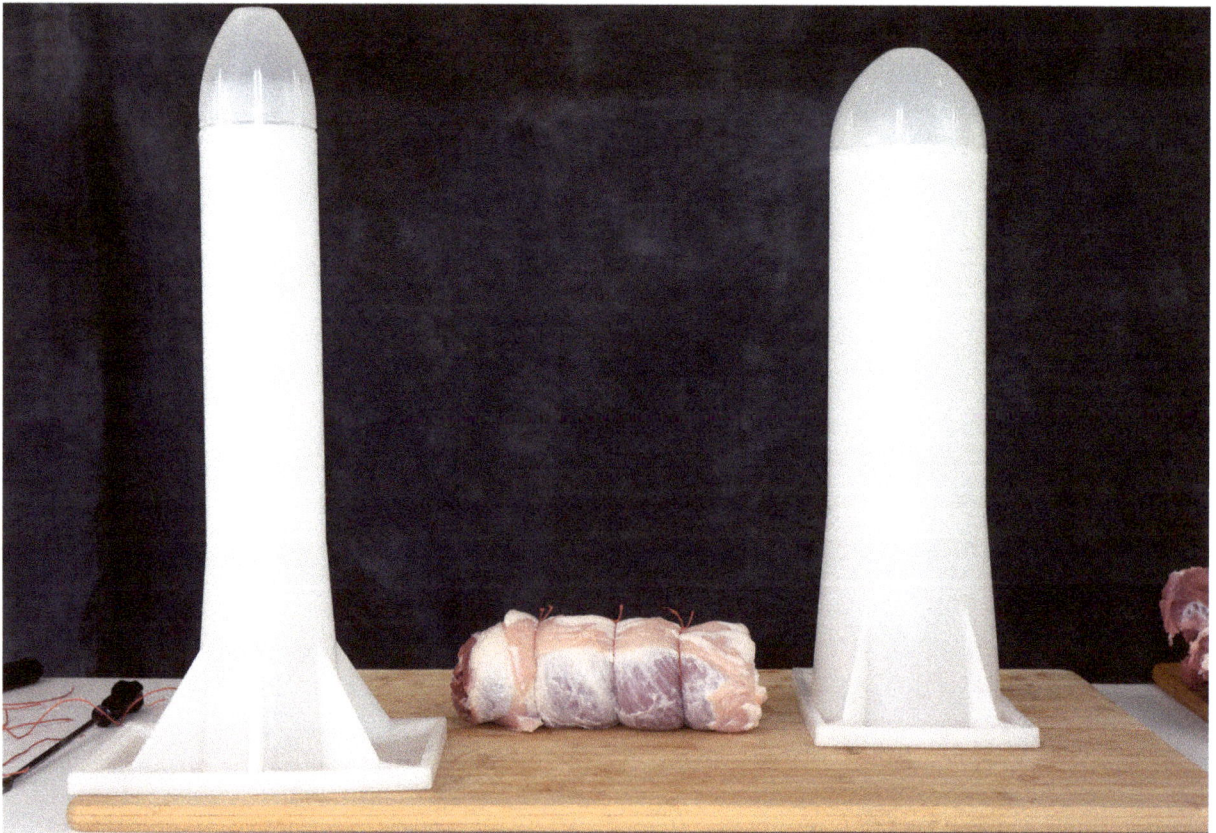

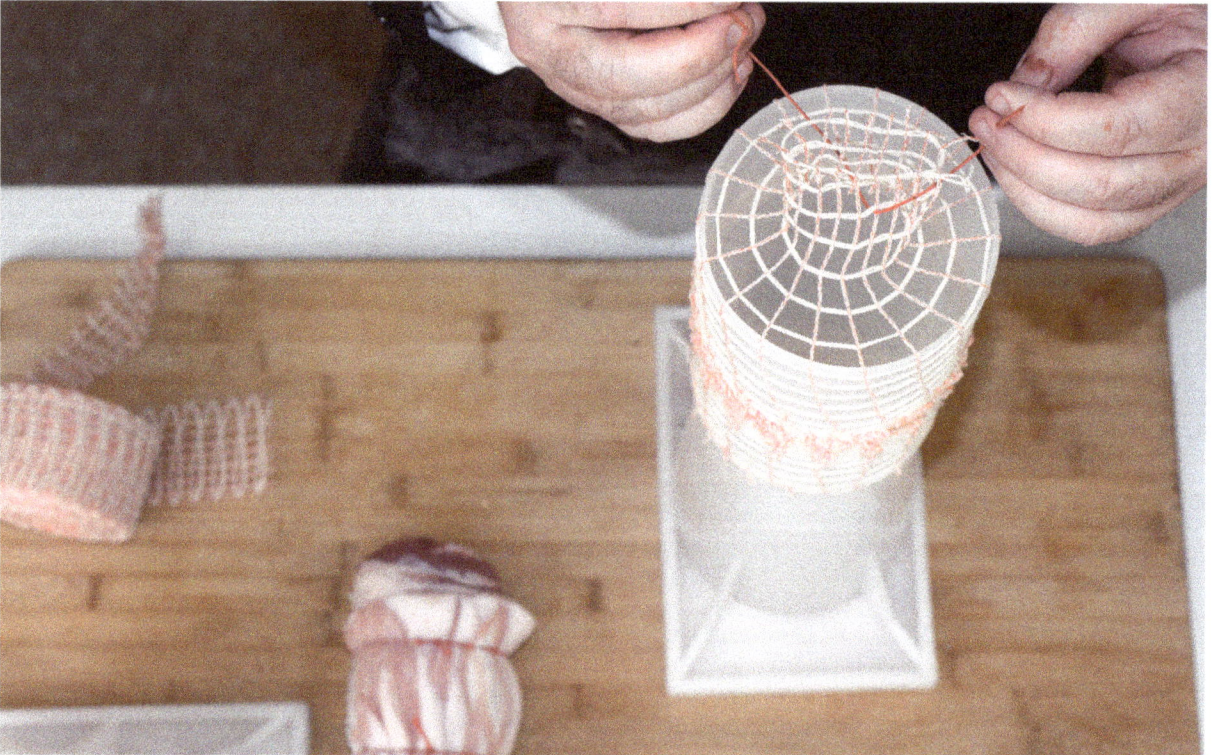

Once the netting is in position, in its desired length, it needs to be pushed below the cone. The cone is then removed. The netting is eased up over the entrance and the opening of the netting secured with some string. Use this opportunity to make a loop in the string for the purposes of hanging the product.

Next comes the fun bit or another parlance, the money shot. Invert the netting tube and insert the rolled and tied meat. Hopefully you have chosen a netting tube of sufficient diameter to allow the rolled and tied meat to pass through the tube. If not, then you need to start again. There is no shame in this, it has happened to me on many occasions. It is often the case that ones ability to pass the meat through the tube is not accurately assessed. But I digress. Shake the meat down through the inverted tube and it will enter the cocoon of the netting tube. Cut it off and tie the end. If you are intent on getting a very very tightly compressed product then consider the following ninja step. Twist the meat in the netting and push it back into the tube such that it is wrapped in the netting for a second time. Then it can be tied off. This is the technique I use for rolled pancetta which is a particularly troublesome child and if given any opportunity will open out and spoil from within.

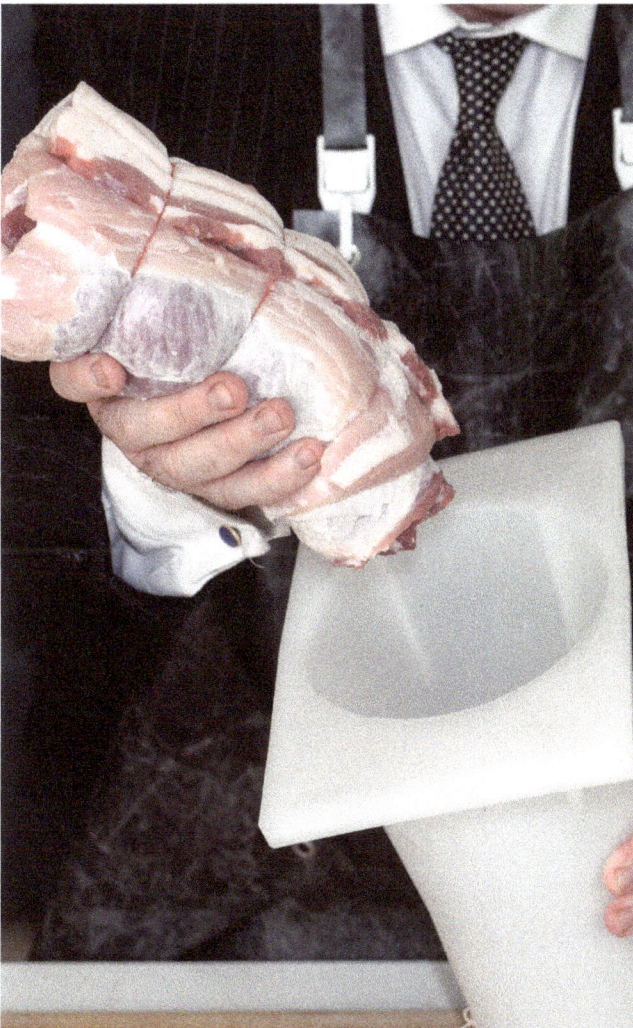

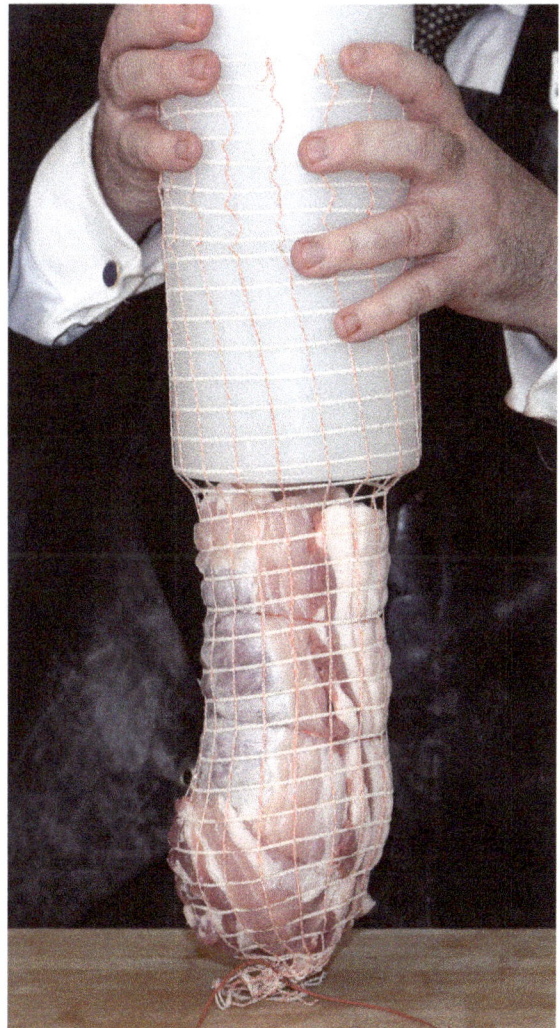

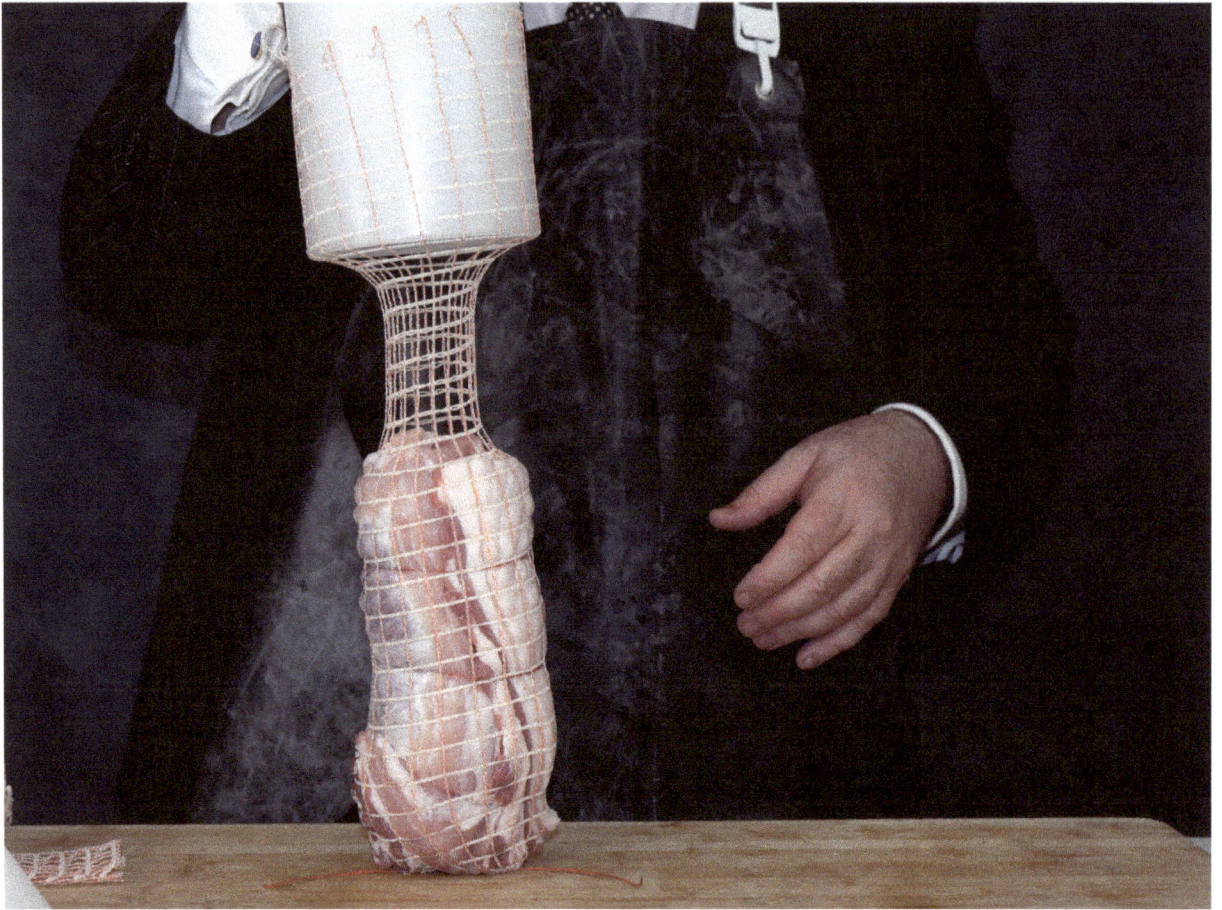

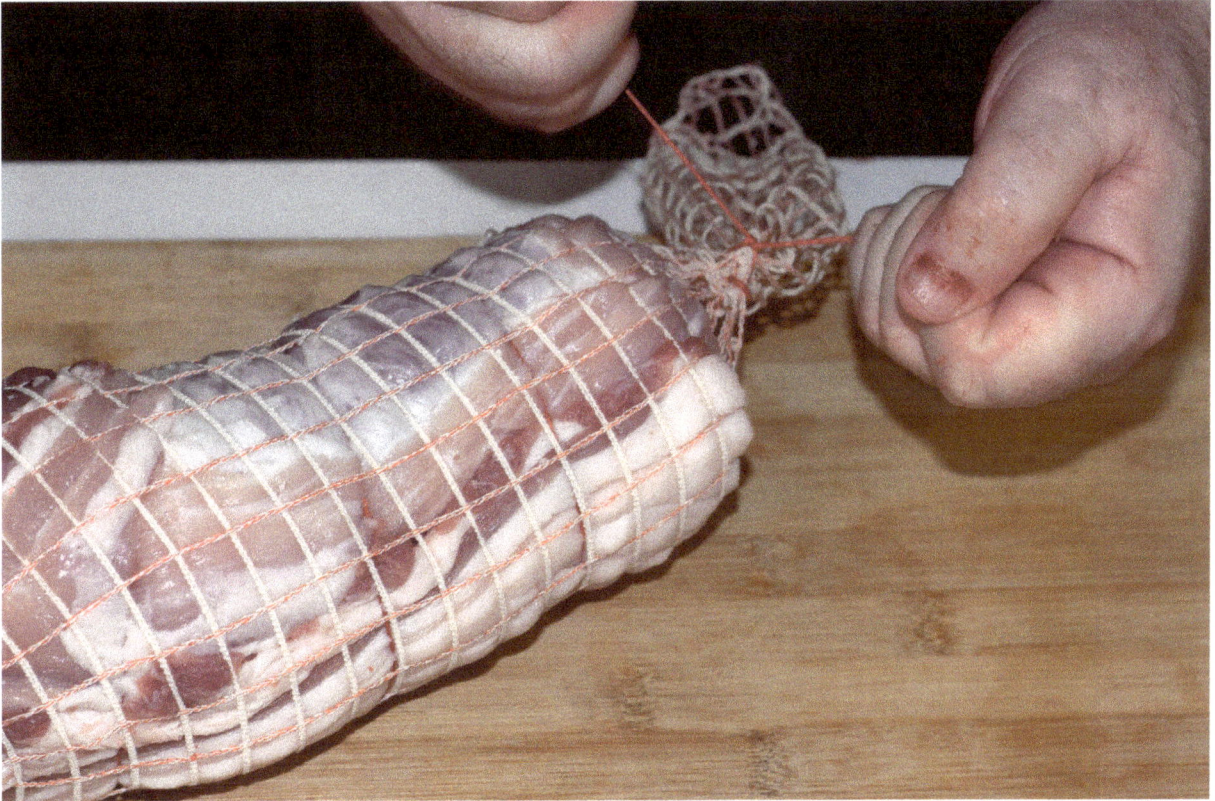

For the purposes of tuition, I also include images of netting a much larger piece of meat, in this case a coppa, for the purposes of capocollo production. The larger diameter of the meat requires commensurately larger diameter of both the netting and the netting to. The principles, however, remain the same.

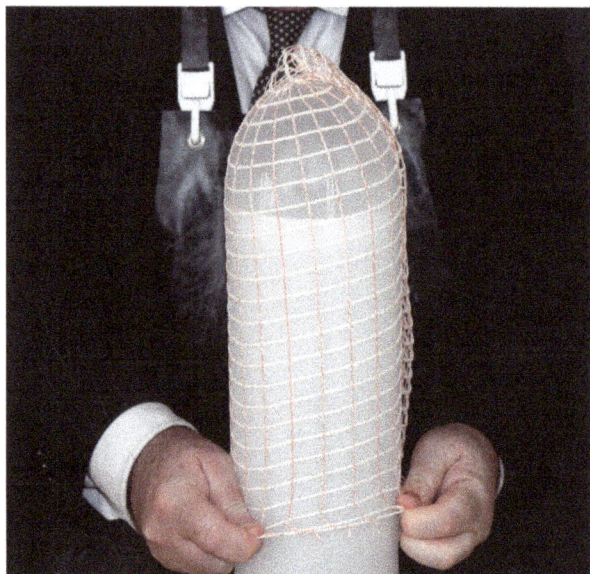

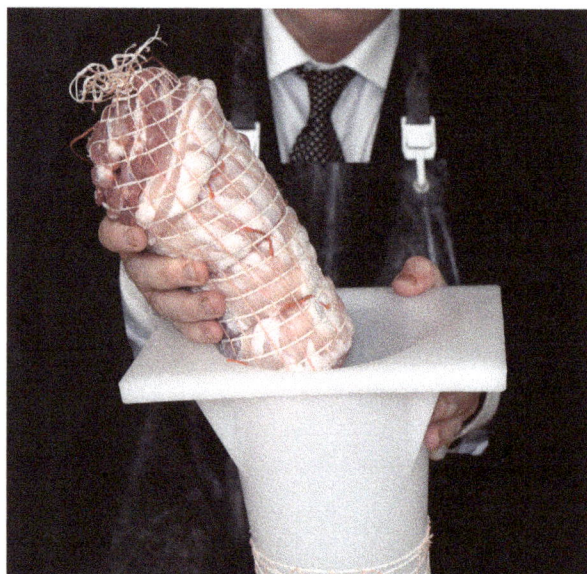

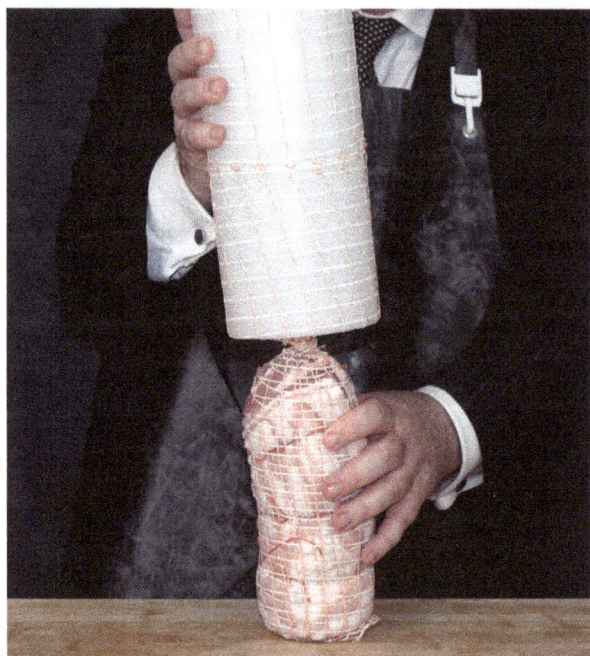

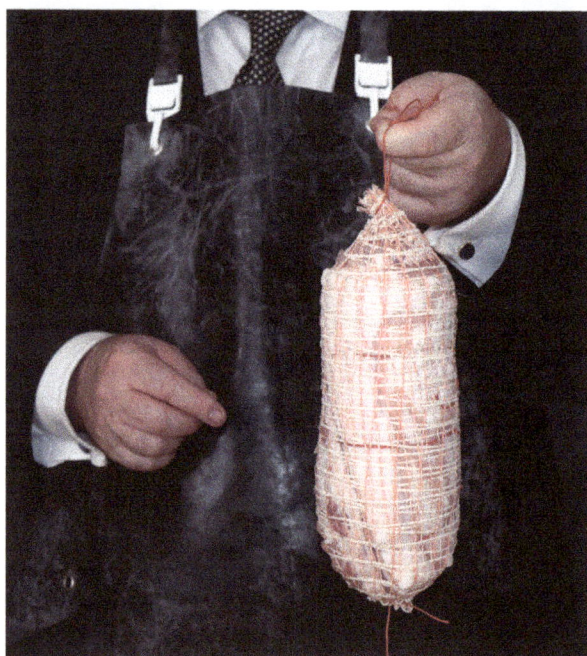

Collagen wrapping

Notwithstanding that charcuterie is an ancient art, modern technology has come to assist in some very useful ways. I have already mentioned elasticised netting and netting tubes. Collagen wraps are the next best thing in your charcuterie armoury. In the same way that fabricated casings made from collagen, but which are not natural casings, are very useful, collagen wraps are sheets of collagen, which are man-made from natural collagen products. They are extremely useful for larger pieces of meat which may or may not be lean, but which benefit from a slowing down of the rate of air drying which a protective covering affords. Plastic will not do, nor will baking paper and certainly not aluminium foil . Natural casings can be split and wrapped around the product, if it was large enough. This no doubt was the way in which delicate pieces of meat were shielded from the ravages of air-drying. Consider for example, cullatello which is classically encased in a hog bladder. The meat is lean, coming from the leg, and is air dried for an extended period, up to 36 months and beyond. It will dry out beyond recognition without some protection. The cured hog bladder provides that protection. Why not use cured hog bladders to protect similar products, I hear you ask? . A very good question and one I would like to be able to answer. Unfortunately hog bladders cannot be purchased in this country. I do not know why. It seems to me that they are no different from any other part of the animal ranging from the brain to the intestines and internal organs, all of which are available in raw form in this country. But not the whole bladder. Clearly this is the beneficence of the authorities keeping us from hurting ourselves. Clearly the beneficence of the authorities knows things that we do not, and that the evilness of the raw hog bladder is something that we must be protected from at all costs. But once again, I digress. Yes you can encase products like cappocollo in raw casings, split and overlapped. This is no doubt the way that it has been done for many years, particularly because there is only one hog bladder in every hog. That is why I mention the intervention of modern technology and in particular collagen sheets or wraps. They are made from natural collagen, I do not know or need to know the process. They come in various sizes. They are like crinkly wrapping paper. Wrap the meat in the collagen sheet, then tie it and or net it. It is worth the effort.

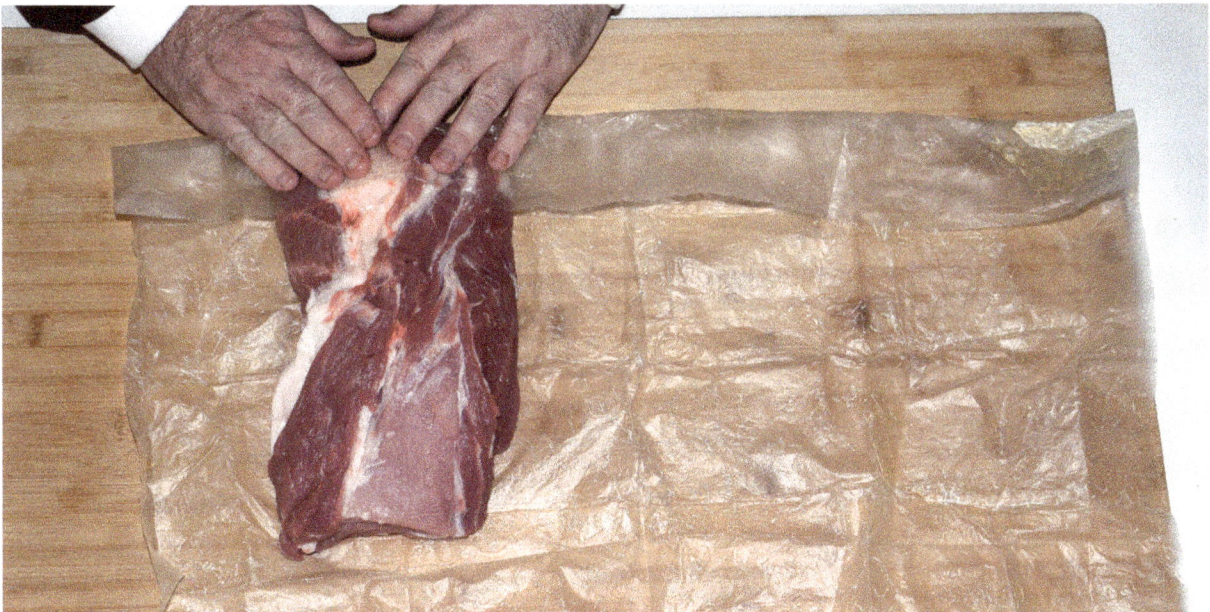

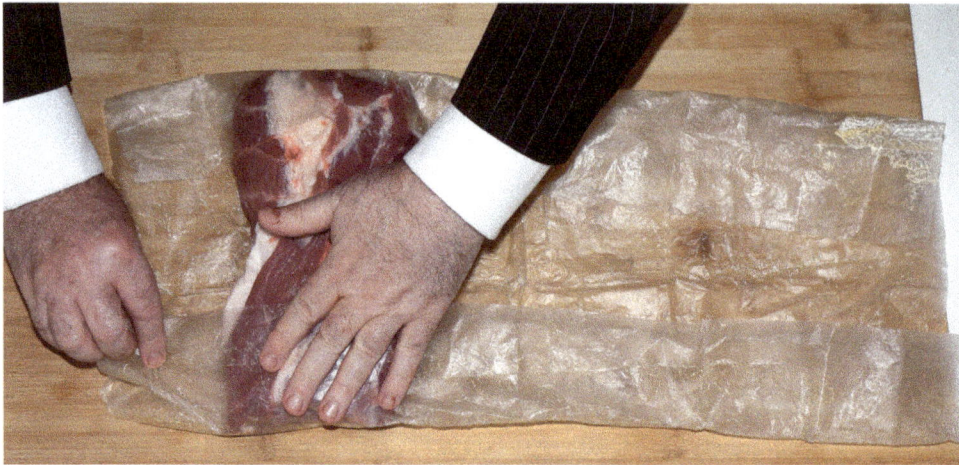
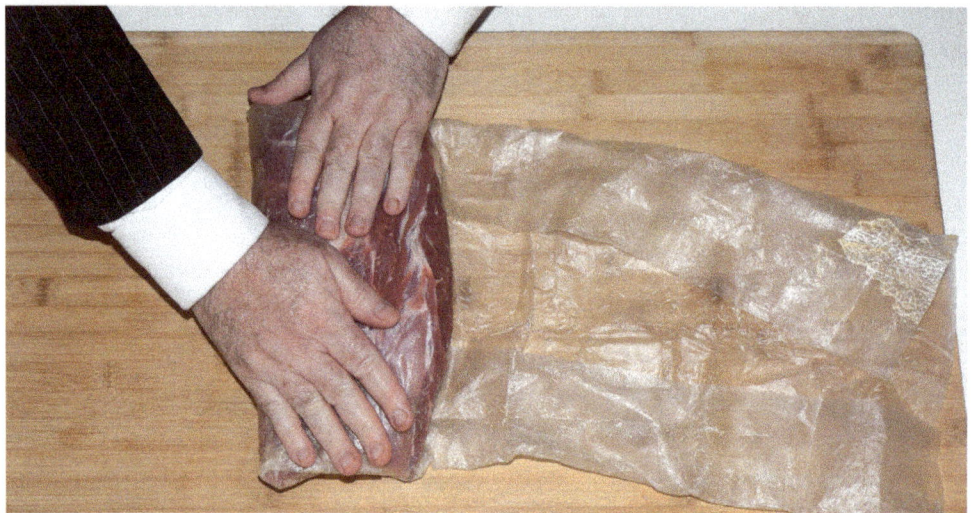
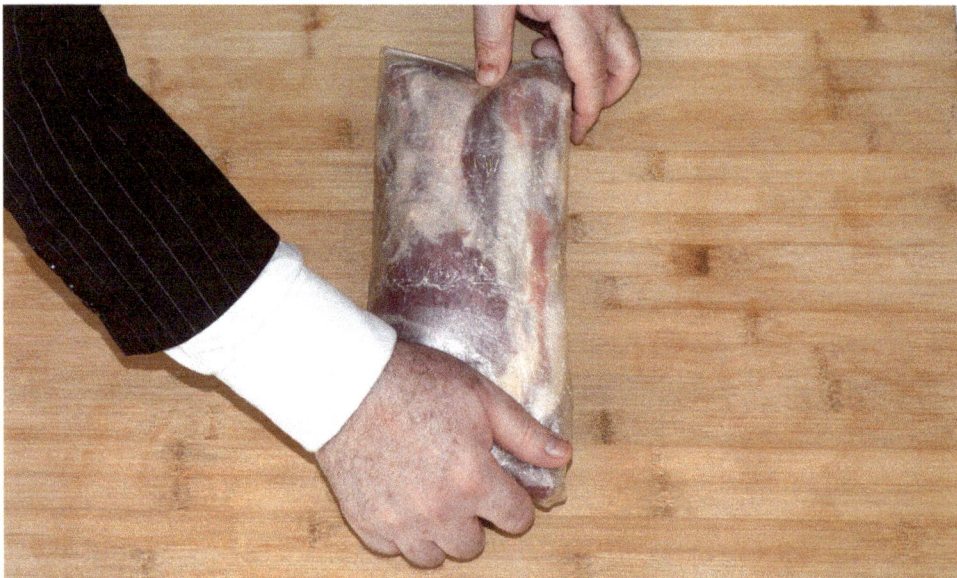

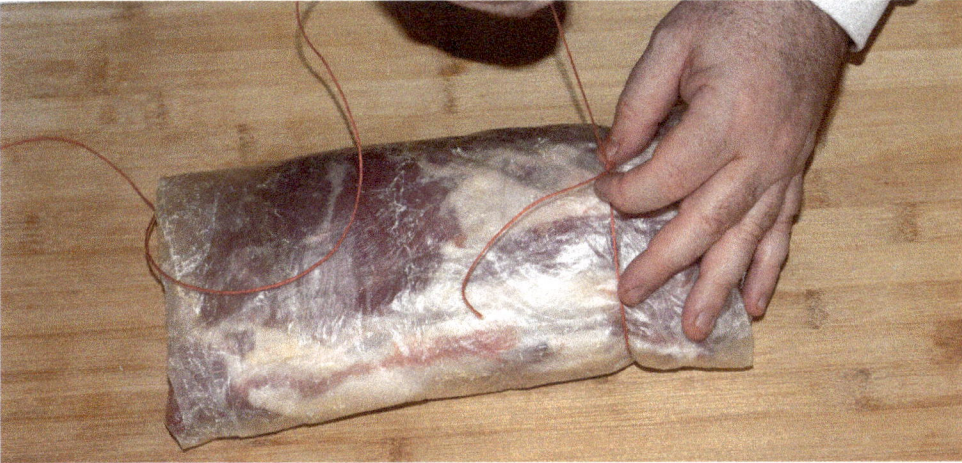

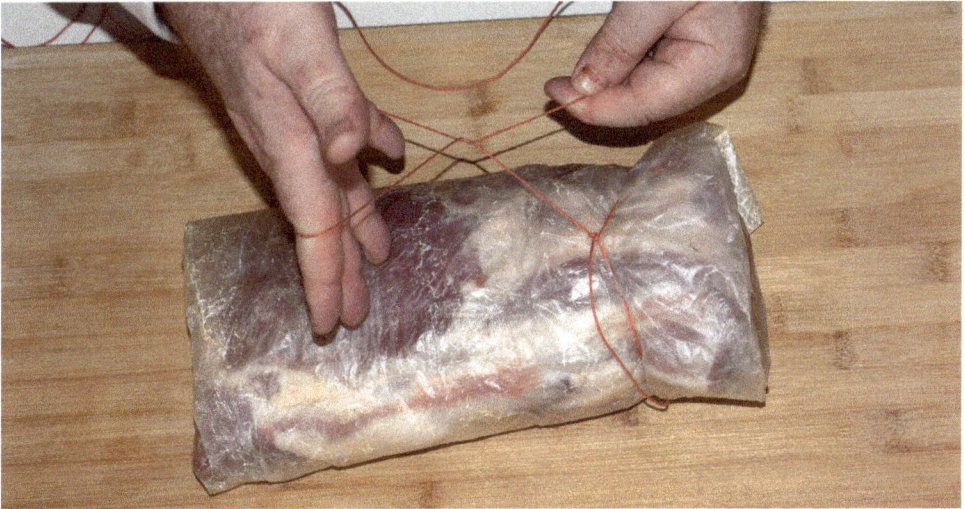

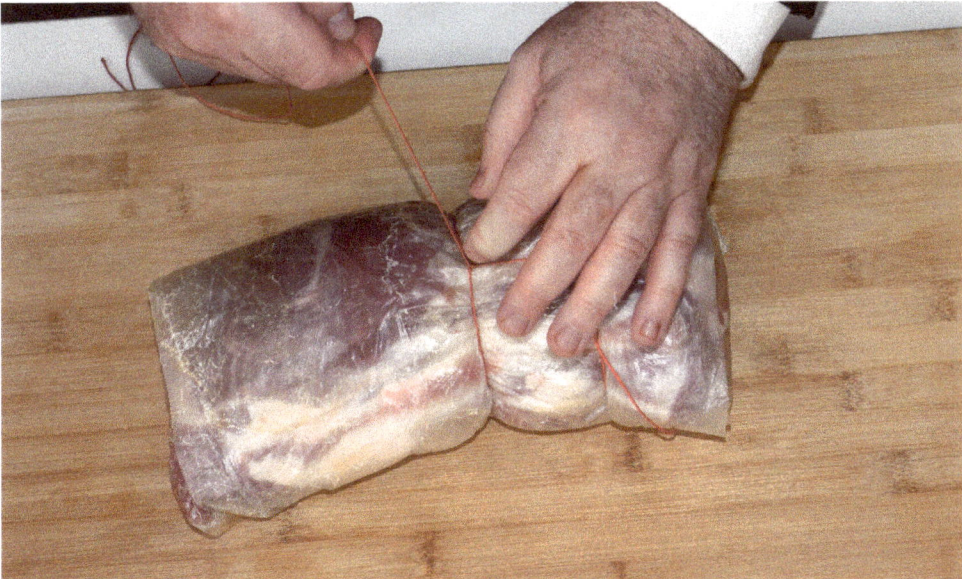

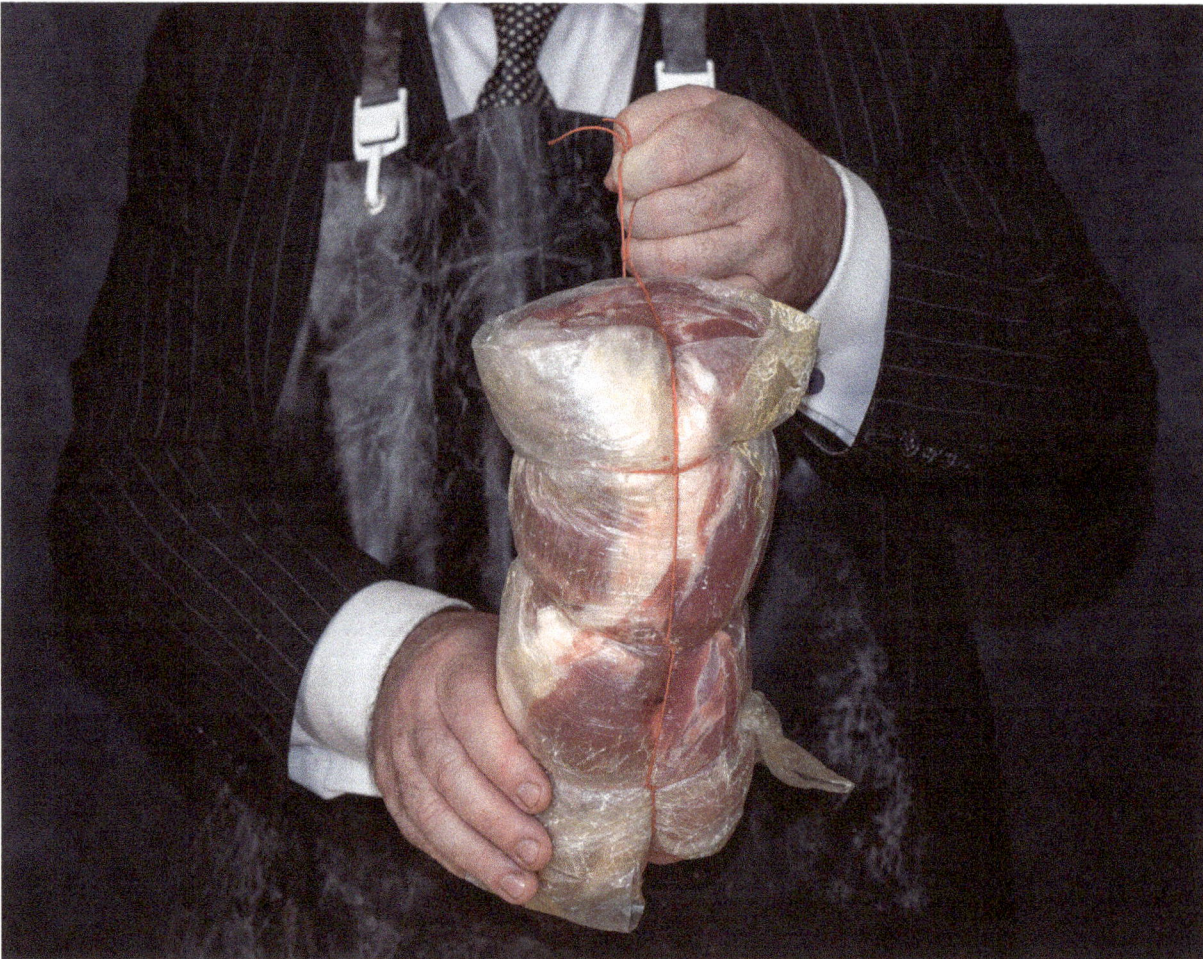

Caul fat-wrapping the meat the original way

Obviously manufactured collagen sheets are a modern innovation. Do not forget the original. The abdominal cavity of a pig is surrounded in a diaphanous membrane made of fat and connective tissue. This is the caul fat. It is a most desirable product for the purposes of cooked charcuterie. A delicate offal rich meatball such as the English faggot or the French version lark sans tete (translated as larks without heads-who comes up with these names?), can be encased in the caul fat. It both provides structure and moisture, as the fat dissolves, whilst the cooking is underway. It can also be used for the purposes of wrapping whole muscle charcuterie, such as capocollo. Consider it but use collagen sheets.They are much more betterer (another new word of which I am quite proud)

Guanciale

The cheek of the pig can be cured and air dried.It is used by our Italian cousins to make carbonara sauce for pasta. It is called guanciale. It is easy to prepare.

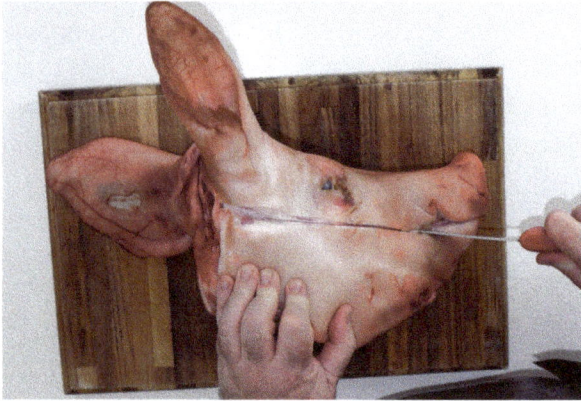

Make a cut from the base of the ear to the corner of the jaw.

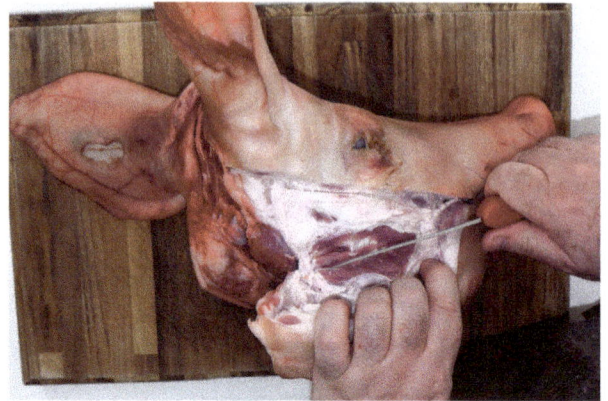

Peel back the cheek from the bone

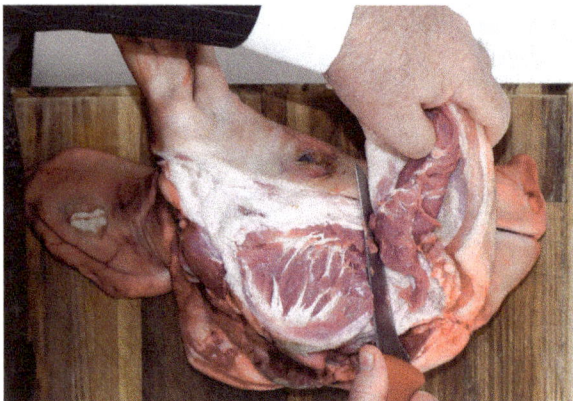

Keep as much of the cheek muscle on the cheek as possible.

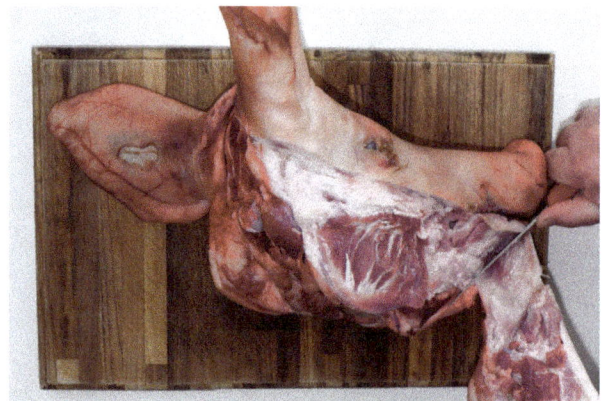

Keep cutting until the cheek is separated from the head

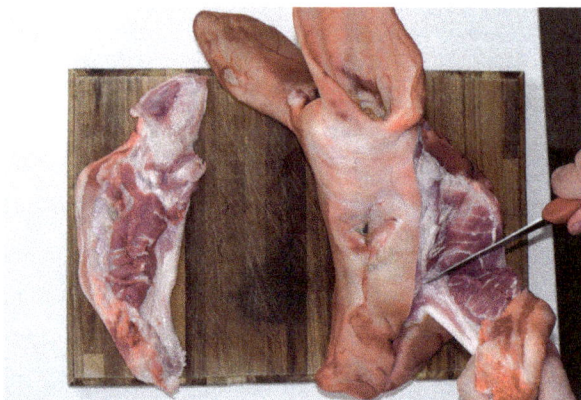

Repeat with the other side

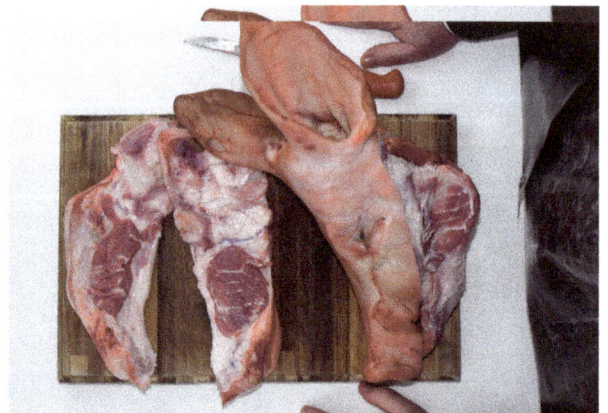

You will now have two separated cheeks

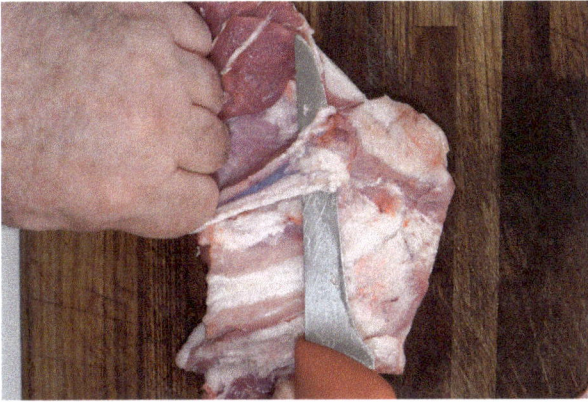

You have not finished yet. Trim the cheeks to remove blood vessels and any nasty bits

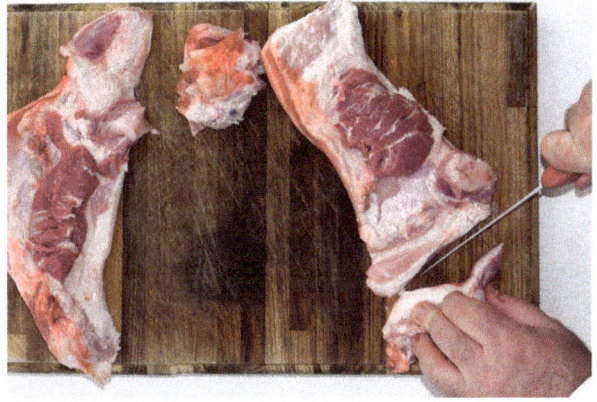

Square up the cheeks and remove any ragged parts which may provide safe haven for bugs.

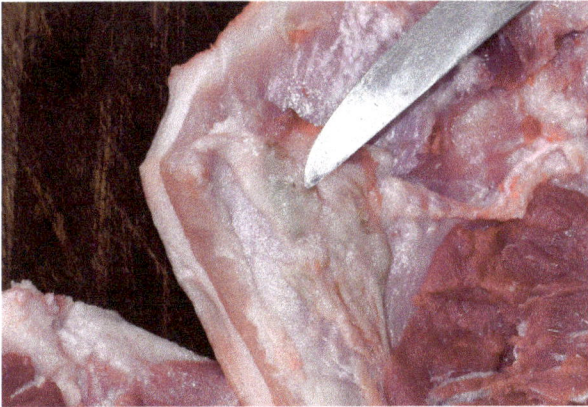

Remove any glands. These are small grey jelly bean shapes. They will be found near the corner of the jaw and on the other side of the ear where it joins the head. They are often covered with fat. They are no good to eat.

Rolled pancetta

Rolled pancetta can be tricky. The problem is if the meat has any internal gaps then the product will spoil from the inside and you will not know until it is too late.

Take a piece of boneless pork belly with the skin removed. Cure it as described in the recipe with salt, curing salt and the usual suspects. Remove the meat from the cure and after rinsing dry it well.

Roll it such that when it is sliced you will be cutting across the grain

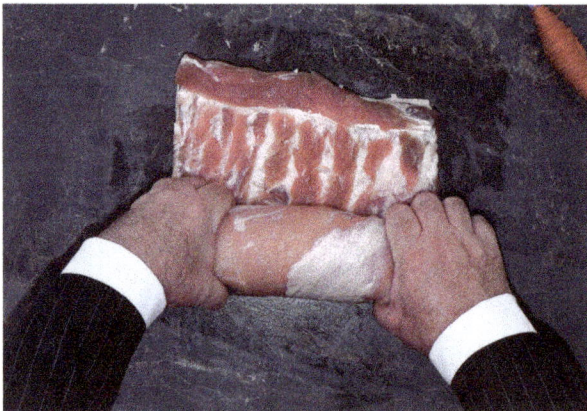

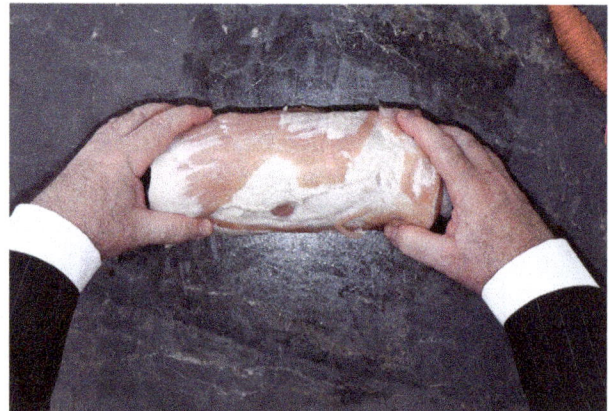

Tie it tightly with string starting in the middle, then at both ends, then evenly fill in the gaps with string.

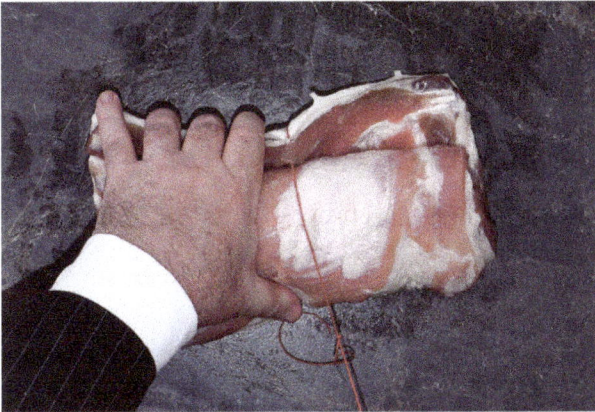

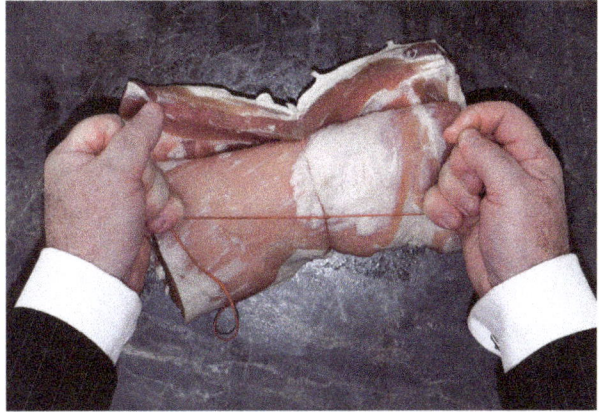

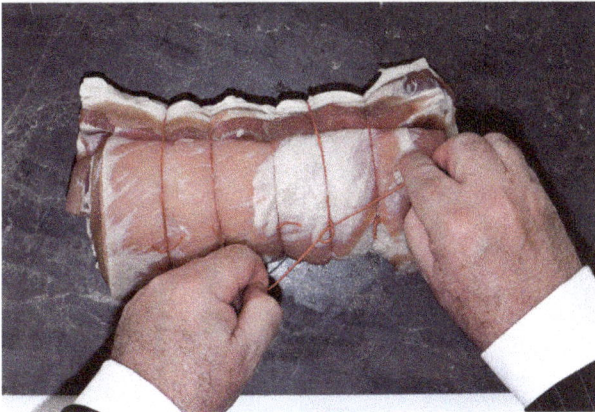

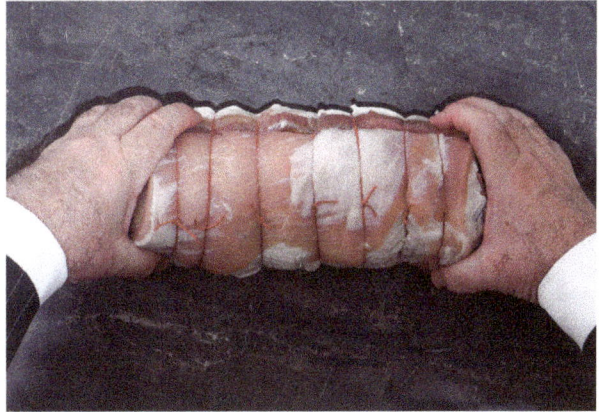

Square off the ends by trimming with a sharp knife to remove ragged bits which will act as bug havens

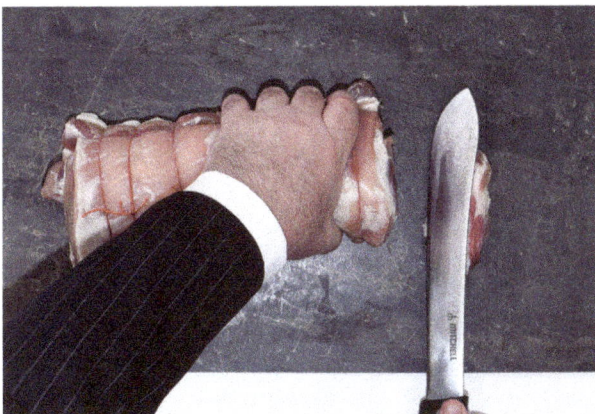

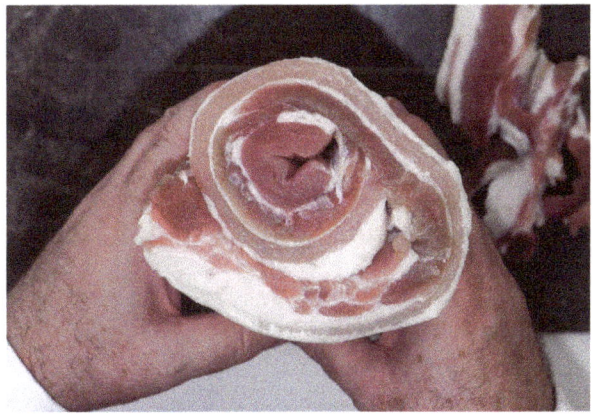

However even with your tightest knots you will observe there are still gaps inside the rolled, tied meat. If you cure it like this then if it does not spoil, you will get dry bits through the interior which look most undesirable.

The secret technique which I am prepared to share with you on the basis that that you do not tell anyone else is to now net the product as tightly as possible. Once you have passed the meat into the net once, do not cut off the net, twist the net tightly and passed the meat back into the tube so it is netted for a second time.

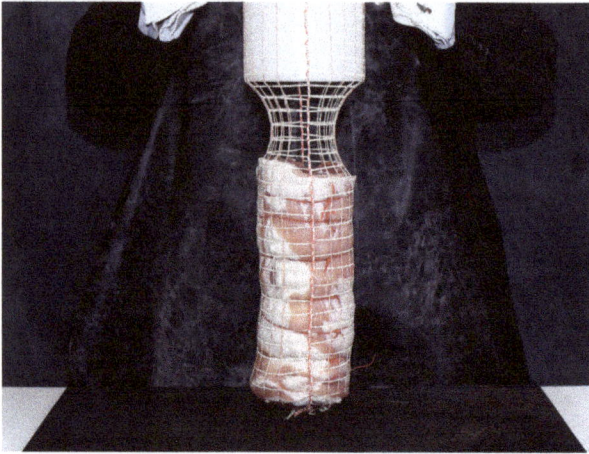

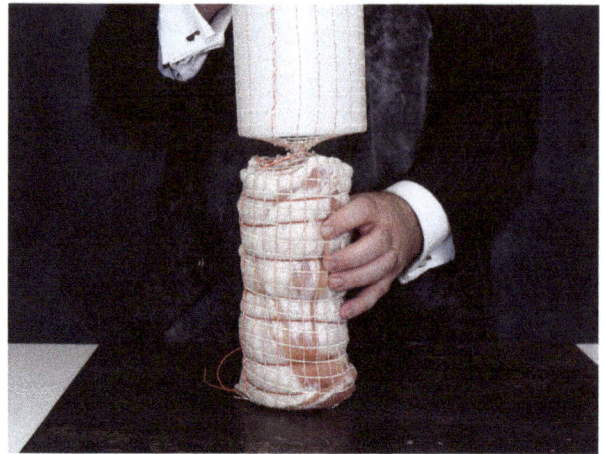

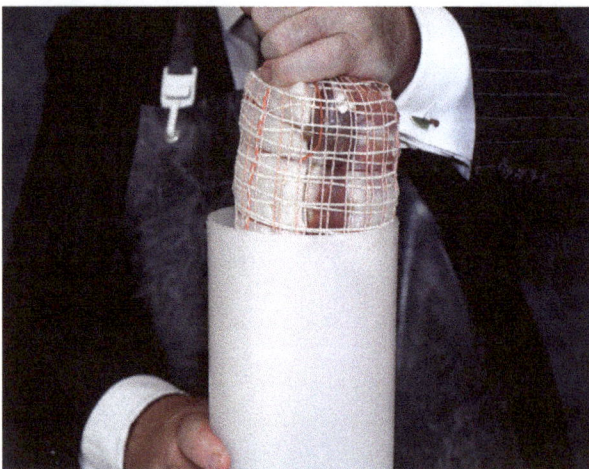

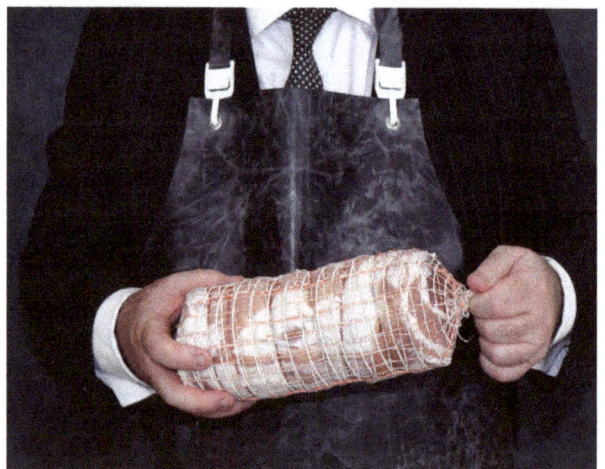

Weigh the product, record the relevant details on a tag. Now air dry for the requisite period of time. This method whilst not perfect, usually results in a product without any internal gaps.

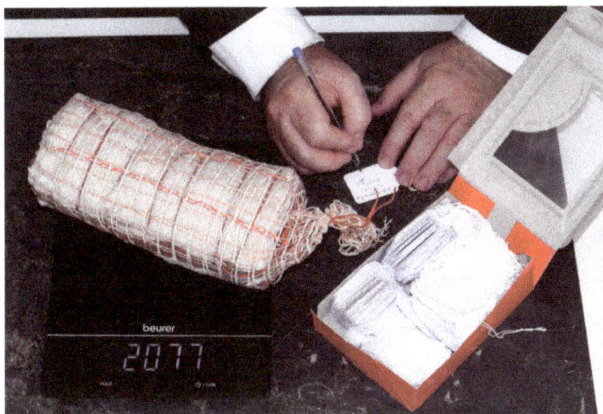

Basturma

Basturma is one of my all-time favourite products. The Middle Eastern cured and air dried beef product heavily flavoured with fenugreek. Take a good size piece of beef. I prefer using the eye of the silverside from the leg, often in Australia called the girello. I do not know what it is called in other countries. Cure this as for bresaola according to the recipe. Then wrap it in collagen wrap and air dry for approximately 2 weeks. Remove the wrap and string.

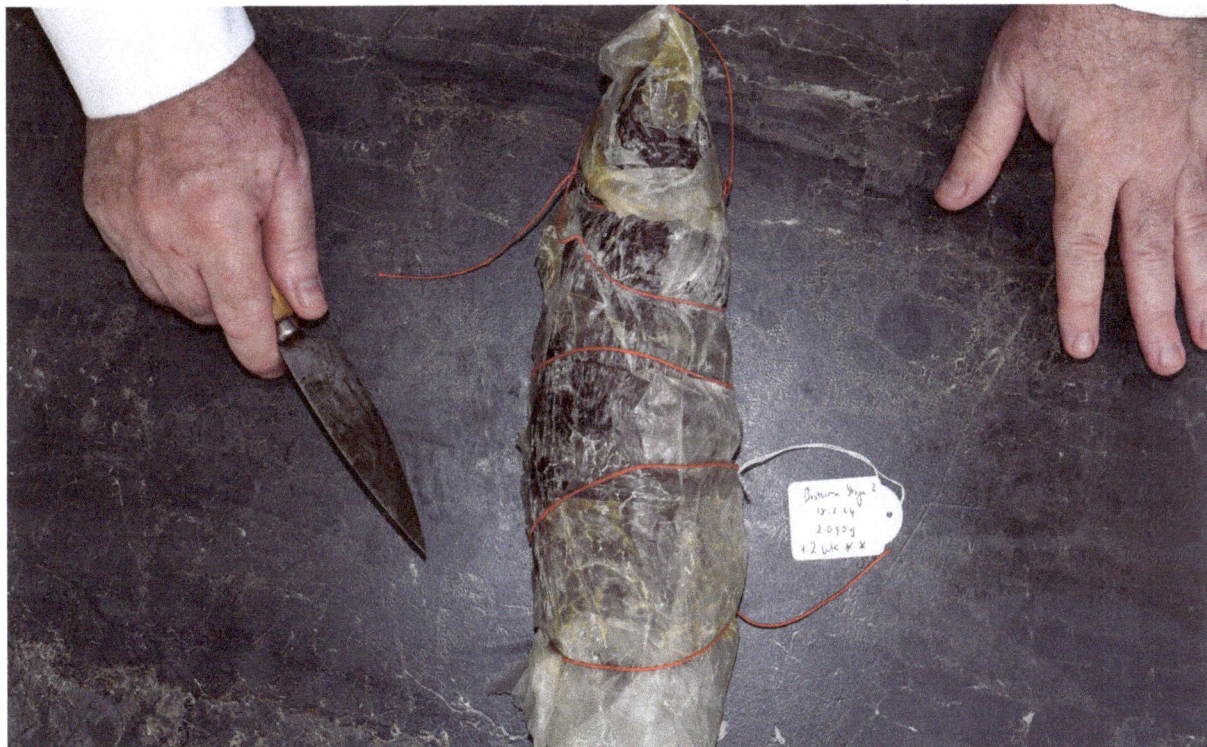

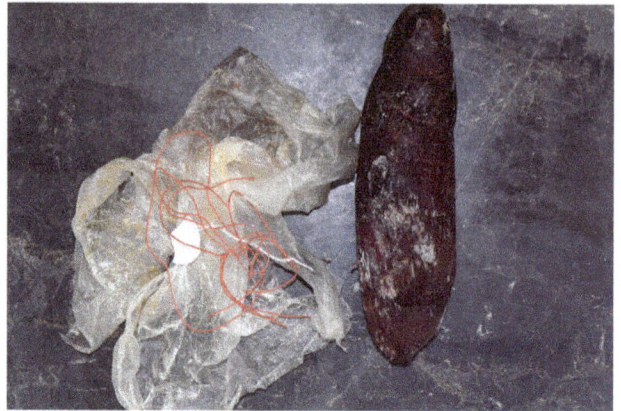

Remove any surface mould.

Make a paste according to the recipe, it is predominantly powders of fenugreek and paprika, onion garlic and white pepper. Add sufficient water so it is able to be evenly coated on the meat.

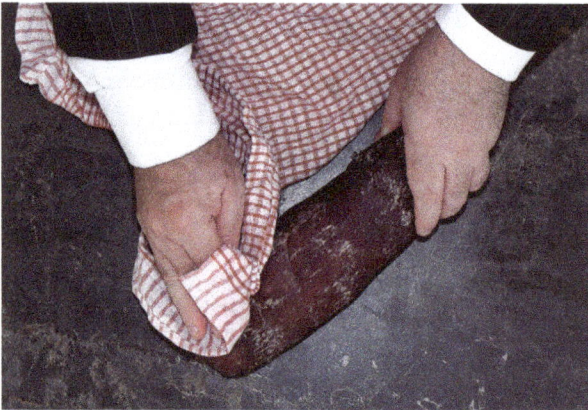

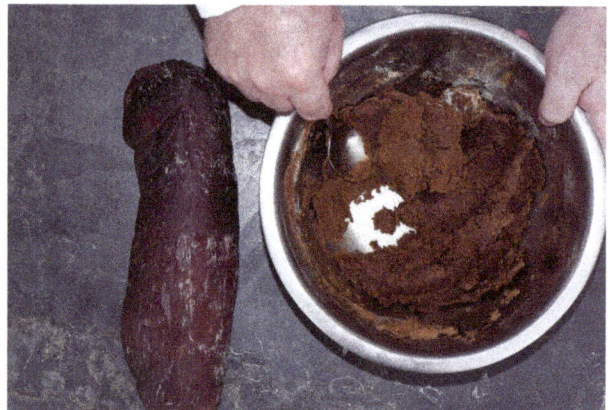

Using the butcher's needle, before the paste is applied, pass string through the meat so it can be hung for air drying.

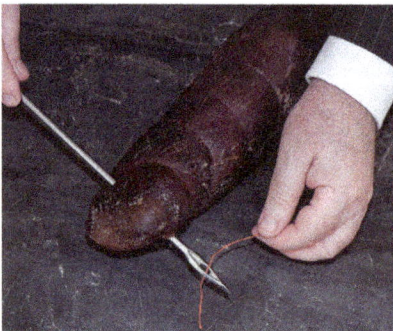

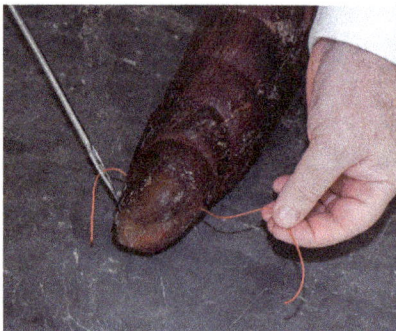

Using gloves apply the paste so that the meat is completely covered, damp hands will make it easier to give a nice smooth finish. You do not have to use gloves but if you do not then your hands will be the colour of the paste and smell like fenugreek for ever.

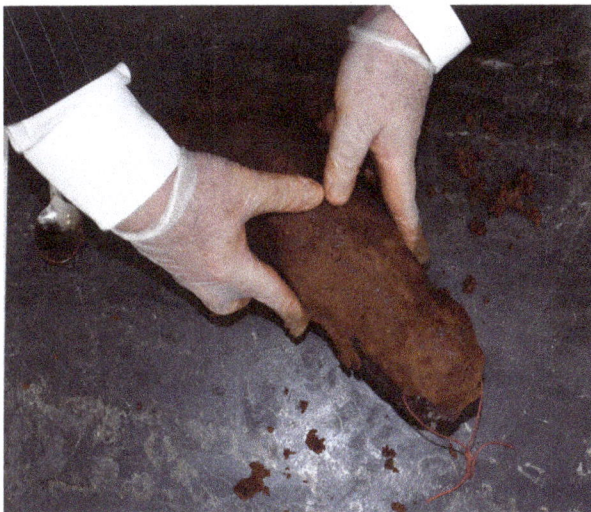

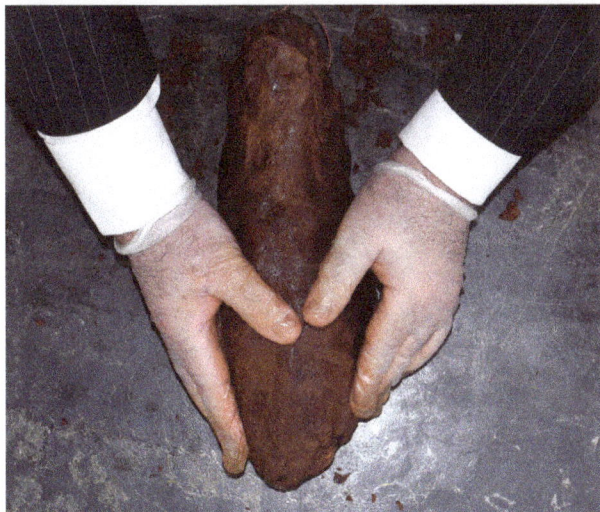

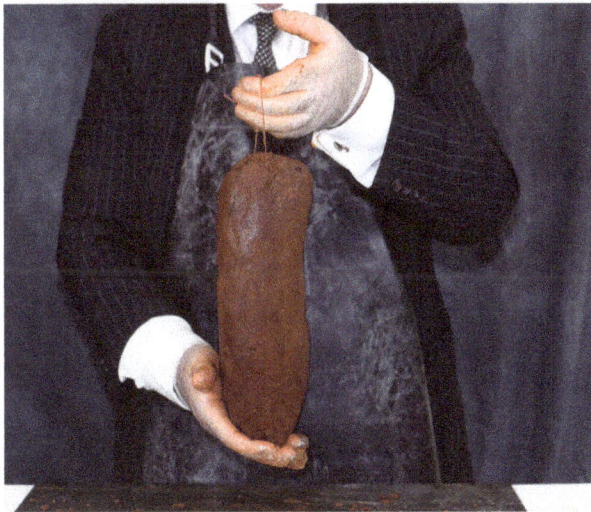

This story is finished

The introduction to charcuterie butchery is complete, at least for present purposes. Thank you for your attention and I hope that it has been of some utility, if not of some interest.

Gods speed to Vous et Votre.

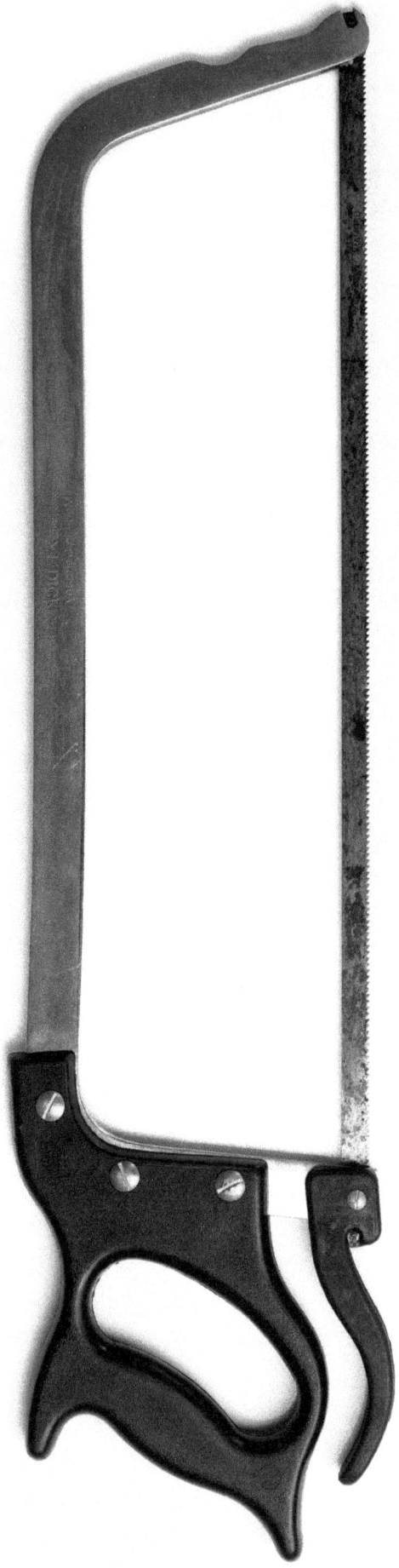

THE STORIES

THE STORIES

PORKZILLA AND BOAR TAINT

I was asked whether I would be interested in a half share of a pig. This is not an unusual thing. I have been asked this on many occasions. You may think this is an unusual thing, but you need to get into the groove. Naturally I said that this would be acceptable. I asked the usual questions about weight, price per kilo and expected delivery date. The answers were broadly acceptable although the weight was a bit curious, 200 kg dressed weight may be 250 kg dressed weight. Now gentle readers, I have been offered this sort of proposition previously and, as you recall, it was not a normal outing. It was the so-called salami pig which, frankly, I still have nightmares about. I asked the obvious questions. The questions are answered, the gender of the animal was avoided. Under some intense cross examination, the answer became apparent, it was a boy pig, not a girl pig. This was immediately of some concern because I have read the literature, over the years, as you have done and was full of knowledge about the undesirability of male pigs and the inherent unfortunate characteristics which you know has boar taint. The literature made it clear, the books made it even clearer, male pigs are bad, they smell bad, they eat badly, and they are generally bad individuals. Why else would the markets always have the appellation that the meat that one is buying is "female" and not "male"?

I communicated these reservations to my source, and I was told that the price was so good it did not matter whether the pig had some boar taint or not. I did find this to be a somewhat unsatisfactory response. However, I must say the price was pretty good and I decided to do it on the basis that I would assist in the butchery and only partake of the product if I thought it was desirable and did not smell like you know what. This was an acceptable proposition and before I knew what I was doing I was once again in the Gulag chopping up endless quantities of meat. As an aside I have spent many hours in the Gulag and was somewhat resistant to return to it . Nonetheless if one has sharp knives then the sharp knives need to be utilised. Once again, we entered the uncharted territory of butchering a very large animal, with primitive resources but some very sharp knives. It became a test of physicality which I was somewhat unprepared for. Many hours later, with much spinal soreness, bad knee playing up and the rest, I was released.

There are several interesting matters which I can share with you because of this experience. First, the meat was not of the normal pale pink character that one would expect from commercial female pork. It was much darker, closer to yearling beef than one might expect. So far, so good . This is neither more nor less than one might expect from the male iteration compared to the female persuasion. The thing that I was looking for and would be ultimately disappointed by was the lack of the so-called boar taint. I had read about it. I was concerned about it. I was looking for it. The books told me it would be an unpleasant barnyard, outhouse, smell that one would not forget. I needed to find this to justify my reticence at taking on a male iteration of the pork persuasion.

I am extremely pleased to report that the meat had no odour, unpleasant or otherwise, there were no outhouse reflections, no barnyard computations. It just smelt like good, fresh meat.

Not to be outdone, I insisted that we cook some raw meat. If there were concealed barnyard or outhouse

odours, surely, they would reveal themselves on the hot plate.

Sadly, tragically, that was not to be the case.

At the end of the day, it was apparent that the much-maligned male pig was indeed overly maligned than did not reveal himself during the butchery experience.

What did I glean from this?

Well, once again some modest research, as always Internet-based, disclosed the following. Boar taint refers to the off odour and off flavour produced while eating meat from some un-castrated male pigs. Castration prevents boar taint.I am informed that it can be attributed to the presence of the compounds skatole, androstenone and to a lesser extent, indole . These compounds are mainly located in adipose tissue and have been associated with odours described as "perspiration like" or "urine like" in cooked pork. In particular androstenone has a definite urinary odour, skatole exhibits an intense faecal or manure like and to a lesser extent like naphthalene. At usual slaughter weights the incidence of boar taint is very variable, ranging from 10% to 75% according to different studies. Because of the large variation in the incidence of boar taint, and because of the variety of culinary habits between countries, the acceptability of boar meat, as measured in consumer surveys, can be quite inconsistent between studies. Interestingly, research suggests that 75% of consumers are sensitive to boar taint and,that white women and certain ethnic groups showed a higher degree of sensitivity than men.

In summary, boar taint is a bad thing, but it does not occur in all uncastrated male pigs and not everyone can detect it. Certainly, in my experience I could not detect anything unusual about the meat neither could my associate.

The desirability of using boar meat, however, for charcuterie is a different issue. The meat was very lean, dark ruby red in colour like yearling beef and firm or tough. The hot smoked bacon was darker colour than normal, good flavour profile but quite tough. In my view its use would be limited to that of a condiment, lardons to be included in the casserole or something of that nature. The minced meat, with added pork fat was a completely different proposition. It is made into a good, air-dried sausage but you must add at least 20% extra fat to it, maybe 25%.

The other thing to observe is that boar meat is very inexpensive. This is no doubt due to the foregoing issues, namely possibility of boar taint, lack of fat and toughness of the meat. The Porkzilla in question cost approximately $75 for a 200 kg – 250 kg carcass. It was an experiment, and much was learned. Would I do it again? Probably not.

Truth begins in lies.

The copperware

Before lock down, but mostly during and afterwards I became interested in antique copper cookware. I am not sure why; I think I have always thought of them as desirable pieces and the fact that they related to cooking made them interesting to me. I looked at modern iterations of copper cookware, with stainless steel interiors and was not terribly interested. There were two reasons for this. I am not particularly good at or interested in using stainless steel cookware for anything other than boiling vegetables or making sauces. I am sure this reflects my inability to get the best from stainless steel cookware. But it did mean that expensive copper cookware lined with stainless steel did not really appeal to me. The second reason was these products are extremely expensive and I could not overcome my inherently parsimonious nature sufficiently to purchase them.

Having discounted modern iterations of copper cookware I became interested in antique copper cookware, usually of the French persuasion. There are a number of reasons why I like these products. First, they are pieces of history which you can still buy and use in everyday life. Secondly, I like the idea that they are made using different techniques, often, than those in current use for production cookware. I will return to this later.

The first technical question which arises is why copper cookware was used at all.

The answer that requires some explanation.

Once again McGee comes to the rescue.(He really is a sterling chap). McGee observes that copper is unique amongst the common metals because it can be found naturally in its metallic state. He opines that it is prized for its unmatched conductivity which makes fast and even heating a simple matter. However, it is expensive and difficult to keep polished because it has a high affinity for oxygen and sulphur which forms a greenish coating when exposed to the air. It can also be harmful; the human body can excrete only limited amounts of copper and if sufficient is ingested it can cause significant physiological issues. To overcome this, McGee stated, manufacturers lined copper utensils with stainless steel or, more traditionally, with tin. Tin, however, has some significant disadvantages. Whilst it binds with copper very well, the best example of that which is the alloy referred to as bronze, it has a low melting point (approximately 230°C) which can be reached in some cooking procedures and a softness that makes it very susceptible to wear.

However tin lined copper pots are such lovely equipment to use and represented the most technologically advanced form of cookware available at that time.

The methods of construction of copper cookware are also interesting to me.

Because of the risk of toxicity from copper cookware the cookware has been lined with various compounds for many years. Historically copper pots were lined with nickel or, more often, tin. Indeed at one point in time nickel cooking pots were the next best thing and better than copper. The expense and unavailability of nickel meant that did not last.

 Lining copper pots with stainless steel is a very recent innovation. Modern trademarks reflect the various styles of lining copper pots. Cupretam is trademark which refers to copper lined with tin. Presumably it derives from the French words cupro (copper) and andetame (tinned) . Cuprinox is a different trademark used to refer to copper lined with stainless steel, again presumably from cupro and inoxydable (stainless steel). Cupronil is a trademark which presumably refers to copper lined with nickel, presumably derived from cupro and nickel. All these terms have recently been registered as trademarks but the methods, with the exception of stainless lining, are very old. Allow Moi to explain somewhat, but not from a position of any expertise (Vouz will be accustomed to Moi position in   such matters).

Early copper pots were made by hammering sheets of copper into the desired shape and then riveting the two ends together. These are rarely seen, in my experience in Australia. One of the next iterations was joining two different pieces of copper often the base to the shape of the pot with dovetail joints. Coppersmiths referred to these as cramp seams. These can be seen as a zigzag line around the base or in a vertical seam both of which have a yellow brass line running through it. The method of manufacture was to beat the zigzag piece together with the other piece after overlapping. The seam was then further sealed by application of molten brass which joined the crevices. This is called brazing.

The handles of old copper pots are also quite interesting. They are in different shapes and metals. Early handles were made from low carbon wrought iron; later iron handles were high carbon cast iron handles cast into moulds.

Other handles are made from cast bronze or brass. They are a characteristic gold colour.

The handles are fixed with copper rivets. These can be seen as circular shapes on the interior, covered with the relevant lining.

Lastly, the pots are often stamped with the manufacturer's name or trademark. There are websites which can help in translating the manufacturers' mark or name. This is quite a useful and interesting thing to do to try and gauge the country of manufacture and approximately the age of the piece. For example, several of my pots are stamped "PETER 'and "BRUX ". This is the mark of a manufacturer called PETER, who made copperware in Belgium from the mid-1800s to the early 1900s.

Some copper pots are unlined. This is curious because of the well-known toxicity of copper once exposed to acidic foods. Why are some not lined? The bowls which are affected are those used in making jams and preserves, zabaglione pans and those used for whisking egg whites. Copper bowls for whisking egg whites as described by McGee is a French invention dating back to the 1700s. As explained it turns out that along with very few other metals, copper has a useful tendency to form extremely tight bonds with reactive sulphur groups, so tight that the sulphur is essentially prevented from reacting with anything else. The presence of copper in foaming egg whites essentially eliminates the strongest kind of protein bond that can form and make it harder for the proteins to embrace each other too tightly. Egg whites whisked in the copper bowl achieve the desired texture very quickly, stay glossy and never develope grains or that gritty texture. Also, copper is not exposed to acidic foods, so the risk of the toxicity associated with copper ions is negligible.

The use of unlined copper pans for making jam and zabaglione is somewhat different. As near as I can tell copper is considered desirable because it assists in the gelling of the jam or zabaglione, and sugar interferes with the acidity of the environment and reduces the risk of toxicity. Accordingly, it is said that one should not macerate the fruit in the copper pot, one should not add the fruit into the copper pot without sugar and that one should only add the fruit to the copper pot once it has been combined with the sugar.

Retinning is a special process, modern electroplaters can do it but most do not care to do it. I think this is because it is quite tedious. The surfaces which are not to be retinned must be masked or they too will be coated in tin.Your beautiful copper exterior will be , pretty much irrevocably coated in tin. Then the interior, once retinned, needs to be polished and made smooth and nice. The exterior is then polished including the handles, whether of steel, brass, or bronze.

A lot of work, and which is reflected in the price for each piece.

Can this be justified on any rational basis I hear you ask?

The answer is that there is no need to be like that.

Such a response ignores the pleasure of owning a copper pot which is probably more than 100 years old, has been restored to its former glory, is a direct link to history and a way of life which is unlike any other piece of kitchen equipment you are likely to own. They can be re polished with lemon juice and salt in your study on a wet winter afternoon. These things are without price or if price can be quantified, they make the refurbishment process cheap by any measure.

At least this is the published response.

I acknowledge, but only to you and it cannot be repeated, that modern stainless-steel pots live forever and are cheap. Modern stainless steel lined copper pots are quite expensive but not when compared to restored antiques of the same persuasion. They also last forever but are soulless.

What would I rather have?

Restored antique copper every time, but maybe some nice modern stainless steel lined copper for every day.

As an aside the antiques shop owner, where I have bought many old pots, recently justified her use of unrestored pots at home, by informing me that she had used them for many years and " I am not dead yet ". There is something to be said about that.

The pots which I recently bought at auction are extremely heavy, probably commercial quality such as I have never seen before. My assumption is that they have been discarded for risk management reasons.

On any view I have been the beneficiary. Nonetheless I will have them restored as and when means are available.

This leaves me with one final practical point. Keeping the pots looking nice. After all you have paid a reasonable amount to purchase the pot and a lot more to refurbish it. It deserves to look nice, at least I think so. There are two aspects. The copper exterior and the tin interior. I deal with each in turn. You can buy commercial copper cleaning products from the supermarket. They do a good job. I cannot add anything that you will not read all the directions on the tin. There is another way and one which I quite enjoy. Lemon juice and salt or vinegar and salt create a cleaning solution which gives a result very close to the commercial copper cleaning products. However, I like to think it is more friendly than copper.

You can cut a lemon in half, dip it in salt on the cut side and rub it onto the copper. Alternatively, you can make a paste of lemon juice, salt, and some flour. Apply the paste to the copper surface and then wash off with hot water. Another variant is to use equal parts lemon juice and salt and baking soda. Using a cloth apply this to the copper surface and polish. Rinse off with hot water.

Avoid using abrasive cleaners, they will work but scratch the tin surface in an undesirable way.

The brass or bronze handles can be cleaned in the same way.

Iron handles are tough and stain resistant. You can be robust with them.

The tin interior is a different matter. Tin is notoriously soft so abrasive cleaners should not be used. The tin interior should be washed with a soft cloth, using hot soapy water. Allow it to dry well.

If it is very stained then a paste of baking soda and water, used with a soft cloth this will clean the interior up quite significantly. However, it is in the nature of the tin interior to tarnish over time and to wear. That is the reason why it has deteriorated, and you had to pay a significant amount of money to re-tin the interior of the pot. Forget trying to keep it looking brand-new. That is unachievable in my experience. And in any event, the patina of the tin is quite a desirable feature.

Remember the melting point of tin is 231.93°C. This is achievable in a domestic oven. It is certainly achievable on a gas or electric cooktop. Be afraid. Be very afraid.

Defeat is always momentary.

THE OLIVES

Lockdown had finished but we were still making up for lost time and looking for new projects. We have looked at olives before but did not know what to do with them. The time came when we decided that the olives looked so good that we had to do something with them. Part of that reason was because fresh olives are not often seen in the market, I do not know why. Perhaps most people are like me and unsure of what to do with them. Nonetheless the olives looked good. There were three types. Small green olives, medium size green olives, and a much larger green olive. The latter boxes had a significant number of olives with varying degrees of purple, ranging from blush to a reasonable purple colour. However, they were not soft as black olives are want to be.

I asked the market stallholder which type would be best, small medium or large. I told him that I was lleaning towards the big ones because I like colours and bigger is always better. He explained that with olives bigger is not always better and that his father preferred the medium-size olives because they cure more evenly. What is one to do in those circumstances? The answer is obvious, follow the advice of the Greek or Italian market stallholder's father, whom one has never met.

I brought the 10 kg box of olives home and proceeded to ascertain how to deal with them. I contacted an Italian restauranteur, who coincidentally had recently returned to Italy on an extended sojourn. He was kind enough to provide his family recipe by email from Italy. The number of steps and complexity of the process was frankly most disheartening. I thought about it and decided that there must be an easier way.

This, after unsatisfactory responses from Italian and Greek colleagues, led to the Internet once again. The variety of methods to cure olives was quite staggering. The techniques range from a series of water changes and increasing salinities of the brine to pre-salting and other complicated techniques.

I went to the website of an Australian olive oil producer who also commercially produces cured olives. I was familiar with both products and use them reasonably regularly. To my enormous delight there was a recipe for curing olives. The recipe was very simple, and it seemed to me that this was something that I could deal with.

The recipe is as follows. For 5 kg of olives, wash the olives well in fresh water and drain, make 10 L of a 10% brine solution (1 kg of salt in 10 L of water), add 100 mL of vinegar to the brine solution. Add the drained olives to the brine. Place a weight or cover such that the olives are fully submerged in the brine, put a lid on the container (which should be non-reactive, such as plastic or glass). Come back in two months. Well, I did and after 2 months the green olives had changed colour and become a mottled khaki colour but were tough and inedible. I asked whether I should change the brine solution, which by now was quite dark in colour. I was told that it was not necessary. I continued. After about 6 or 7 months the olives were a uniform khaki type colour , did not have the raw bitter taste of fresh olives and were considerably softer.

The recipe then required one to drain the solution, rinse the olives and replace them in a new brine solution of 5% with a splash of vinegar as advised. The recipe then called for a layer of oil on the top of the containers to prevent further oxidation.

What I did at this point was to place the drained and rinsed olives in containers added dried aromatics such as chili, peppercorn, mustard seed and the like. I filled the containers with vegetable oil, although I could have used an expensive olive oil.

These containers of home cured olives then became gifts.

THE NTK PRINCIPLE

Allow me to introduce the NTK principle. We have used it for many years, and it has never let us down. The acronym, I think that is the correct grammatical term, stands for Need To Know, hence the NTK principle. The principal stands for exactly what it says. It is the release of information on a need-to-know basis. This follows from the modern insistence from all manner of people to demand answers to all manner of things. In truth they do not need to know these things but they only desire to know them for their purposes. The response to this has been the development over many years of the NTK principle. They are only told on a need-to-know basis , usually they do not need to know much. The protestations and allegations which follow from these people who demand to know things only underline the fact that they do not need to know. We have applied the NTK principle unfailingly, and without fear or favour. It is a principle which is applied to all things in modern life and is not something which can be avoided. As an aside it is a sad reflection on modern life that all manner of people demand to know all manner of things when they are clearly not entitled to do so. Hence the importance of the unflinching application of the NTK principle. Let me give you an example. The modern predilection and insistence on passwords and usernames, expressed as a security issue for your own protection, is in fact nothing of the kind, it is all about the person insisting on such matters trying to protect their own database. What is the likelihood of someone hacking your information when you are buying a T-shirt online from a domestic website? The answer is that it is extremely unlikely. It is all about the vendor or ensuring the purity of their own bodily essences rather than yours. Similarly, the practice of workplace cyber security experts insisting on brand-new passwords and usernames every three months, and one cannot use a variation of the previous one, only reflects their inability to guarantee the security of the network, rather than a real desire to ensure that your own details are protected henceforth hereafter.

On a more prosaic level the NTK principle extends to people who, in everyday parlance, demand to know what one is doing, intends to do, or did yesterday. Allow me to illustrate. Bureaucrats want to know if one is divorced, is of particular ethnic origin or even better is from a culturally "diverse background". The latter is as irrelevant as it is offensive. Of course, I am, the English language is a blend of English and French words, my Anglo-Saxon heritage is complicated, rich and of long standing. The prominence of English spoken worldwide is a reflection of many things if not the rich British heritage of maritime exploration. But this is not the answer these people are looking for. The question is as loaded, irrelevant and offensive as it can be. I do not respond to these questions. The interrogators do not need to know. As an aside previous secretaries or " P A's ", and there have been quite a few, would always innocently ask where I was going, where I would be, and how would be contacted. This is a much more benign example of the modern demand for information. If I decided that information was necessary to be shared then I would do so. Hence a positive application of the NTK principle. If I decided that it was not necessary, and the High Court would be unlikely to need to contact me urgently then I would explain to them that the answer was "NTK". Invariably the officeholders, paid employees, were unsatisfied with this. This illustrates the true and correct application of the NTK principle.

The truth is out there.

THE TOKYO EXPEDITION

I recently had an opportunity to travel to Tokyo with Number 1 Son. It was a boy's own adventure comprising mainly of food tours. Token visits to culturally significant sites were made for the purposes of reassuring our handlers but were kept to a minimum. One outing was noteworthy for present purposes. It involved a trip to Kappabashi Street, between Asakusa and Euno in Eastern Tokyo. The street is in a quiet area and is approximately 1 km in length. The street is entirely populated by retail vendors of kitchen ware and hospitality supplies. Accordingly, it was a pantheon of pots and pans, commercial appliances, napery and the fascinating plastic food reproductions which adorn the windows of many Tokyo restaurants. It is referred to by the locals as kitchen Street, for obvious reasons. My principal reason to visit kitchen Street was to investigate the many knife vendors. Whilst many of the shops sold kitchenware including knives there are approximately half a dozen dedicated knife shops in Kitchen Street. Kama Asa, Kamata, Tsubaya , and Seisuki to name a few. These range from relatively small retailers to much larger very upmarket retailers including those offering extremely expensive, high-end Japanese knives. I am very fond of Japanese knives and I own several of them. I was interested in purchasing some more knives when I was in Tokyo. Interestingly the shops were laid out in a very similar way. At the entrance to the shop the knives on display were all Japanese knives but made in a very familiar Western style. They were characterised by stainless steel double edged blades and a curved cutting-edge like the German knife, unlike the flat edge of a Japanese knife. They also had Western-style wooden or plastic handles with rivets secured to an exposed tang. In other words, they looked like Western cooking knives. They were very nice and often had interesting wood for the handles, unlike German or French cooking knives. Some handles were quite brightly coloured. They were all extremely expensive. There were many of them and they seemed to dominate the retail space at the front of the shop. Upon entering the shop I would be directed to these types of knives by the staff. Their obvious assumption was that a Westerner would be looking for a Western-style knife. Indeed, most of the customers were Westerners and they were all focused upon the Western-style knives.

I was not there to purchase a Western-style knife. I explained this to the shop staff. They were somewhat confused by the concept of a Westerner seeking to purchase a Japanese style knife. Once they understood the concept they directed my attention to some of the knives in the front part of the shop which they thought might satisfy my enquiry. These were straight edged, double bevel knives but made of stainless steel and all with Western-style handles and exposed tang. I explained to the staff that I was not interested in those knives but rather I was looking for traditional single edge, mild steel Japanese knives with the Japanese handle. This concept took a little explaining. Ultimately, I would be ushered to the rear of the retail space to a much smaller area in which were displayed traditional Japanese knives. There were only a few knives on display, much less than the Western style knives. It was in this area that I investigated and ultimately purchased two very nice knives from different retailers. First a short bladed knife predominantly used for peeling vegetables or fruit. It is referred to as a petty knife, perhaps a reference to the French "petit ", meaning something small. The second knife is a longer rectangular bladed knife, it has a straight edge and no point on the end. Rather it has a square end. This is used for slicing vegetables very finely. It is called a nakiri.

I came away from the knife purchase experience very happily with my two new knives but also with the clear impression that the Japanese either do not value their own traditional knives much anymore or commercial retailers have decided that the best market is in imitation Western-style knives. Either way a somewhat disappointing state of affairs.

I also bought a Japanese pocket knife. They are different to Western pocket knives . They have a flat metal housing for the blade and a rectangular blade. Vey small and lightweight.

Two other purchases were noteworthy from general cookware shops. First the square high sided pan for making the Japanese rolled omelet. The pan is called a makiyakinabe, I think. The omelet is called tamagoyaki ,I think. The pan is made of copper with a tin lining and a raw wooden handle. I have been too scared to use it. Secondly a cutting board made of rubber. It is stiff and inflexible like a wooden board but is very kind to the knife edge. I have never seen anything like it anywhere else in the world. It is a pleasure to use.

Ps: The former wholesale fish market, now a food destination , Tsukiji Outer Market is a really good food destination but also has some very expensive knife shops- Masamota, Minamoto, Aritsuga and Nenshi. Take votre credit card. They are beautiful but very expensive. They make German knives look cheap.

Sayonara.

> *Do not imagine, comrades, that leadership is a pleasure. On the contrary, it is a deep and heavy responsibility. No one believes more firmly than Comrade Napoleon that all animals are equal. He would be only too happy to let you make your decisions for yourselves. But sometimes you might make the wrong decisions, comrades, and then where should we be? (George Orwell, Animal Farm)*

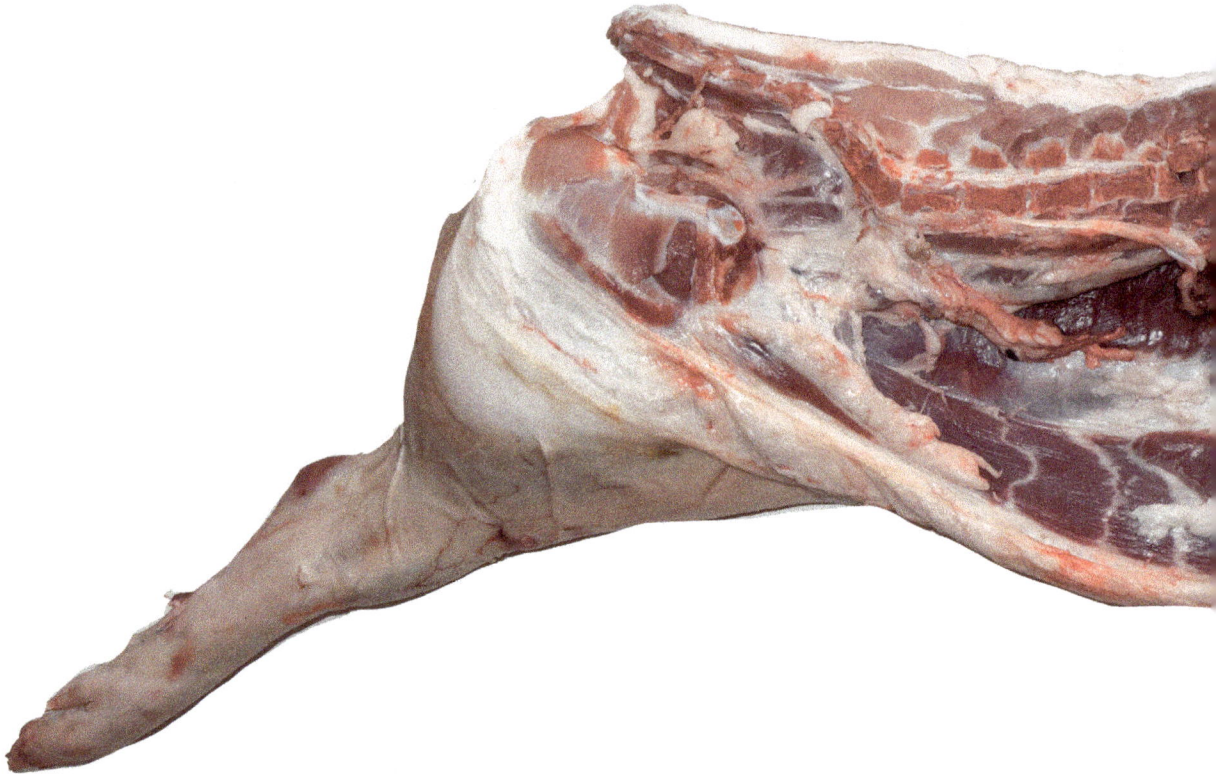

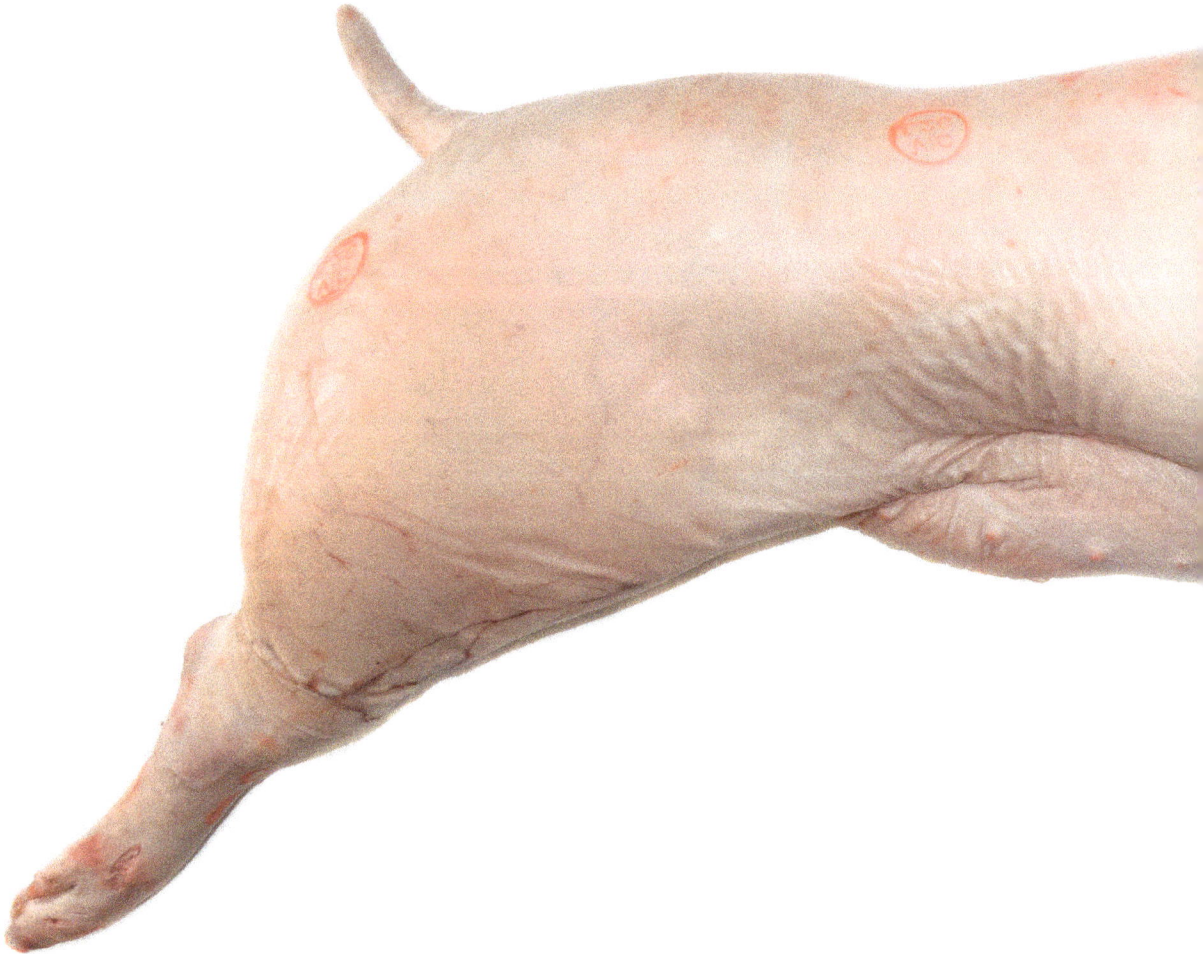

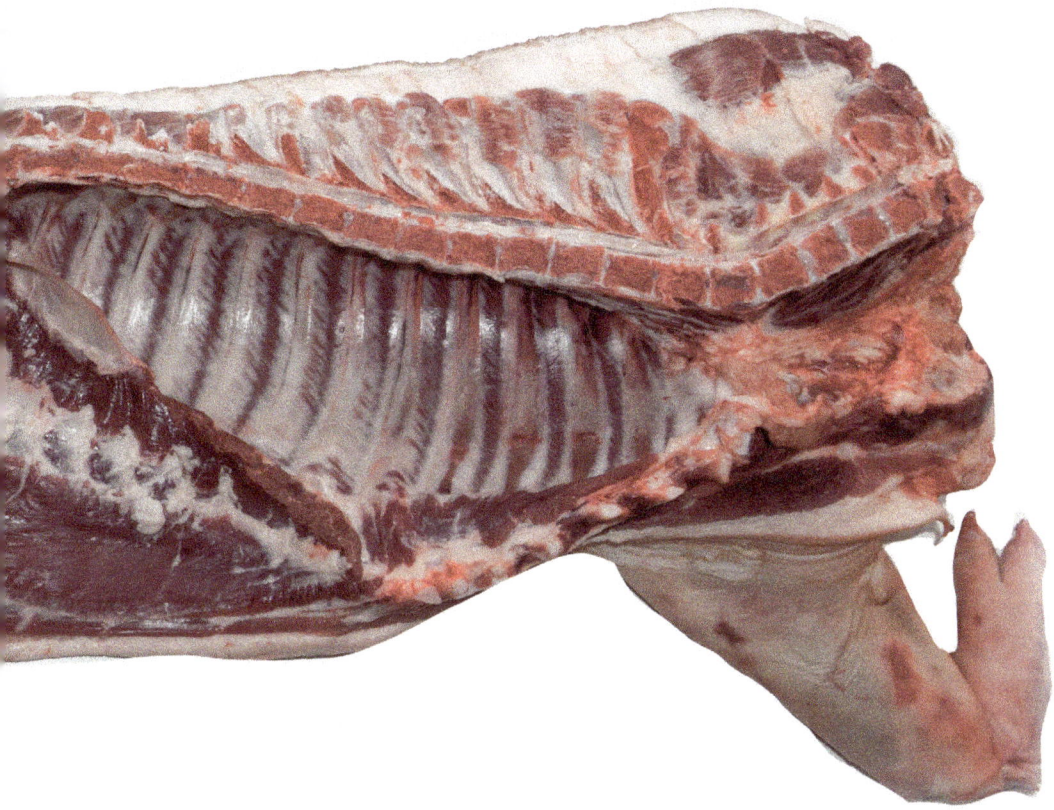

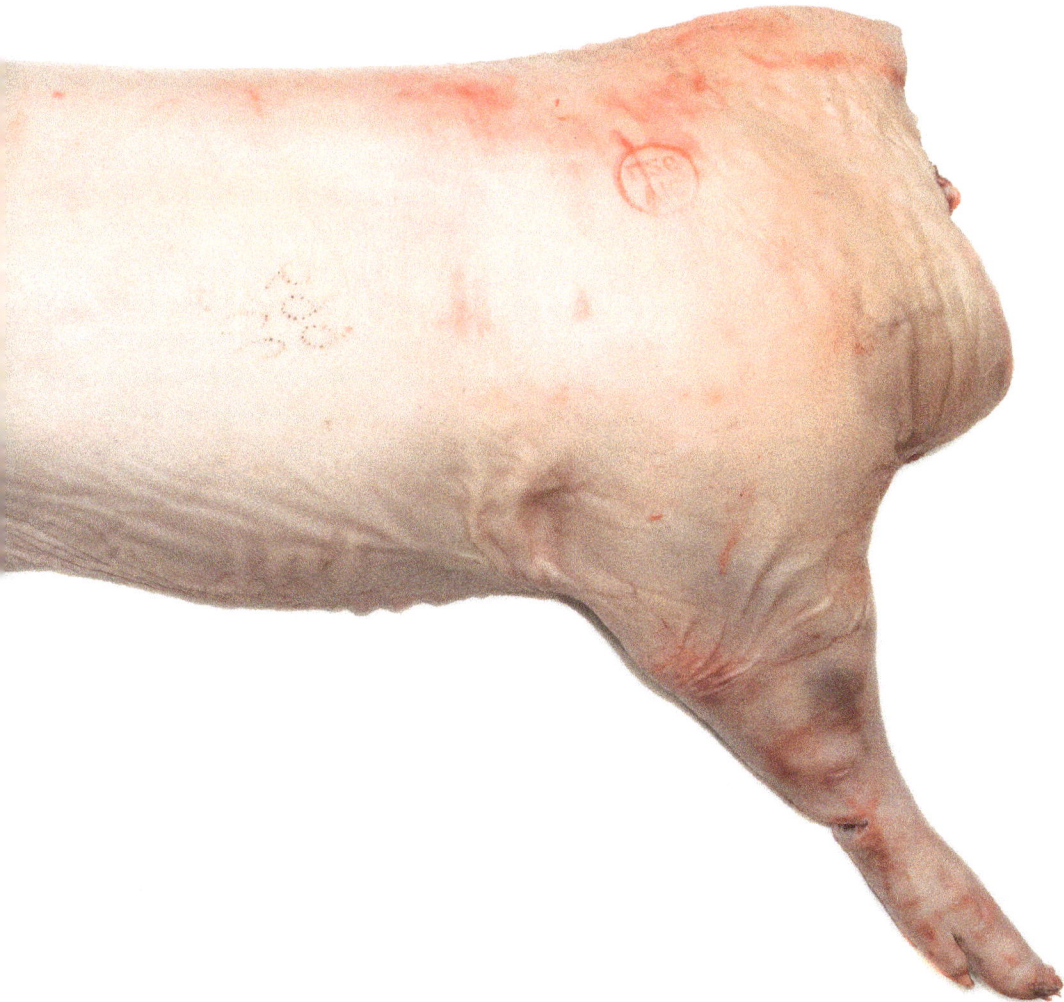

THE INTERMISSION

THE INTERMISSION

KNIVES AND SHARPENING, THE TECHNICAL STUFF

I decided that this section, in relation to sharpening and the tools which are required in relation thereof, should be a separate section, because it did not fit logically into the equipment section. The other more significant reason is because I think sharpening knives is a very specialised state of mind and is not to be confused with buying a sharp knife. A sharp knife lasts as long as it can, depending on the available circumstances. But ultimately a sharp knife will become a blunt knife. The really important issue in knife husbandry is maintaining a good edge or acknowledging that the edge has not been maintained properly and then setting about fixing this most unfortunate circumstance. I have had to deal with this for many years because evil people in my household will use knives until they are utterly unusable and then complain that they are blunt. I, on the other hand, test the blade before I use it, sharpen it, if need be, test it throughout the butchering process, sharpen it again, if need be, and then usually sharpen it before I put it away. The other issue is that occasional sharpening whilst one is preparing to cut some meat is a transient but necessary phase of mind. The holy dedicated, Zen situation in which one finds oneself, usually in one study in the depths of winter, to resurface all available knives is a completely different situation. I acknowledge that this is often aided by fermented fruit juice if not organic preparations made from barley and the water from organic mountain streams in the Scottish highlands or on an island. This, I think, should be the counsel of perfection and the counsel to which vouz should aspire.

Happiness is a sharp knife.

But I digress, with the introduction and enough thereof. I proceed to the carefully thought-out narrative.

Knives are the most important things in butchery. Forget all the other stuff. Without a sharp knife it is very difficult to cut anything. Without the right knife is very difficult to cut according to the meat's requirements. I have many knives. They are of many different types, shapes, steel quality and sizes. I like them all. But some I like better than others. I just do not tell the other knives which ones I prefer.

a) The types of knives

The many different aspects of the knife need to be considered. I will deal with each in turn.

i) The first consideration is the type of steel. It is a decision between stainless steel and so-called carbon steel or mild steel, curiously so called because all steel is made from carbon. Why do these people say this?. Carbon steel is not coated in chromium and is less shiny, it is softer than stainless steel and will react with its environment. It will require more maintenance than a stainless steel blade, but the great benefit of a carbon steel or mild steel knife is that it will be razor-sharp with a few passes over the sharpening steel. The other issue with carbon steel or mild steel knives is that they do discolour and develop some surface rust but this can easily be removed with some steel wool or other abrasive product. They develop a patina with age which I like.There is nothing like the razor-sharp edge of a carbon steel knife. They do tend to be lighter weight than a stainless-steel knife, but this can often be an advantage if you are undertaking a lot of cutting in one session. Some cultures prefer carbon steel knives notably Asian countries, French to some extent and some other European countries like Spain and Portugal. Our German cousins only want high end very hard staless steel. What can I say? They are German. Carbon steel knives tend to be cheaper than stainless steel knives but will not last as long as a good quality heavy stainless-steel knife.

ii) The next issue is the hardness of the steel. Stainless steel knives tend to be made of harder steel than carbon steel knives . This explains the ease of maintaining a razor-sharp edge on a carbon steel knife compared with the difficulty of getting a good edge of a stainless-steel knife. However, the benefit of the hardness of the steel is that a good stainless-steel knife will maintain its edge for a lot longer than a carbon steel knife. However, in contrast, while a carbon steel knife will lose its edge relatively quickly it is far easier to regain the razor edge of a carbon steel knife than that of a stainless-steel knife.

iv) Blade shape is another point of difference between knives. A knife with a flat blade is designed for repetitive slicing or cutting on a board. Most Asian knives, especially Japanese, are designed with very flat blades which are for the purpose of repetitive vertical movements to facilitate chopping and slicing. Some European knives are also like this, notably French.

A rounded blade edge or belly is better for the rocking motion of slicing through meat or vegetables when the blade really does not lose contact with the cutting board surface to a great extent. They are designed for a different form of cutting or slicing which perhaps involves less effort because the knife blade does not lose contact with the cutting board surface significantly. However it may be less precise.

v)Different knives also have different blade thicknesses. Thinner knives are easier to make and better suited to slicing where there is liable to be low resistance. Thicker knives are better for more robust conditions and where the slicing might be through more resistant materials.

vi) The edge of the knife is fashioned by creating a bevel either one side or as a double bevel. Most knives regardless of country of manufacture or style use a double bevel. Japanese knives use a single bevel, and this can be either for right-handed use or left-handed use. Japanese single bevel knives are very sharp and very useful for quite low resistance foods such as vegetables or fish. However, a single bevel knife is very delicate and requires special sharpening techniques. The other downside of single bevel knives is that they tend to want to cut towards the straight edge of the knife therefore they can be difficult to use if a long straight cut is required.A slightly different technique is required.

A double bevel knife however will cut a very straight line because of the properties of the double bevel, they are also easier to keep sharp. A butcher sharpening steel can be used on a double bevel knife, it cannot be used on a single bevel knife because it will ruin the cutting edge. The double bevel knife is also designed for either a right- or left-handed person to use as the case may be, whereas a double bevel knife can be used by either.

vii) Blade length is also important, very long knives are used for cutting large animals like tuna or other large fish, or for cutting steaks through large cuts of beef, in either case the length of the blade is needed because of the thickness of the meat. However, they tend to be specialist knives and have obvious disadvantages with smaller meat thickness. Most knives in the kitchen have lengths depending on the intended application. Small knives, often referred to as paring knives are good for peeling vegetables and fruit, slightly longer ones can be used for chopping slightly larger vegetables, a 6 or 8 inch (most knives are described in inches rather than centimeters for some unknown reason) tend to be good as general-purpose chef knives.

viii) Knife handles are also different. Good knives are constructed of a single piece of steel which continues into the handle. The handle end of the knife is often referred to as the tang. The style of construction is either a hidden tang or full tang knife. Hidden tang knives of which Japanese knives are a good example have the handle of the knife as a graduated point which is inserted into a, usually, round, or oval wooden handle. The tang of the knife cannot be seen because it is buried within the handle. There are usually no visible securing rivets or pins. The full or exposed tang knife, of which German knives are a good example, have a much thicker tang which is not of a graduated point, and which is sandwiched between the handle material, which can be either wood or a synthetic material such that the steel the tang is visible. It is secured with visible rivets or pins.

The differences in these methods of construction gives a different balance to the two styles. The hidden tang knives tend to be front heavy or blade heavy, which is more advantageous for a slicing, cutting motion because the blade is driven by the forward heavy weight of the knife. The exposed or full tang knives are more handle heavy and perhaps better suited to chopping motion or slicing motion. Further the hidden tang method of construction is less designed for heavy duty use, whereas the exposed or full tang method is more suitable for heavy cutting or chopping.

ix) Knife handle material also varies between countries of manufacture. Asian knives, particularly Japanese, tend to have unvarnished wooden handles. These are easy to use, non-slippery , and especially the case in Japanese knives, fashioned to suit a right- or left-hand grip and oval in profile. European knives tend to be, in modern times, of synthetic, food grade materials which can be a little slippery to use but are robust and have significant longevity. Often, especially in the case of brands which are specially designed for heavy commercial use, they are of food grade plastics which can be subjected to high temperatures for ease of sterilization and food safety. In passing I observe that your good knives should never be put in the dishwasher. The conditions are too extreme and it will all end up in tears.

Older European kitchen knives tend to have wooden handles with brass rivets or securing pins which are elegant and disclose their age or antiquity. There are also differences in the shape of the handle. Japanese knives have oval handles which are oriented either for left-handed or right-handed use. They do not have any return end on the handle to stop your hand slipping backwards. German knives like Wustoff, tend to have a profile which has a return at the end which stops your hand from moving backwards but also a fuller section in the middle which accommodates the contour of the palm of your hand. French knives like Sabatier, tend to have relatively flat handle with no contour to fit the palm of their but also a return on the end. This prevents your hand from moving backwards. The other thing is that different cultures tend to have knives which fit the physiognomy of their own people. That is to say Asian knives, I find have handles which are too short, they have been designed for people with small hands . German knives seem to fit my hand quite well, French knives tend to be a little short but not a short in the handle as Asian knives for my taste. No doubt your preferences will be different. The only thing to do is to pick up the knife and see how it feels in your hand.

x)The end of the blade closest to the handle is the thickest part of the blade and the longest part. It is often referred to as the bolster ,sometimes the heel of the knife. Different knives have different bolsters or heals. German knives have a bolster which flares out becomes thicker and is a guard to stop you from cutting your fingers as you deploy the knife. It is also angled forward, that is to say away from the handle and therefore away from your fingers slightly. This design means it is difficult to nick your fingers if you are holding the knife by the handle as it should be . French knives tend to be have no flaring or thickening at the end and very straight, 90° bolster or heel which can mean that you can nick your fingers when you are using them . Asian knives generally are made with a bolster which is not flared and 90 degrees against the handle. The downside with the flared German bolster is that it is difficult to sharpen the blade completely up to the commencement of the bolster. In contrast at Asian knife can be sharpened perfectly up to its conclusion, the 90° end of the blade nearest the handle.

In summary a German chef's knife will be a heavier thicker blade than a French chef's knife, and the curve of the blade will start about in the middle of the blade. The curve in a French knife is shallower and commences closer to the tip. Japanese knives tend to be thinner, lighter, and made from softer steel. They have one bevel and usually have a straight edge. Unlike both French and German knives, a Japanese knife has no bolster at the handle end of the blade. German knives have a bolster which blends into the blade such that the blade end at the bolster is not sharp. A French knife will have a bolster, but the blade is sharp right up to the bolster.

I prefer different types of knives for different uses. Each is different. None are better. At least that is what I tell them.

b) how to sharpen a knife

Knife sharpening is a necessary skill if you are going to embark on any type of butchery, whether it be red meat, white meat , fish or poultry. My mother showed me how to sharpen a knife, you might think this is somewhat unusual but she did grow up on a sheep property in central west Queensland together with her four sisters. In essence the process is very simple regardless of the type of sharpening implement which is used. It involves using a long slow path across the sharpening surface or polishing surface at a very shallow angle. This is required to achieve a very shallow angle on either side of the edge which creates the double bevel in most knives. Single bevel Japanese knives are different proposition and I have described them separately. The motion, for a double bevel knife , involves pushing the knife blade away from you such that the abrasive or polishing surface runs evenly across the blade, this is best achieved by using an angle of 25° or 30° across the face of the abrasive or polishing surface. Then the knife is flipped over such that the cutting surface is facing away from the handler and drawn backwards across the abrasive service at the same angle to create the bevel. Ultimately the knife bevel will create a roll of very, very fine metal on the bevel, this is the bur, the roll of metal which is created because of the sharpening process. The process continues until the bur is removed.

The process of sharpening or repolishing a knife edge depends on the state of the knife blade. Knives which are very blunt, or which have nicks or damage must be subjected to a more rigorous grinding process using hard grinding stones. The hard grinding process removes much more metal from the edge of the blade and returns it to its original profile. This may take some time and is because of heavier pressure on the grinding surface. Such grinding stones usually use oil as a lubricant rather than water. Such

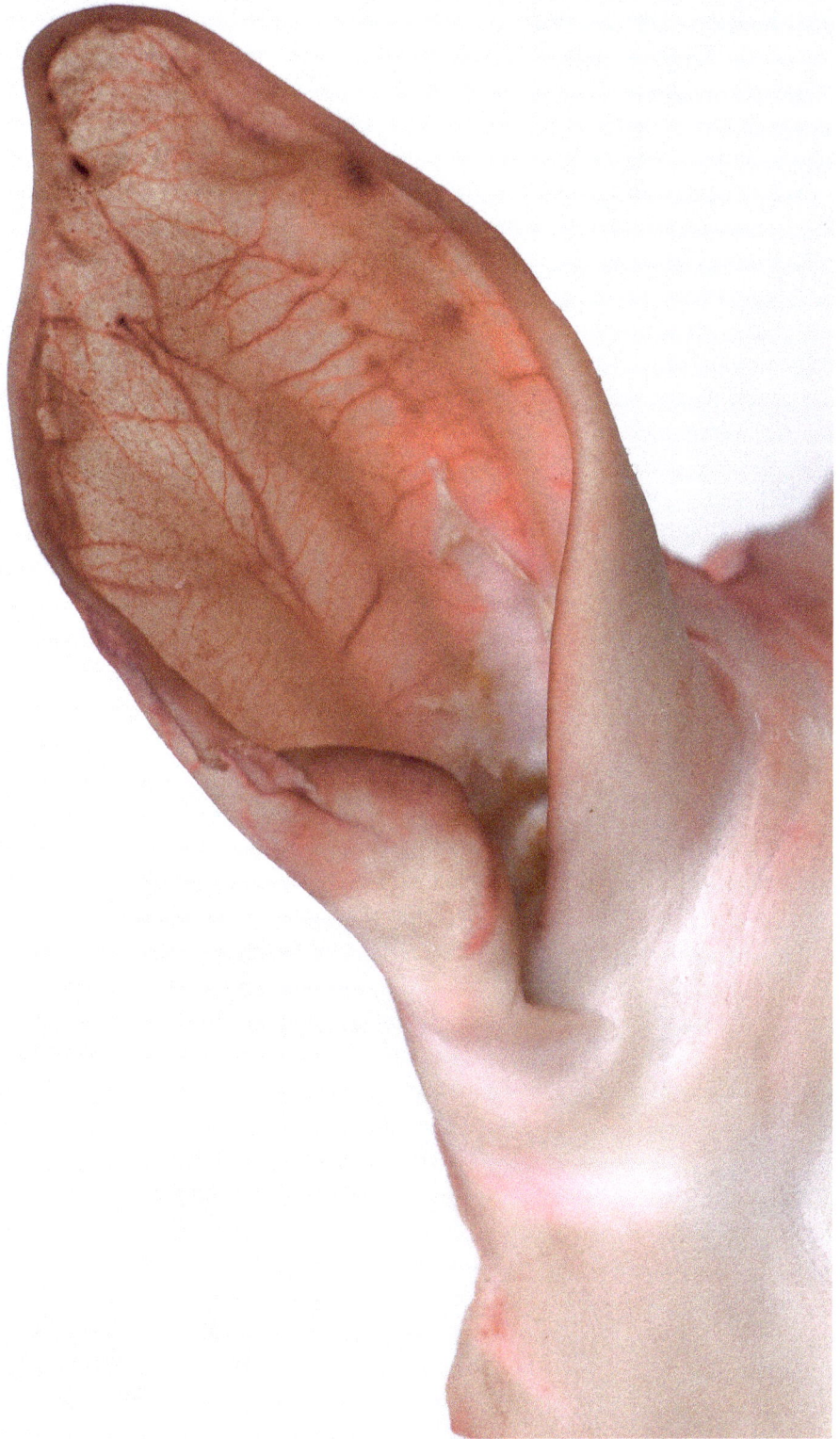

is the pressure and friction which is applied by the heavier motion and the rougher surface. Once the nicks or problems with the edge have been corrected, and this may take some time, the blade is ready to be sharpened and polished. The sharpening and polishing occurs using water stones or mudstones, and often collectively referred to as whetstones. Whilst they are slightly different it is a reference to an old form of expression which was whetting the blade which was a reference to the sharpening process.

I have some very old mudstones which use water as a lubricant, they create a dark muddy slurry of fine abrasive paste. These were originally made from river sediment stones or other extremely fine grade abrasive stones and their primary function is to polish the blade to a fine edge. Arkansas mudstones are a very good example of this although they are much harder than other mudstones and do not create the dark grey slurry of other mudstones. They are more of a polishing stone.

The modern equivalent of water stones or whetstones are to be found in Japanese sharpening stones which are synthetic but derived from very fine abrasive compounds. They are conveniently stipulated in the polishing number or grade. They are also very conveniently double sided and in a narrow rectangular form which is ideal for the long slow angular process which is required to polish the blade edge. They are not useful for rectifying blades which are very damaged , or which have nicks or imperfections. I have many Japanese whetstones. They are a pleasurable thing to use, they need to be soaked in water for at least 5 minutes before using and then one starts from the lowest grade, perhaps 900 and progresses through the different degrees of polishing strength up until polishing grades of 6000 and up to 10,000. If done correctly and with the proper Zen frame of mind, you can achieve blades whether of single or double bevel which will cut through a sheet of paper like a razor. Don't you worry about that.

I can tell you that the process of bringing a very good quality knife from less than ideal in sharpness to a knife which will cut paper effortlessly, achieved in my study on a wintry afternoon, is one of the best things that one can do. You need to trust me on this and try it. If you do not try this then I will find you.

b) The other sharpening devices

There are many devices and therefore ways to sharpen a knife. Let me discuss some of the other popular methods to do so. They mostly involve stone surfaces, I have already discussed metal surfaces, but also include leather surfaces. Let me deal with them one by one.

i) The strop

You have all seen images or videos of the barbershop with a cutthroat razor sharpened on a leather strap. This is called a strop. A strop is a polishing surface rather than an abrasive surface. It takes advantage of the rough side of the leather to do a rough polish and then finishes the process with the smooth side which is a finer polish. The honing or polishing is not about resharpening but is more to do with realigning the bevel on each side and thereby creating a sharpened blade . Polishing or honing a knife edge using a strop involves long slow draws across the surface of the leather at a very fine angle and then repeating it in the reverse direction to polish the bevel. It is not a technique that will recreate a bevel edge for a knife which is very blunt or has significant intrusions into the bevel edge, that is to say nicks or cuts. These cannot be rectified by the process of using a leather strop. The surface is a polishing action and will not recreate or regenerate a blade which has a significantly deteriorated cutting edge. It is very similar to the effect of a honing butchers steel but much more subtle and to be used with finer edges like a barber's straight edge razor. Hence the predominance of a leather strop in a barber's situation rather than in a butcher's situation. The use to which a barber's straight edge razor was put was far more subtle than that which a butcher's knife was put. Nonetheless a leather strop can achieve a beautiful fine edge on a good quality steel knife in a way that other hard surfaces cannot. I have used a leather strop to finish fine quality Japanese knives or, curiously, mild steel French and Italian pocketknives. I do not understand the difference between the two, but I do say that the process of using leather strop on a wintry afternoon in my study to create a really satisfying edge is something that I do enjoy. Do not tell the other knives about this. They will only become jealous and needy. No one needs a needy knife.

ii) Steels

You will often hear the term "using a steel ", in reference to sharpening a knife. This can be somewhat misleading. Allow me to explain. There are two fundamentally different types of knife steels. The traditional, old-fashioned, knife steel does not sharpen blade. It is only designed to polish or hone the blade. Its purpose is to redress any minor irregularities in the blade profile and retain the angle which gives the blade its sharp edge. That is why a traditional knife honing steel does not have any abrasive surface, is circular in profile and has a series of fine ridges running down its length designed to return the blade to its original level angle by removing any minor irregularities. It is designed to be used on multiple occasions while one is using the blade, classically before and on many occasions whilst using the blade. It is a polishing tool.

Knife honing steels do not wear out, they will outlast you and your children. That is why antique knife honing steels are not only desirable because of their patina but because they still work.

The other type of steels are true sharpening steels. These are a more modern tool. These are designed very differently, often oval in profile and made of a material which is harder than the steel of the knife. They work by abrading and creating a new sharp edge. They are a modern iteration of the traditional knife steel but operate very differently. They are essentially of the same length and characteristic of a honing steel that is to say they have a handle with a guard and a long metal surface, usually oval in profile and sometimes round. They are made of different materials to a traditional honing steel, sometimes ceramic oor if made of steel are often diamond coated. The ceramic steels are very hard and durable although quite brittle. They can break which can be most unfortunate, if not expensive. But they are reasonably durable and long lasting. Diamond steels are made by coating a steel rod with industrial diamond fragments or powder which abrade and sharpen the metal of the knife because diamond is the hardest substance known to man. They work very well and give a good edge very quickly, but the great downside is that they wear out. The diamond fragments do not wear out of course but are dislodged during the physical process of running the knife blade along the length of the diamond steel. However, they are not brittle like ceramic steels, a positive advantage. I have owned many diamond steels and they have been very good at sharpening knives in their early days however they wear out surprisingly quickly. Ceramic steels are much better but far more expensive. In my view honing steels are very good for everyday use, a diamond or ceramic steel is very good for occasional use to bring back the edge of the knife to the sharpness that one might need. However, there is no substitute for slow and careful re-fabricating of the edge of a cooking knife through the process of using abrasive compounds such as a whetstone, an oil stone or a water stone. I will describe these below.

iii) Sharpening stones

As discussed above I have many polishing stones. The use to which I put them depends on the condition of the blade. A very blunt blade with imperfections requires a grinding stone. A blade which is without imperfections but requires some technique to bring it back from quite blunt to extremely sharp requires a Waterstone or an oil stone.

iv) Waterstones or whetstones

My waterstones are Japanese and uniformly of 180 mm in length and 60 mm in width. They are of 30 mm in thickness. They are of various polishing combinations because they are dual sided, there does not seem to be any method in the dual sided grading other than from a rough grading through to a higher grading. Let me explain by reference to the whetstones which I have, the first is to 240 x 800, the next is 1000 x 3000, the next is 1000 x 6000 and the final is 5000 x 10,000. There appears to be no particular reason why any two surfaces are combined other than they represent a lower and then a higher grade of polishing whetstone.I infer that they can be used sequentially. They all require water to lubricate the surface and the manufacturers reccomendation is that they are soaked in water for approximately 5 minutes before use. This results in water penetrating the compound, the visual representation of this is that the whetstones fizz and bubble because the water is penetrating the compound. They are then removed and lightly dried. Thereafter water is required to be added little by little as the lubricant for the polishing action of the blade on the compound. Most of these products are sold with a wooden or metal cradle which elevates it from the bench and has a nonstick surface on the underside such that the smooth polishing action of the blade across the whetstone does not drag the whetstone across the bench surface. They are very pleasing to use.But they can be also tricky to use. The worst result is that the edge is destroyed.

The polishing of a blade with a double bevel using Japanese whetstones is more or less the same as the polishing action required of a double bevel knife on a grinding stone. Japanese single bevel knives should never be resurfaced on a grinding stone, the edge is far too fragile and will result in nicks and imperfection which are very difficult to remove.

The polishing of a Japanese single bevel knife on a whetstone is a bit more difficult than the process for polishing a western double bevel edged knife on a whetstone. In essence, however, it is the same .The bevel edge is progressed across the whetstone in a smooth even process at about 25° across the polishing surface. However, when using longer blades and because of the single bevel extreme care must be taken in order that the blade remains parallel to the whetstone surface albeit at a slight angle. If the blade does not remain parallel to the whetstone surface is very easy to mark or nick the blade because of the 90° edge of the whetstone surface. If this occurs, then one must take a deep breath and start again. As usual the process requires moving through the whetstone polishing surfaces from small numbers, for example 240, up until the highest number that one has, for example 10,000. If this is done correctly then the edge will be extremely sharp and will have significant longevity. The trick is not to allow the blade to become extremely dull or nicked. It must be re polished at high polishing grades often, after use such that the razor edge is maintained. If the razor edge is allowed to be degraded substantially then it is a very long road to return to its appropriate form.

vi) Grinding stones or oil stones

Grinding stones and oil stones are very old tools for resurfacing a very blunt blade. They are exactly what it says on the tin, they grind the metal and remove particles of the metal and thereby reform the bevel edge, usually a double bevel edge in Western knives. They are very harsh and require oil as a lubricant because they grind the metal from the blade edge. They should only be used in the most extreme circumstances when the knife is beyond repolishing and has significant damage to the cutting surface. They often come in the same configuration as whetstones, about 180 mm in length and 60 mm in width, and with approximately 30 mm thickness. They are usually double sided. A course grind on one side and a finer grind on the other side. As with whetstones usually come in holder which enables the knife to be resurfaced on a bench top without sliding away during the process. The holder can be made of wood or often, in modern times, of a plastic product. If you are using a knife correctly and repolishing them as required, it will be most unusual for you to need to resurface the whole blade. If this is the case, then it might be preferable to give the knives to a professional re-sharpener although in my experience they do tend to be very harsh on the blades and I do not use them. I would prefer to take the time of taking the knife through the process of reforming it with a grinding stone or oil stone and then repolishing the edge using whetstones or water stones. Apart from anything else I do find the process to be extremely satisfying. As discussed above, do not tell the other knives this.

vii) The linisher

Another type of grinder used to fashion and shape a blade is a belt grinder. These are motorized belt grinders or shapers. They are not the usual type of electric belt grinders. They operate at variable speeds with variable grade grinding bands. Professional knife makers use them to fashion the shape of the blade and its profile. You will probably not use them for this purpose, but they can be used to create a new edge on a blade which has been so degraded that a stone will not fix it. They are referred to as linishers. Mine has a variable angle and speed, as well as being used with various grades of abrasive belts. They will not give the best edge but will shape and profile a degraded edge. They can be a useful tool but are quite difficult to use. I think I need lessons on how to use it properly.

The mind of man is capable of anything. (Conrad, J, "Heart of Darkness ")

IN THE MATTER OF STEEL

Knife blades are made from steel. However not all steels are created equal. Let me explain in brief the different types of steel and their different properties in the context of knife blades.

First some terminology. Hardness is the ability of the blade to resist deforming, it is measured by reference to a hardness scale, the Rockwell scale designated as HRC. Toughness is slightly different; this refers to the ability of the blade to resist cracking. Wear resistance refers to the blades ability to withstand abrasive and adhesive wear. Abrasive wear refers to surface coming into contact. Adhesive wear refers to debris being dislodged from one surface and attaching to the other where is generally synonymous with hardness. Edge retention refers to the ability of the blade to retain a sharp edge despite use.Different types of steel will be described by reference to these parameters,but that is beyond the scope of this work.

One essential difference is the difference between so-called carbon steel and stainless steel. All knives are made from iron and carbon so why carbon steel knives referred to as such? I do not know. However some explanation is as follows.

Carbon steel is usually made with a carbon content of between 0.5% and 2.1%. Carbon is the common factor which gives knives their hardness. Carbon steel knives , so called , have a higher percentage of carbon and are therefore softer which means they are easy to sharpen but it also makes them somewhat brittle. These knives are also prone to rust and discolour.

Stainless steel is steel utilising not more than 1.2% carbon and at least 11% chromium. These knives are harder than carbon steel knives because of the lower percentage of carbon and stain resistant because of the addition of chromium. Chromium is the metal which gives these knives their bright shiny silver finish. Chromium is also resistant to rust. Their hardness means that they retain a sharp edge for longer but are harder to resharpen, also very durable and not brittle like a carbon steel knife. Other elements are also added such as vanadium, molybdenum, titanium, nitrogen, or silicon. These also contribute to hardness and longevity.

Cooking knives are sometimes made of Damascus steel. This is more a method of manufacture than anything else. Two different types of steel are used in alternative layers. They are forged together. Then the blade is edged during which the lower carbon percentage steel stays a light colour, the higher percentage carbon steel goes a darker colour.

Damascus steel was used in the manufacture of edged weapons. They were reputed to hold a keener edge than other edged weapons of the times and were more robust. I do not know who first applied the technology to cooking knives. Presumably the rationale is the same as when Damascus steel was preferred for weapon making.

They are distinctive in their wave pattern. You either like them or not. I am not quite sure; on balance I think that I like them, but they are much more expensive. A matter for Vouz to decide upon.

The Japanese can also be very picky about the types of steel used for their cookware, presumably from the samurai influence. Aogami steel is made from a very pure type of steel from iron rich river sand to which carbon is utilised as an alloy. It is often also referred to as Blue Paper steel, because it comes in blue paper packaging. There are 3 grades : #1, #2 and Super.

White Paper steel is the same as Blue Paper steel but does not have chromium and tungsten added.

AUS 10 is made by a particular manufacturer and is a stainless steel with chromium, molybdenum and vanadium added. Traces of nickel, manganese and silicon are also added. It is very hard (60 HRC).

X 50 Cr MoV 15 is the common form of steel used for most stainless-steel knife blades. I have many hard stainless-steel knives. They are durable and stain resisitant. Perhaps lacking in a little character but one cannot be judgmental in respect of one's knives. They are all equal.

1.4 116 is a high carbon content stainless steel. It is very similar to X50 Cr MoV 15 however it is very hard to sharpen but holds its edge for a long time. The steel choice for good pocketknives. It has good stain resistant qualities. It is the steel of choice for Swiss pocketknives.

Sandvick 12C27 and 14C 28N are stainless steel's which hold a good edge but are not overly hard and therefore can be sharpened easily. It has quite good stain resistant qualities. It is the steel of choice for French pocketknives.

As you now know, not all steels are created equal.

Trust me, I write books about meat.

THE RECIPES

There are no recipes. Those days are gone.

Suck it up cupcake.

One can't live with one's finger everlastingly on one's pulse. (Conrad, J, "Heart of Darkness ")

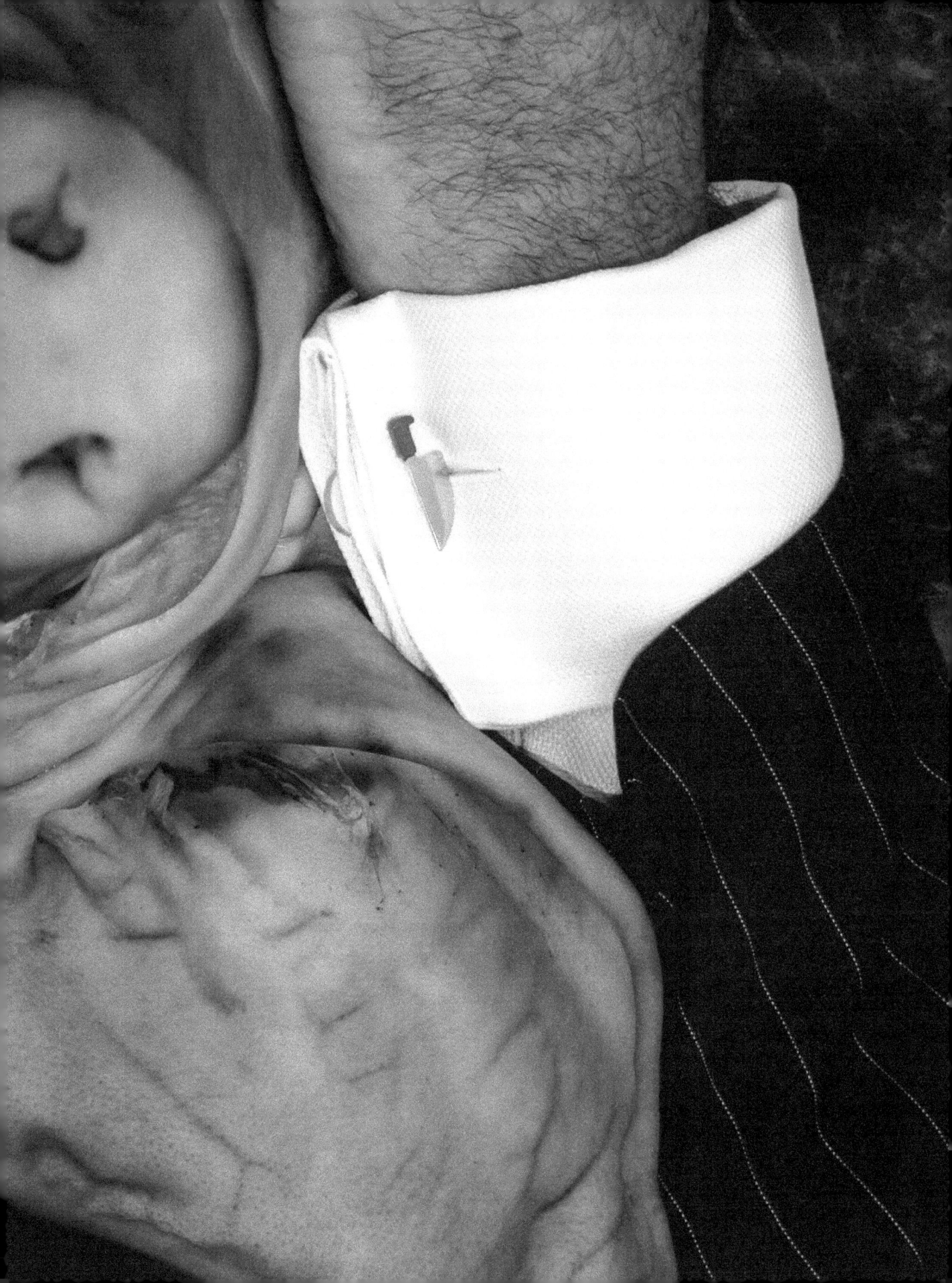

THE APPENDICES

THE APPENDICES

POCKETKNIVES

I have long had an interest in pocketknives. I remember well being given a miniature pocketknife by my late aunt when I was about 6 or 7 years old, it was intentionally blunt so I could not injure myself or anyone else. It was silver with a nice green cover, and I enjoyed opening it out to expose the blade which was only probably 1 ½ inches long. But it was a very important thing to me, and I was very keen on sawing anything that I could find on my grandmother's property.

I have purchased many pocketknives since then.

Currently I have many antique French pocketknives, just because I like them. I have several Italian pocketknives which are very different. I have a few American pocket knives . The latter are in a very different style, short, thick blades with a very curved edge. I quite like them. I like them all, nonetheless. I have never told any pocketknife that I prefer that over the others. Sure, the others would be very disappointed if I were to say that. But I mean them no disrespect. Each is important in their own special way. There are no real favorites. At least that is what I tell them. They are silent which Moi takes as an acknowledgement. Pocketknives are like this. I use pocketknives every day to cut cheese, fruit or cured meat while I am working in my study. They are also very important to have available when one is travelling. Although these days they are somewhat of a liability insofar as on-board luggage is concerned. That is not to say that they are not extremely useful when one is at one's destination. A good knife is extremely useful to cut fruit, cheese, bread, or meat when one is in foreign accommodation, far from home, when the available knives are somewhat disappointing. The addition of a corkscrew has historically been useful, although less in modern times with the addition of the Stelvan seal, an Australian invention ,I am pleased to report.

The French pocketknives which I have collected over several years are in many different styles and sizes. The predominant brand which I have collected is Laguiole. I do not know how to pronounce this name. Nonetheless they are characterised by a blade of varying lengths and colored handles either made of wood, bone, or metal. They all have a characteristic embroidered metal spine with a bee image relief at the pivot point. Some others are from Italy. Others still, are from Spain , Portugal, or America.

I do not know whether they have any relevance to charcuterie butchery, but I do know that I have many of them and they are valuable to me. Forgive me for including them in this narrative. They are knives which I like. It is my book, and I can do what I want.

In the matter of the butcher's apron

When researching topics for this book I became interested in the history of the butcher's apron. Why is it always blue, why is it always striped? Unfortunately, few answers can be found. Some research disclosed that in the United Kingdom an organisation of butchers existed as early as AD975, The Butcher's Guild, the modern iteration of which is The Worshipful Company of Butchers, one of the Livery Companies of the City of London. The Butcher's Guild was incorporated by Royal Charter in 1605. I found an email address for the clerk of the Butchers Hall, which seemed to be an iteration of the current Secretariat of the Worshipful Company. I sent an email introducing myself and the purpose of the inquiry. I explained that I was interested in the history of the butcher's Guild and of the history of the apron and other livery. I asked if they could refer me to any literature which would inform me of these matters including the significance of the apron colour and the various stripe configurations. Sadly, I did not receive a reply. I sent another email. Still no reply. Who are these people ?

I decided to undertake some further research. The results were colloquial and lacked the detail I was hoping that the Worshipful Company could impart. Allow me to share with you that which I have discovered with some modest research. The blue striped apron was the uniform of the trade originating from at least the 16th century and is carried on today. The broad stripe identifies a master butcher from the apparel of an apprentice. The term "earning one's stripes" may refer to the transition from apprentice to master butcher. Although as an aside I have heard this expression attributed to achievement of certain military rank as a non-commissioned officer namely the stripes on the uniform. But I digress.

The term "apron" refers to a garment that protects the wearer's clothing but may derive from the mediaeval French word "naperon" meaning a small tablecloth. I do not speak mediaeval French but observe that the modern French word for apron is "tablier", not so similar to "apron ". (Maybe).

The best source of information was an article in the Sydney Morning Herald published in September 2008. The author is not identified. The article explains that the blue apron has been an industry trademark since 1540. The Butcher's Guild, an Associate Edition of butchers in York, dictated that a butcher's uniform or livery should include hat, coat, and apron. The striped apron designated the progression in the trade from apprentice to master butcher. Pinstripes distinguished a master butcher from the apprentice. The master butcher wore a broad striped apron but only if he progressed in the trade without an apprenticeship. If he had trained throughout an apprenticeship, then the broad stripe was accompanied by a narrow stripe. Apprentices wore narrow-striped aprons. The Butcher's Guild determines the apron's colour. It was often referred to as butcher's blue, also the colour of the Butcher's Guild crest and coincidentally the best colour to conceal blood stains.

I remain interested to receive a communication from the Guild which may explain something which they clearly value for its historical significance if nothing else.

We wait with faint but eager anticipation.

"The creatures outside looked from pig to man, and from man to pig, and from pig to man again; but already it was impossible to say which was which." (George Orwell, Animal Farm)

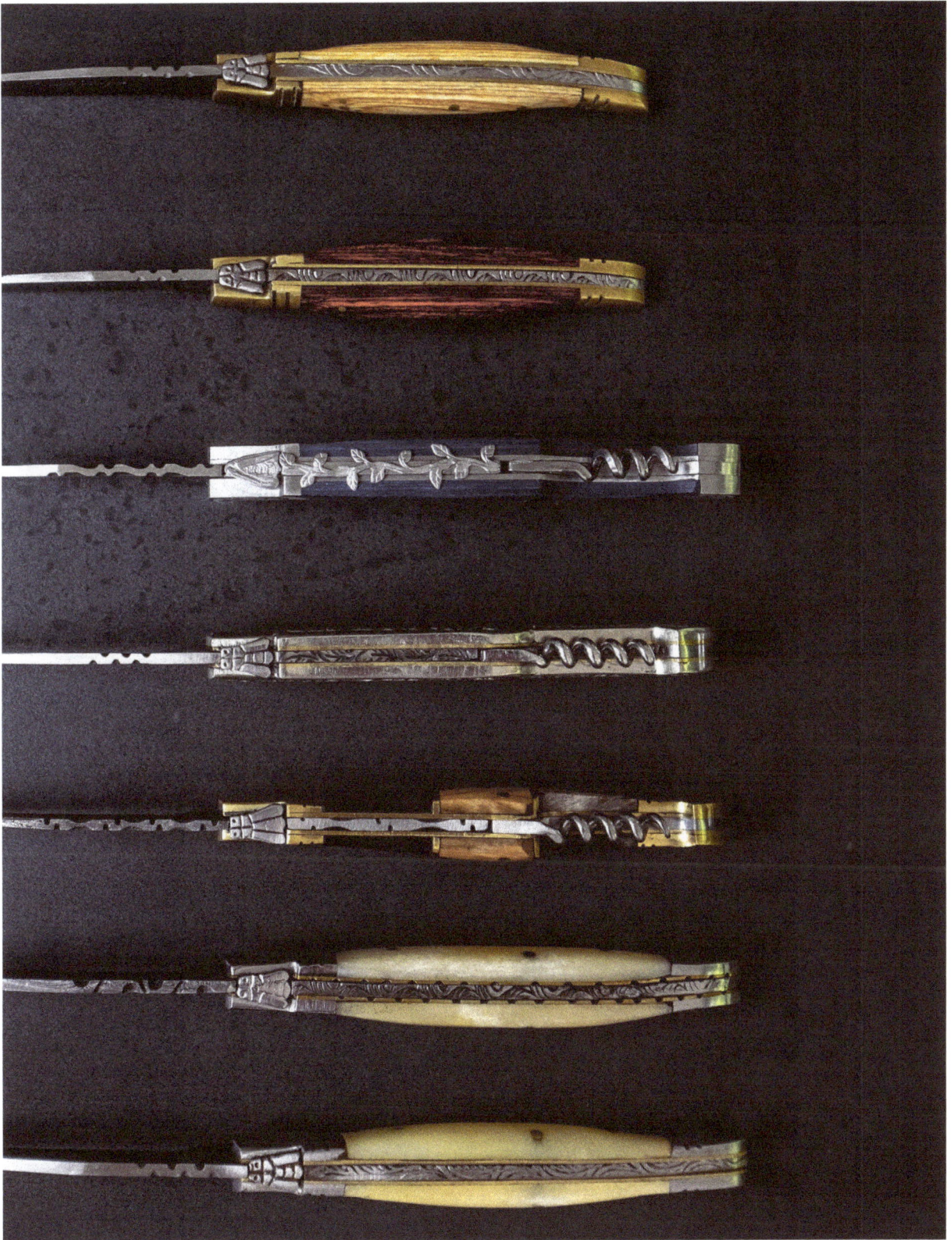

THE NEW BLACK DOG

The One True Dog went to the big kennel in the sky. Vouz knows this. The apprentice is of the same colour but of a different, smaller, persuasion. I held out for a like for like replacement as long as Moi could. However, in the face of trenchant opposition, non-Geneva Convention tactics and worse if not worserer (a new word, see a previous book) torture, Moi gave in. No one can hold out forever. I do apologize for this, but it was real world terrorism, not pretend war games. Moi says again, there must be an end. Moi accepts that Management has vetoed a proper replacement. Nonetheless the new black dog has tried to adapt to the gap left by The One True Dog. This has taken several years. She now sleeps in the study when Moi is working or writing, she now snores almost as loudly as did her predecessor, she now bumps open the closed study door, as did The One, she also looks for crusts from the lunch time sandwich. However, she is yet to contribute to editorial, grammatical or layout matters as did The One. On a positive note, she does not have the downstairs issues which plagued a sleeping black Labrador of aged proportions. These were quite significant and would often result in The One being ejected from the study. This is a positive benefit for Moi.

Standby for further updates.

Perhaps.

We are but microbes in the dust of charcuterie.

THE FRENCH AWARDS

You may have noticed that two of my books have red stickers on the front cover.

What do they mean ?, I hear you ask. Moi is tres glad that vouz has asked. Allow me a moment of ego in order to explain.

The red stickers represent awards given by an international cookbook competition, based in France. The Gourmand World Cookbook Awards were started in 1995 by Edouard Cointreau. They are designed along the lines of the Olympic Games and entries are categorised on a country basis and then in various subcategories. One may be awarded as the best cookbook in, for example, Australia in a particular category. Thereafter the winners in each category are again reviewed in order to find a global winner in that category. Ultimately the best cookbook is identified.

A Charcuterie Diary was awarded a special award of the jury, in Australia, in 2018.

Feathered was awarded best single subject award in Australia in 2019. Ultimately it was awarded one of the best 3 cookbooks in the world in that category.

I was astounded by the success of both books and remain so today. The Gourmand Awards have been described to me as what the Sundance Awards are to film, but in respect of cookbooks. The awards have also been compared to the Oscars for film but in respect of cookbooks. It does not matter to me of any comparison. I am delighted to have received recognition for books particularly in such a rich field of international competition.

Sadly , tragically receiving the awards has not translated into financial success but, as I often say, I did not write the books for financial reward and they have not disappointed me.

My earnest hope is that one day there will be an Australian cookbook award. Maybe one day.

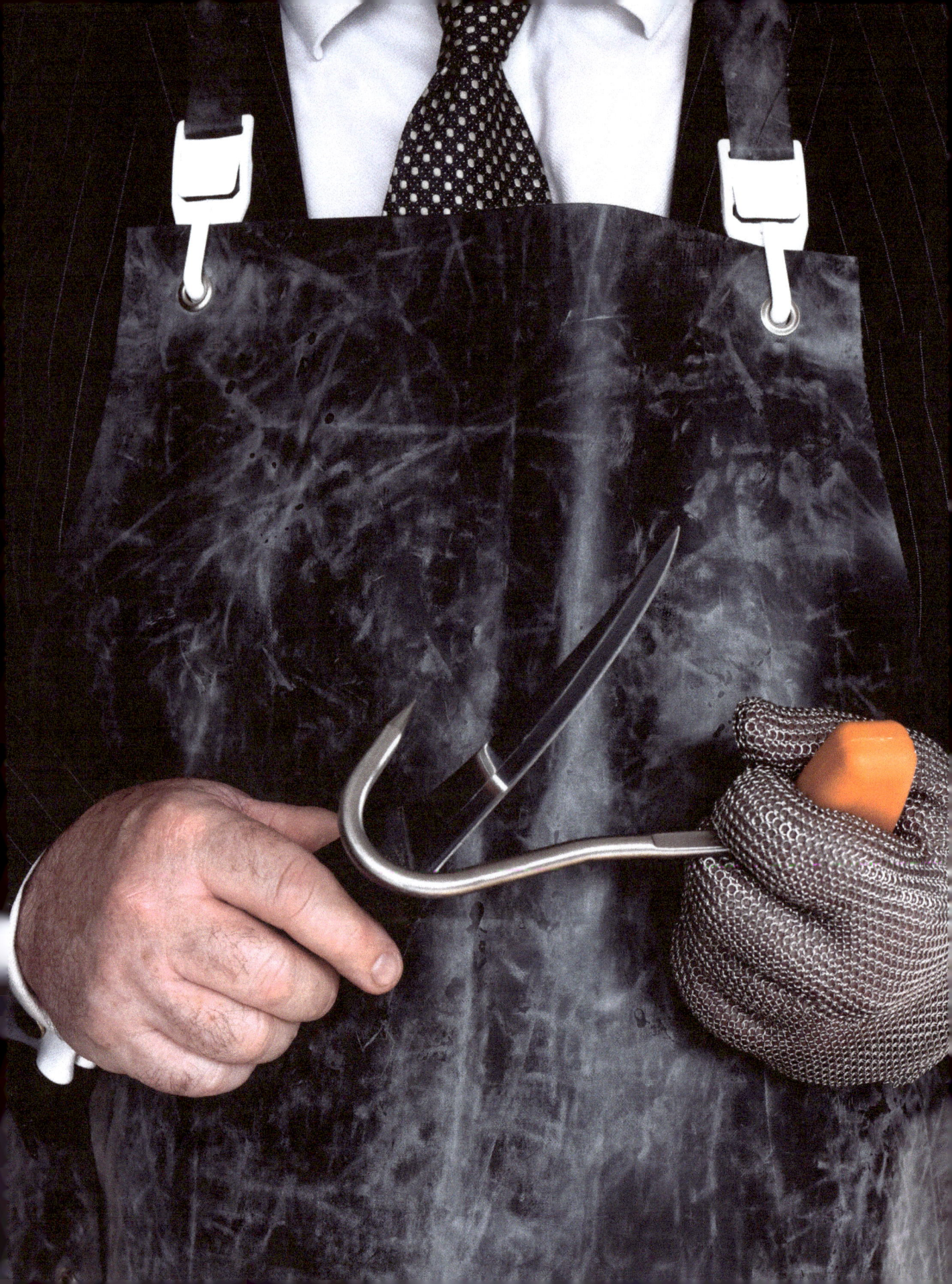

THE EPILOGUE

I did say that I would not do another charcuterie book. I really meant it. You will observe that there are not any charcuterie recipes in this book. This is just other stuff that I needed to tell you.

In fact, this book is a distillation of the classes which I have been fortunate to conduct in many places over the last 10 years. There are some extra bits and some bits have been expanded, but that is normal for this type of thing. Therefore, and henceforth, I have not done that which I stated that I would not. So there.

Do not be afraid of charcuterie, it is certainly not afraid of Vouz.

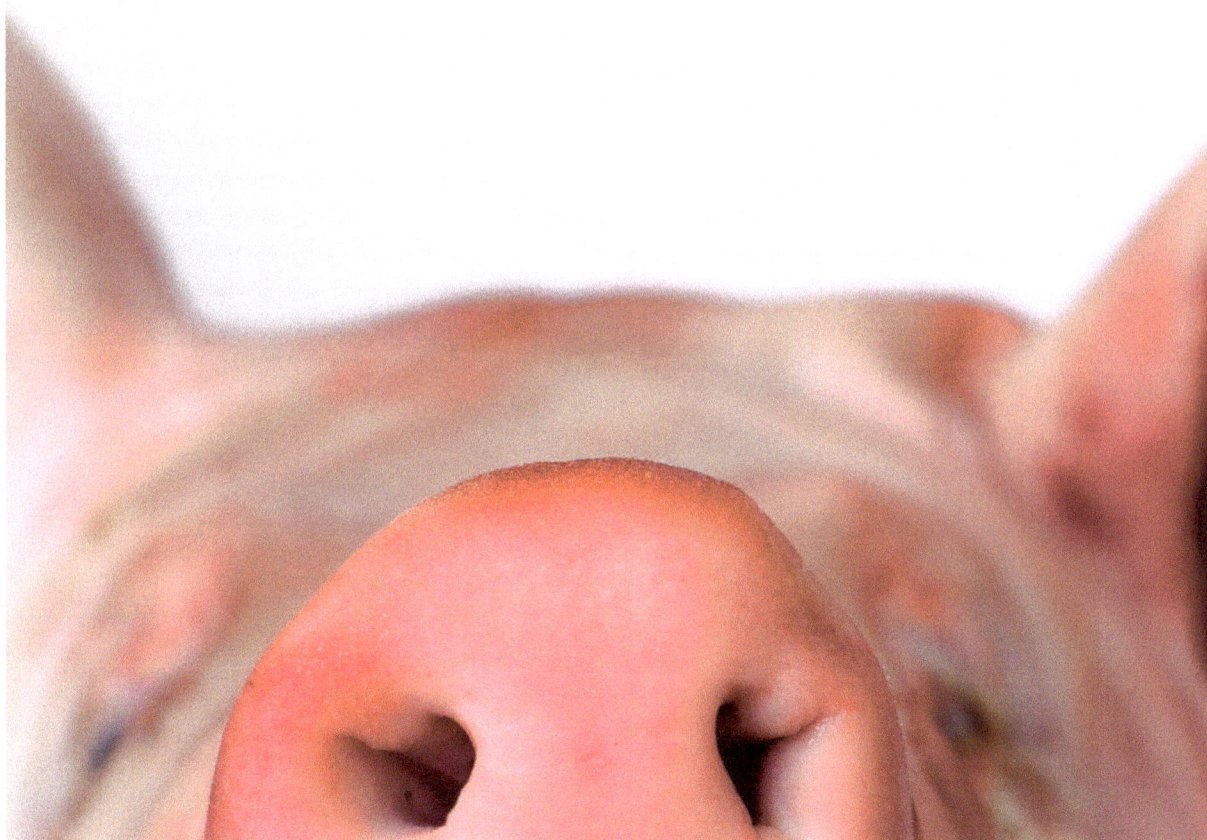

THE BIBLIOGRAPHY

These are the books and other resources which I have had regard to in writing this book or which have otherwise been a source of inspiration if not comfort. Use votre knowledge for good, not evil.

1. Barlow, J, "Everything but the squeal ", Wakefield Press, 2009.

2. Barrett, J, "Sustain ", Hardie Grant, 2023.

3. Bernado, P et al "Nitrate is nitrate: The status quo of using nitrate through vegetable extracts in meat products ", Foods, 2021, 10 ,3019.

4. Blot, P, "Handbook of practical cookery for ladies and professional cooks ", Applewood Books 2008, originally published in 1868.

5. Bonneau M, et ors, "Boar taint – causes and management", Encyclopaedia of meat sciences, 2004.

6. Booth, P, "A charcuterie diary", self-published ,2017.

7. Booth, P, "Feathered", self-published ,2018.

8. Booth, P, Slackwater", self-published ,2020.

9. Booth, P, "Squeal" self-published, 2022.

10. Buford, W, "Heat", Vintage publishing, 2007.

11. Burke, J-L," Flags on the Bayou ", Hachette UK, 2023.

12. Burroughs, W S "Naked lunch ", Penguin Books, 2001.

13. Child, L "Echo Burning ", Bantam Books, 2011.

14. Conrad, J, "Heart of darkness ", Popular Penguins, 2011.

15. Craig, E (Ed), "New standard cookery ", Oldham's Press, 1933.

16. Danforth, A "Butchering", Storey Publishing, 2014.

17. Dardick, G, "Home butchering and meat preservation", McGraw-Hill Education, 1993.

18. Davies, E, "Gohan ", Smith Street Books, 2023.

19. Davies, M, "Manual of a traditional bacon curer", Merlin Unwin books Limited, 2009.

20. Davies, M, "Secrets of a bacon curer", Merlin Unwin Books Ltd, 2007.

21. Davies, M, "Adventures of a bacon curer", Merlin Unwin Books Ltd, 2007.

22. Disher, G, "The way it is now ", Text Publishing Company,2021.

23. Farr, R "Whole beast butchery", Chronicle Books, 2011.

24. Fearnley – Whitingstall, H, "The River Cottage Meat Book", Random House USA, Inc, 2007.

25. Feiner, G," Salami- Practical science and processing technology ", Academic Press, 2016.

26. Fleming, I, "On her Majesty's secret service ", Nelson Thornes, 1991.

27. Fleming, I, "Live and let die ",Nelson Thornes, 2012.

28. Fraioli, J "The home butcher", Sky Horse, 2019.

29. Fitzharris, L, "The butchering art", Penguin Books Ltd, 2018.

30. Fulton, A W, "Home pork making", Orange Judd Company, 1902.

31. Green, A , "The butcher's apprentice", Quarry Books, 2012.

32. Green , G , " Our man in Havana " , Macmillan, 2015 (First published 1958)

33. Gott H et al, "Hawksmoor at home", Preface Publishing, 2001.

34. Gott, H et al, "Hawksmoor restaurants and recipes", Preface Publishing ,2017.

35. Govari M, Pexara A ," Nitrates and nitrites in meat products" , J Hellenic Vet Med Soc , 2015, 66 (3): 127-140

36. Gilmore, P, 'From the earth", Hardie Grant, 2023.

37. Hasheider, P "The complete book of pork butchering, curing, sausage making and cooking", Voyageur Press, 2016.

38. Hastie, L, "Finding fire ', Hardie Grant, 2017.

39. Hayward, T, "Knife", Quadrille Publishing, 2016.

40. Heath, A, "Pig curing and cooking ", Faber and Faber, mcmlii (1952 for non-Latin speakers)

41. Heyrman E et ors, "Developing and understanding olfactory evaluation of boar taint", Animals (Basel), 2020 Sep; 10 (9): 1684.

42. "Il Salumi d 'Italia- Le Guide de L'Espresso" –GEDI Gruppo Editoriale SipA, 2020 .

43. Kunstgemasse garnier ung Von Schusseln – " Allagemeine Flieschier Zeitung ", publication details unknown[1]

44. Leigh, M, "The ethical meat handbook", New Society Publishers, 2015.

45. Keenan, D F, "Boar taint ", Encyclopaedia of Food and Health, 2016.

46. McGee, H, "McGee on food and cooking", Hodder and Staunton, 2004.

47. Moore, K L, "Immuno castration, physical castration, and meat quality of male pigs", Reference Module in Food Science, 2022.

48. Mountain, J, "Pig: cooking with a passion for pork", Duncan Baird, 2021.

49. Mrs Toogood, "The Treasury of French Cookery ', Richard Bentley ,London , 1866.

50. Nicols, G J, "Bacon and Hams ", Pranava Books, 1917.

51. Niland, J, "Fish butchery ", Hardie Grant, 2023.

52. O'Meara, R, "Wild meat ", Hardie Grant, 2022.

53. Orwell, G, "Down and out in Paris and London ", Harvest books, date unknown.

54. Redzepi,R, et ors, "Vegetable , Forest, Ocean ", RRover Aps, 2022.

55. Smith, I and Schneider, S (Eds), "1001 Movies you must see before you die ", Pier 9 ,2019.

56. Squires E J and Bonneau M, "Boar taint", Reference Module in Food Science, 2022.

57. Tanty, F, "La Cuisine Francoise ", Rand McNally & Company, 1896.

58. Thompson, H S, 'The rum diary ", Bloomsbury, 2011.

59. Tsuji, S , Japanese Cooking , Kodansha USA Publishing ,LLC, 1980.

60. Uglow, J, "The lunar men ", Faber and Faber, 2002.

61. Ude, L E, "The French Cook, system of fashionable and economical cookery, adapted to the use of English families ", John Ebers and Co, London, MDCCCXXIX (1815 to you).

---

[1] "Artistic garnish bowls" appears to be the literal translation. A book with delightful full-colour hand drawn plates of charcuterie arrangement and presentations"

"Some who have read the book, or at any rate have reviewed it, have found it boring, absurd, or contemptible, and I have no cause to complain, since I have similar opinions of their works, or of the kinds of writing that they evidently prefer." (J R R Tolkien)

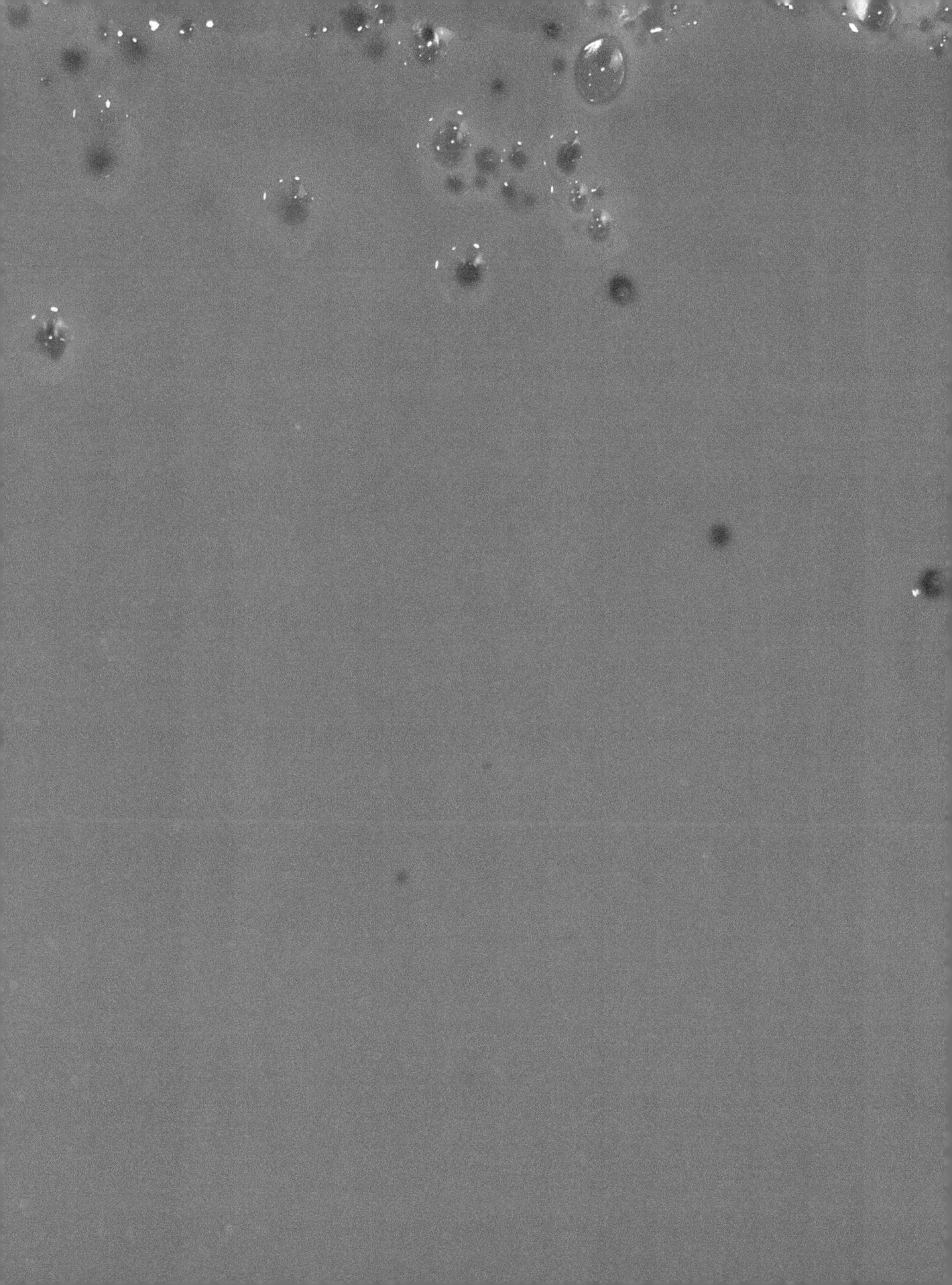

THE ACKNOWLEDGMENT

Once again Amy Gubana has put in an enormous effort in delivering great images, both in terms of time and attention to detail together with creativity. This modest work could not have been achieved in its present form without Amy's enthusiastic collaboration. You can view more of her work at www.amygubana.com.

Ben Taylor did a fantastic job of the layout and graphic design. He transformed an extraordinary complex manuscript with more than 350 images in to a living breathing book. You can see more of his design work here: www.taylordesign.com.au

Do yourself a favour.

Happiness is a sharp knife.

THE POST SCRIPTUM

The first entry in the first notebook is dated January 2013. Accordingly I have been experimenting with this stuff and writing down my observations for more than 10 years. What have I learned over the last 10 years? Allow me to try and answer.

In the beginning all the books told me that I had to start with a whole pig, preferably one that I had raised myself, slaughtered humanely myself and done everything in between. Indeed it would be considerably advantageous if the pig had a private school education followed by a degree in the humanities. I acknowledge that this culinary backwater has emerged from the smallholders need to utilise and preserve food when it is in abundance for the times when it is not. I also understand that there are significant economies of scale when purchasing a whole or half a pig compared to purchasing individual cuts. However, for most people breaking down a 35 kg or 40 kg half pig is an almost insurmountable task, certainly a task which requires significant fortitude and conviction. If one is not a smallholder and there is no survival imperative, then my advice is start small and end up big if you feel the need. By way of example, I can break down a half pig into the relevant components for charcuterie in about an hour and a half. The next steps of preparing each cut for curing, making up curing mixtures and the like, mincing meat, stuffing, tying, weighing and all the rest of take the remainder of the day and then some. Accordingly, if I am working on my own, as I usually am, the process of breaking down one half pig really takes two days. You may have two days to spare. I usually do not. Therefore, these days, I usually take the easy way out. If I want to make bacon, then I purchase sufficient pork belly in order to do so and process it within an hour or so. Similarly, if I want to make prosciutto then I purchase a leg of pork, cut to my specifications, and process it in 20 minutes. Air dried sausages are even easier. The butcher will mince meat to order or will add fat to my specifications in the already minced meat. When I return home with the quantity of minced meat, with fat added to my specifications, I can add spices, stuff casings and hang the meat in a few hours. Of course, it costs more to purchase meat this way, but I get the pleasure of making it myself without the heavy lifting of butchering the meat and separating it into its component parts .The added benefit is that I can make only the products that I require, in the quantities that I require, and it does not take very long to do so. I do not get the added pleasure of butchering the meat myself, but I can live with that. I commend this method of domestic charcuterie production to you.

Secondly, one does not need to embark on commercial quantities of charcuterie production. My acquaintances, I have no friends as you know, seem preoccupied with vast commercial quantities of domestic charcuterie production. I do not share their fervour. There are several reasons for this. If you make a mistake in the production, and ever it is thus, then you have ruined a significant quantity of raw materials. Also, because I give most of my production away, I do not have sufficient acquaintances to whom to give a vast quantity of product. Lastly, 10 kg or 15 kg of air-dried sausage require a significant curing cabinet or facility to ensure that they cure properly and do not spoil. Most domestic facilities cannot accommodate this.

Thirdly, it was also apparent in the beginning that one must use rare breed, organically raised, ethnically slaughtered, university educated pigs and only while reciting verses from an organic manifesto. I have used such raw materials and, in my view, whilst they may make one feel better and perhaps taste slightly better, the economic reality is that normal, commercially produced, retail pork is perfectly good. Apart from else if you make a mistake with organic, university educated, et cetera, pork then you are wasting a lot of money. There is no reason to do this. On any view that products that one makes using basic retail pork will be far better than the products you purchase as completed commercial charcuterie. In my view life is too short to be shouldering the burden for organic, University educated pork for the purposes of domestic charcuterie. However, if you feel the need to do so then by all means.

Next, in the beginning it was clear that one had to use natural casings to produce air-dried sausages to the exclusion of everything else. This is because the books said so and because it has always been done this way. Therefore, it was the only legitimate way to produce air dried sausages. The problem is fresh casings are nasty, slimy, slippery suckers and difficult to use. True it is that once loaded up on to the stuffing nozzle they run off very nicely, but they are slippery and difficult to use. Further, when making larger diameter single length air dried sausages, natural casings require that one stop, tie, cut, retie, and continue for each individual air-dried sausage. This is time-consuming and prone to mistakes if the knots slip off the extremely slippery casings. It is a slow and, often, frustrating process. There is an easier way. Manufactured casings, but using natural collagen, are easy to use, they require a few seconds softening in water or wine, they are very strong, and most importantly for air dried sausage production come in single lengths of varying diameters but each length has a sealed and has an open end. This means that they can be put on the stuffing nozzle quickly and only require one open end to be tied. These are very quick to use, very reliable and productive of significantly less frustration than the fresh counterparts. Unless I am making fresh sausages, when I use fresh casings, or much larger individual casings like cotechino were I use sheep or beef bung, I always use manufactured, natural collagen, single casings with one open end for air dried sausages.

Fourthly, whilst I have acquired a great deal of equipment over the years, and you have seen the photographs of my armoury, in truth one only needs a few tools. For butchery I only use a six inch semi - flex boning knife, a boning saw and a sharpening steel. I could use many other things, but I really do not need them. It is difficult to avoid the need for a good quality mincer, and I have several of them. My mincers range between a small handheld mincer which I used in the beginning, to the mincing attachments to an American brand domestic mixing machine, a one horsepower Chinese electric mincer of one horsepower or the same powered but more sophisticated Italian mincer. An electric mincer of approximately 0.5 – 1 horsepower capacity will be more than ample for what you will need . Indeed, my 1 hp mincer would mince your mother-in-law happily and not break a sweat, don't you worry about that. Depending on the quantities that you intend to mince, a manual mincer would also be sufficient. It is also difficult to avoid the need for a mechanical stuffer. It is possible but extremely difficult to manually stuff the minced meat into a casing for the purposes of making an air-dried sausage. Indeed, life is too short to try and attempt this. The modest investment in a manual stuffer is well worth it. Mine is of 4 kg capacity and this is sufficient for domestic purposes.

Fifthly, I spent a lot of time researching the area; books, chatrooms, internet, acquaintances (Moi has no friends) and so much more. This was often instructive, often not, sometimes a tantalising reference to an interesting product but which could not be tracked down with any certainty. However, over the years the vague reference to a product was enough (sometimes) to experiment and extemporise such that a product recipe could be developed. Accordingly, the products may not meet the approval of the traditional owners of the recipe. To them I say, bad luck, write the recipes down so that their purity if not longevity can be assured. There is no property in knowledge in my view.

Lastly, the elephant in the room, as always, is somewhere to cure the end product. I have discussed this in previous works. In the absence of a limestone cave, a temperature and humidity stable shed or something else, a domestic wine fridge, in the house in a dark cupboard, will perform adequately for domestic purposes. I have proven this to be so.

Thus 10 years of experiments, mistakes, tears, fear, and loathing, is reduced to a few paragraphs.

Charcuterie is a broad church; it will welcome even Vouz and Votre.

Give it a chance.

We penetrated deeper and deeper into the heart of darkness. (Conrad, J, " Heart of Darkness ")

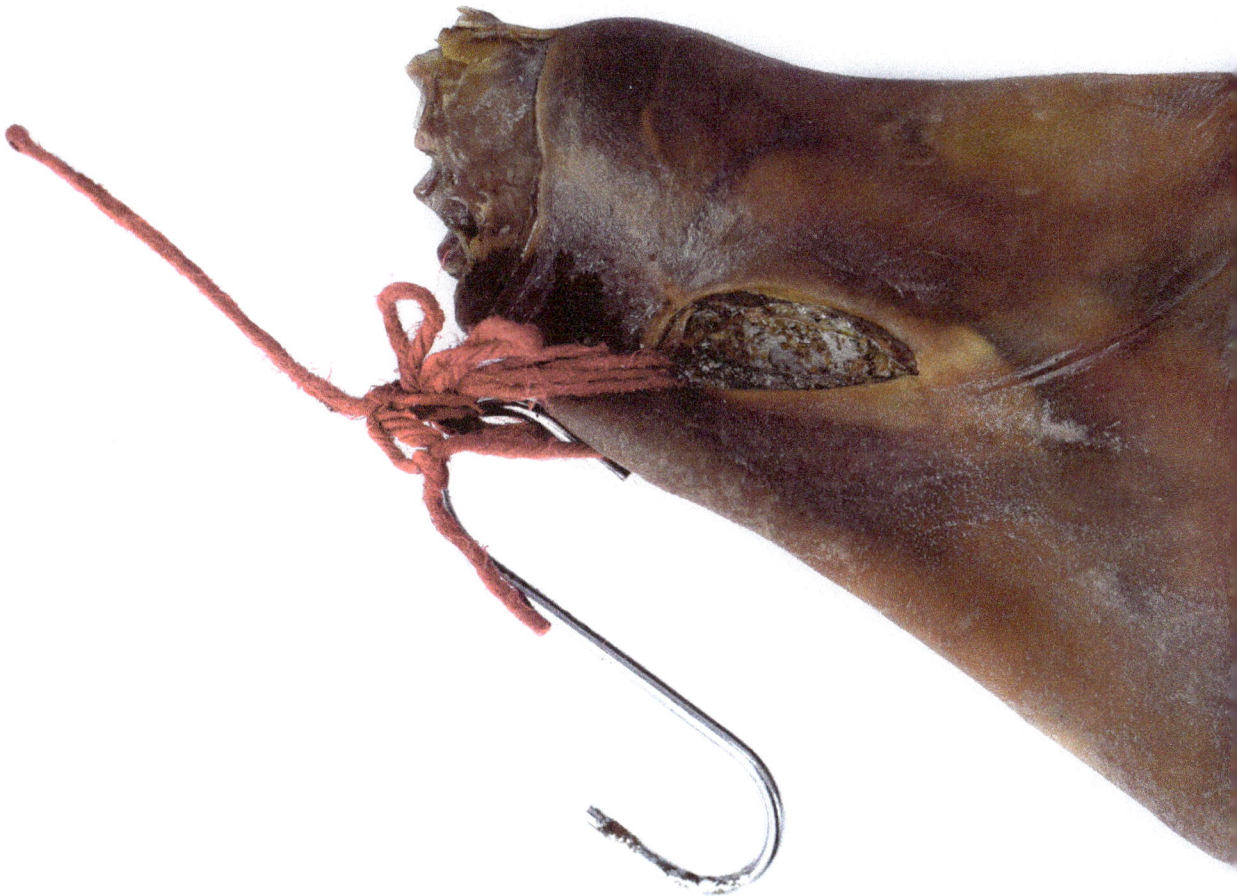

THE POST-POST SCRIPTUM

Two things which I forgot to tell you.

First, I accept responsibility for all errors, omissions, overstatements, understatements, hyperbole, opinion, misanthropy, lycanthropy, and everything in between. As with the last book, the manuscript for this book was dictated by me, in my study with the aid of voice recognition software. Accordingly, there may well be phonetic and other errors. I have checked and rechecked but after a while they become invisible. Such is the process of a self-published book. On the positive side you are the owner of a handmade, bespoke book. Not a ghost-written book which the author just signs off on and might offer some high-level guidance on the way through. This book has not been the subject of focus group testing (except for The New black Dog), workshopped by a committee or spent time in the marketing department.

I have been a nonfiction writer for more than 40 years, although mostly not in this genre. As is my habit, I wrote the book once and once only. I do not write and re write, for better or worse. Once a structure had been devised, the result usually reveals itself. It is just a matter or shaping it as you go. Of course, there was the laborious task of checking for spelling mistakes but that is to be expected. But in my experience, it is better to write what one thinks than to try and improve endlessly upon the expression or the concept. Formatting and layout is best left to others. It is good to acknowledge one's shortcomings, of which in my case there are many.

As the late Ian Fleming explained: *"Writing about 2,000 words in three hours every morning, 'Casino Royale' dutifully produced itself. I wrote nothing and made no corrections until the book was finished. If I had looked back at what I had written the day before I might have despaired."*

Secondly, as I have said before in the context of my earlier books, I owe this book more than it owes me. This remains the same, notwithstanding the passage of time.

Thank you for reading this book. It is the greatest compliment.

I should add that this does not mean that we are friends or anything. Moi has no friends. Ask anyone. It just means that I appreciate your support and fortitude in reading this book.

We have known pain and suffering, fear and loathing and all of their footsoldiers.

We have endured a calling for this that no bayonet can pierce, no bullet can shatter.

We are one.

This story is finished.

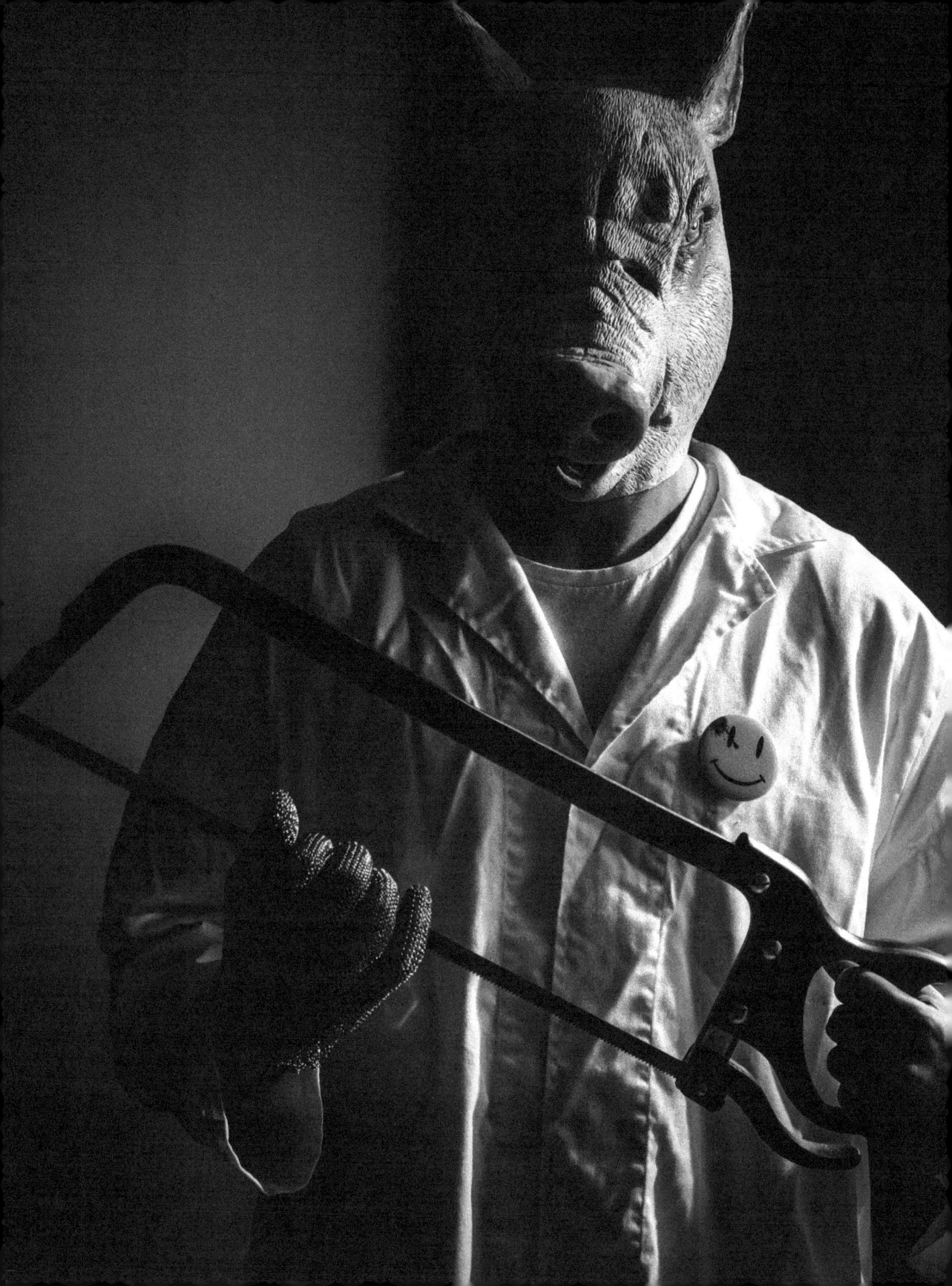

THE REVIEWS

Some reviews for Squeal.

Australian Hunter magazine Volume 15, 2023:

"The front cover delivers a pointer to where the inside contents are likely to take intrigued readers.

The monochrome artwork is highly confronting, featuring a gigantic, semi-deformed pig's head adorned with collared shirt and tie plus cufflinks. Adding to the sense of oddity is that the grotesque subject of the photo seems to have donned a bib with braces as a pair of apparently human hands grasp onto whatever the face is. It is certainly a stark image but in a darkly comedic sense. It looks as though it could fit in as part of a trailer for a macabre horror movie. Indeed, such are the sinister overtures that if Hollywood legend Quentin Tarantino suddenly had the urge to veer off into concocting a cookery manuscript, then this is the avenue that the unorthodox producer/director could ponder.

Once we begin to flick through the pages, we are welcomed by a glowing appraisal in The Foreword from chef and author Matt Stone, who describes the tome as "unique."

"You will not find another collection of such recipes and techniques in any other book," is one of the concluding lines from Stone."

Australian Meat News, April 2023:

"Squeal, the third book published by Peter Booth, takes charcuterie to a whole new level, and assumes the reader has the basics under their belt. Born from a pre-covid trip to Europe and lockdown boredom, Booth explores the more exotic reaches of charcute*rie.*"

Some review for A Charcuterie Dairy.

"Peter Booth is a Melbourne lawyer who's becoming so profoundly immersed in his hobby of charcuterie that he's self-publishing a record of his journey: A Charcuterie Diary. What a project."

"… for anyone who's interested in making sausages, ham, bacon, you name it, at home, this quirky DIY book will be a necessity."

– Weekend Australian Magazine, John Lethlean.

"… this deeply engaging and encyclopaedic tome on all things cured is a joy to read. It's idiosyncratic, funny and earnest in equal measure, filled with inspiration for anyone with more than a passing interest in bacon.

– Herald Sun, Dan Stock

"Booth's enthusiasm for creating beautiful tastes from raw meat, using the preservative properties of salt, is rather infectious as you follow his words through the first part of his book before the recipes start. He has a charm and a wit about his writing that draws in the reader through his journey of charcuterie making.

I feel I know him as a friend."

– Weekly Times, Jeremy Vincent.

"As someone who has recently moved to a small farm and begun breeding Wessex saddleback pigs, I could only thrill to the existence of a Melbourne lawyer's self- published tome, A Charcuterie Diary. Peter Booth is a charcuterie obsessive, and rightly so. His book is smart, eccentric, and neither an academic exercise nor a celebrity chef's outing. He will be my Virgil, going forward."

– The Australian, Geordie Williamson

"Booth's style of writing is highly opinionated, unashamedly tinged with irreverence and he seemingly has no scruples about causing offence as he weaves together strands from his diary of recipes, reflections and results amassed over a period of four years."

"...a volume that succeeds in championing a branch of cooking that even some meat

lovers may at first find rather daunting. This bold, no holds barred crusade deserves much credit for that and for providing plenty of chuckles along the way."

– Australian Hunter, Dave Rose

"It is a beautiful work, with numerous gorgeous photographs accompanying stories and instructions.

"P J Booth's writing style ... is passionate, direct and to the point."

– Victorian Bar News, Natalie Hickey.

"A Charcuterie Diary is a record of the author's four year journey into the art and science of making charcuterie. Starting with a dream – some basic cooking skills but no meat or smallgoods training, Booth learned everything about meat cuts, ingredients, terminology and equipment. The book describes the evolution of his knowledge, and as his skills developed, the products he made."

– Australian Meat News

"Are you afraid of charcuterie? Home charcuterie can be quite an intimidating endeavour, a lot can go dangerously wrong. Grab a copy of A Charcuterie Diary and fear no more! This wonderfully inspiring book is quite literally a diary written by a pork enthusiast chronicling his four year quest to charcuterie enlightenment. P J starts with a highly informative introduction covering the history, science, necessary equipment and techniques of charcuterie along with some humorous meat centric stories. Then the recipes follow; cured, smoked and poached sausages from all over the globe, pancettas, prosciuttos, rilettes, terrines and even a pig head pie for the brave along with much much more. This diary is an essential charcuterie reference guide. Buy some pink salt, pick up some pork, order this book and become a charcuterie artisan today!"

– The Cookbook Review

Winner, 'Australia, Special Interest' 2018 Category, Gourmand World Cookbook Awards

THE END

This is it. There is no more. I have given you all that I can in this area. I would like to do more but my time has come. Use your knowledge for good, not evil.

> *I have wrestled with death. It is the most unexciting contest you can imagine. It takes place in an impalpable greyness, with nothing underfoot, with nothing around, without spectators, without clamour, without glory, without the great desire of victory, without the great fear of defeat, in a sickly atmosphere of tepid scepticism, without much belief in your own right, and still less in that of your adversary. (Conrad, J, " Heart of darkness ")*

THE INDEX

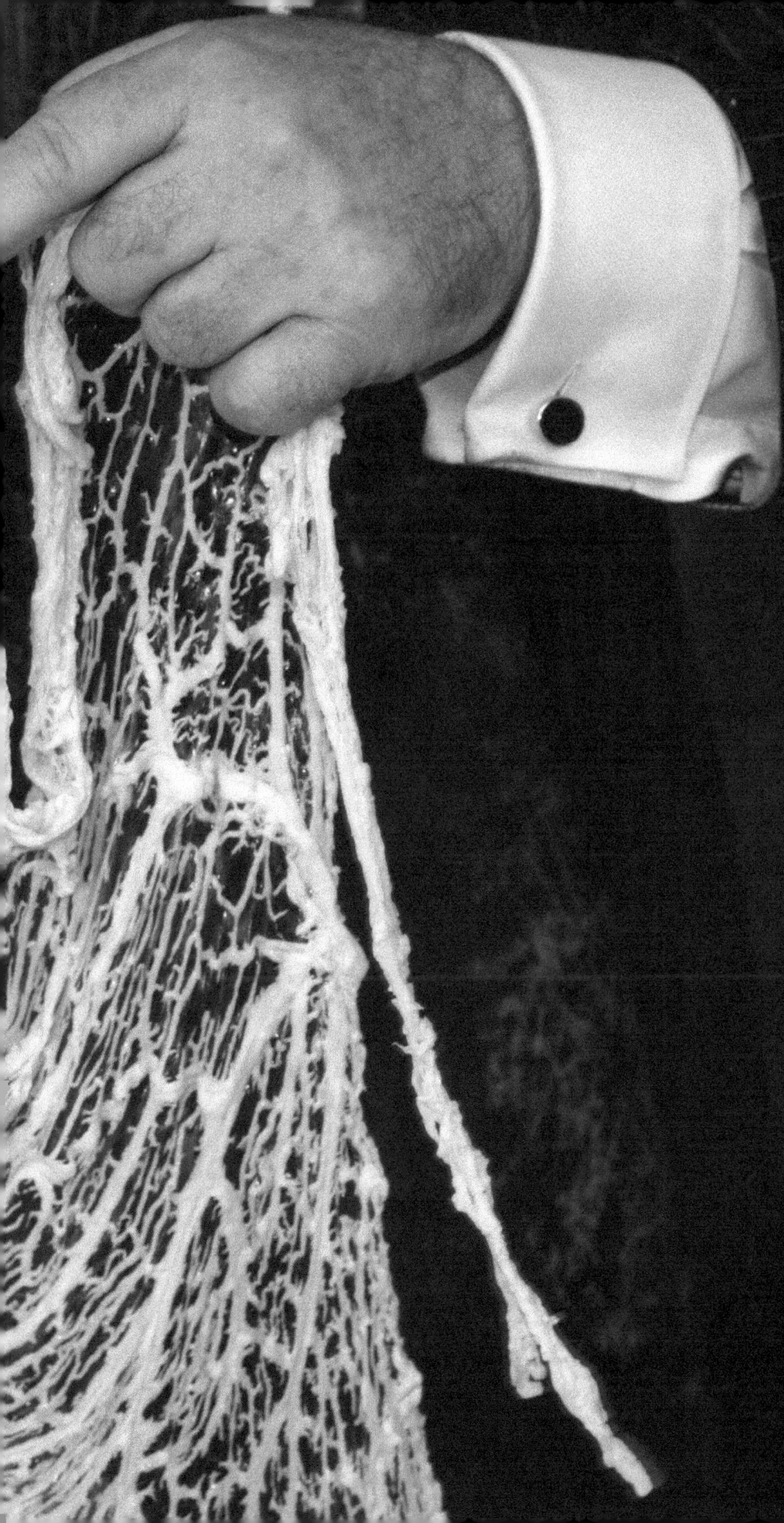

www.ingramcontent.com/pod-product-compliance
Lightning Source LLC
Chambersburg PA
CBHW040255100426
42811CB00011B/1270